A BRIEF HISTORY OF DEATH

A
BRIEF
HISTORY
OF
DEATH

W. M. SPELLMAN

REAKTION BOOKS

In Memory of Edward Spellman

Published by Reaktion Books Ltd
33 Great Sutton Street
London EC1V 0DX, UK

www.reaktionbooks.co.uk

First published 2014
Copyright © W. M. Spellman 2014

Printed and bound in Great Britain
by TJ International, Padstow, Cornwall

A catalogue record for this book is available from the British Library

ISBN 978 1 78023 265 2

Excerpt from 'The Old Fools' from *The Complete Poems of Philip Larkin*
by Philip Larkin, edited by Archie Burnett. Copyright 2012 by
The Estate of Philip Larkin. Reprinted by permission of
Farrar, Straus and Giroux, LLC.

Contents

Introduction 7

ONE
Preliminary Patterns 18

TWO
Thinking Things Through 52

THREE
Extraordinary Narratives 95

FOUR
Adverse Environments 132

FIVE
Modern Reconsiderations 167

Conclusion 205

REFERENCES 212
SELECT BIBLIOGRAPHY 240
ACKNOWLEDGEMENTS 248
INDEX 249

Introduction

The old adage about the certainty of death and taxes is not entirely accurate. There are some in every age who, through privilege or dissimulation, manage to circumvent the latter, but no amount of cunning or pretence has rebuffed the former. Approximately 155,000 people die every day, or 57 million people worldwide every year.[1] If pressed on the matter, virtually all of us will agree that the mortality rate will remain 100 per cent no matter the heroics of modern medical practice, yet few of us are eager to consider our own demise. Today in the developed West death and dying are often kept tidily out of sight, relegated to hospitals, skilled care facilities or nursing homes. Indeed it is not impossible to go through life without ever encountering a dead body outside the cosmetic setting of a funeral parlour. Where once the dying person found solace at home, surrounded by family and friends and in command of the goodbyes, more likely than not the experience today comes at the end of costly treatments, all supervised by professional staff in charge of sophisticated life-sustaining machinery, the dying visited by, rather than living with, loved ones in a familiar setting. And funerary practice – burial or cremation – takes place at the periphery of the community, both physically and culturally. Death today is commonly at a distinct remove from life, very nearly clandestine, almost always unwelcome.[2]

Still, every generation is drawn to the issue of mortality, for the end of life raises perennial questions about human origins, identity and larger purpose. We are naturally curious to understand our place in an enigmatic universe, seeking meaning in life and a wider context in which to play our part as sentient beings. The modern physical sciences have decoded parts of the enigma, but the results offer cold comfort. We know that each of us must die, that species come and go over millennia, but now we also recognize that the entire universe is destined for extinction. Planets, stars and galaxies will, like frail humans, dissolve first into dust and then into naught. Despite major advances in biomedicine and technology over the past century, everyone's natural span remains but an instant when set against the backdrop of historic, not to mention prehistoric time, and coming to terms with this incorrigible personal fact offers perspective and, if we are fortunate, resolution and acceptance. On those quiet occasions when we are able to separate ourselves from the myriad distractions of the day, reflection on death helps us recalibrate our transitory appointment with life. 'What is a man in the infinite?' asked the seventeenth-century philosopher-mathematician Blaise Pascal (1623–1662).[3] Almost 400 years later we are no less impatient for an answer.

This brief, topical survey approaches the subject of death – defined here as permanent loss of neural activity or brain function and the irreversible cessation of biological processes – from a mainly Western perspective.[4] It considers two separate but closely related phenomena. The first involves how individuals understand and come to terms with the fact of mortality, the narratives they construct in order to interpret and provide value within the context of essential loss. Discovering meaning in one's death, or conversely searching and finding no meaning in it, is perhaps the most powerful reflection of our sense of place or condition in life. Attitudes to death shape responses to life, provide grounding for personal codes of conduct and broader ethical systems and afford justification for existing and emergent social and political structures. Second, the book considers the physiological and social processes of extinction: how we die, how the dying are treated, how they conduct themselves in the knowledge of their approaching demise, and how those who remain behind choose to remember them. Remembrance involves what we might term the social context of death. The second-century

Roman emperor and Stoic philosopher Marcus Aurelius (121–180) cautioned his readers that remembrance, like life itself, is ephemeral. 'How quickly all things disappear,' he observed, 'bodies into the universe, memories of them into time.'[5] But in some cases we choose to remember over multiple generations, centuries even. And what we remember tells us much about our own core values, our priorities as a culture, our understanding of what it means to be human.

Irrespective of century, geographical location or culture, peoples around the world seem to have approached the issues of mortality and a potential afterlife of limited or infinite duration from three basic standpoints, and each of these has its contemporary equivalent. A relatively small number of people have concluded that death is the negation of being, the end of life, plain and simple. Modern scientific thinking in general, and neuroscience in particular, tend to point us in this direction, interpreting consciousness as a biochemical activity in specific regions or systems of the brain. Lacking testable empirical evidence of any form of continuity once biological death has occurred, this position, variously described as materialist, animalist, physicalist, mortalist or naturalist, finds no need to explore other possibilities.[6] From the ancient Greek philosopher Epicurus (c. 341–270 BCE) to the modern American humanist Corliss Lamont (1902–1995), recognizing insensibility and extinction as our common destiny has freed humans to centre their attention on the joys – and challenges – of this world, ending what Lamont called 'the dual terrorism of priests and gods'.[7] Agnosticism is the second perspective. While in agreement that inquiry is fruitless and empirical evidence forever lacking, the agnostic finds the mortalist stance too doctrinaire, unduly resistant to the possibility that our sensory reality may be incomplete and perhaps even distorted. Agnostics are willing to allow that our human rational order may be erected on a foundation of mere shadows, a situation memorably described by Plato (427–347 BCE) in his famous allegory of the cave, where the involuntary inhabitants mistake the shadows on the wall for the whole of reality.[8] What that final reality is remains a mystery for the agnostic, above our power to know but not disproved by our limited competence. For most agnostics, the possibility of a hereafter cannot be ruled out without first coming to terms with the deeply embedded human instinct for happiness and self-preservation, and the possibility – however remote – that something external and transcendent, some unseen actuality, exists to meet those needs.

The last and most prevalent outlook comprises mythical, religious and philosophical claims on behalf of some form of continuity, of death denied and surpassed. These claims have involved, most prominently, the unending journey of the immaterial soul as first articulated in ancient Greece, the prospect of bodily resurrection as emphasized in later Jewish, Christian and Islamic traditions, the widely embraced South Asian principle of reincarnation as someone or something else, and East Asian, African and indigenous North American understandings of the role of ancestors in the ongoing affairs of the terrestrial world – the interconnectedness of the two spheres. Western traditions are typically framed in terms of personal immortality, while in general South and East Asian perspectives see individual consciousness dissolving after death and returning to an all-pervasive, impersonal being, the creative force of the universe. Still, at the heart of these religious and philosophical pictures is the assumption of a much greater, albeit ineffable, cosmic order, together with an unshakable human desire to participate at a higher level in that order. St Paul (c. 5–67 CE) captured something of this longing within the Christian experience when he avowed: 'If in this life only we have hope in Christ, we are of all men most miserable.'[9]

We will trace the history and influence of each perspective, recognizing that the commitment to something larger than the traditional three score years and ten has exercised the greatest influence on human cultures, on thought and practice, across the ages. Existing evidence strongly suggests that interest in what becomes of a person after death was of very early origin, and belief in some form of conscious or semi-conscious afterlife for the deceased was typical of ancient peoples worldwide.[10] All societies, it seems, have held a view of post-mortem continuity that is a reflection of the unique human predilection to find fault with its

Post-Mortem Continuity [10]

environment and to wish that things might be otherwise. For millennia, most people compensated for the self-evident limitations of our organic nature with powerful myths and stories about consciousness and identity beyond the grave, in a place whose contours reflected the earthly habitation. Especially in the world's great religious traditions, death as but a stage in life served the cause of justice in an all-too-cruel world, offered reward or reunion with a creator god after the trials of the earthly tenure, and even assured perfection that was withheld from those still in the flesh. For the world's malefactors, on the other hand, the afterlife often meant divine retribution and interminable suffering. The great fourteenth-century Italian poet Dante provided what remains perhaps the most explicit description of retributive justice in the Christian milieu. If nothing else, the author's *Inferno* makes clear that fair dealing is not simply a concern limited to the temporal order.

More recently, mainstream theologians and philosophers have seemed less assured on these matters. While organized religion continues to provide frames of meaning for billions of people around the world, belief and practice are not immune to the influence of wider social and cultural change. The intervening centuries have witnessed the rise of a secular and scientific outlook that largely discounts non-empirical investigations, especially when the results are heavily laden with anthropomorphic references. Why, for example, do formal religions habitually privilege human beings over other animals, forecasting extinction and insensibility only for the latter?[11] The uncertainty has been reinforced by dramatic improvements in the material quality of life, at least for inhabitants of the developed West, which in turn has engendered greater interest in dominion over this world as the path to a meaningful life. The advent of modern therapeutic culture, in particular the aspirant sciences of psychiatry and psychology, has in some quarters trumped pastoral theology, and religious explanations of what happens to the individual personality after the demise of the biological organism no longer command the level of attention enjoyed in earlier centuries. This is especially the case in majority-Christian communities where all but strict fundamentalist churches largely eschew such awkward topics as hell and judgement.[12] Eternal life remains part of the vocabulary, to be sure, but the precise elements of heavenly subsistence are no longer discussed. More common is the sort of language employed by the tortured figure of Shakespeare's Hamlet, who referred to death as the 'undiscover'd country' from whose shores no traveller ever returns.

Even moral theory has been removed from the territory of post-mortem trial, judgement and sentencing. Generally speaking, moral codes in the post-industrial, secularized West find common expression in utilitarian and existential language, relying entirely on this-worldly and narrowly self-regarding formulas.[13] In other words, one follows prescribed norms of conduct to avoid civil and criminal penalties, not to align one's thoughts and actions with eternal directives.

Between an ancient world where notions of continuity first emerged to inform thought, discourse and action over many centuries, and a more recent stage upon which the spotlight has shifted away from all forms of otherworldliness, the account is both varied and instructive. The opening chapter will introduce us to the work of archaeologists and palaeoanthropologists who seek to understand something of the earliest human views of death through the interpretation of complex burial customs and physical remains. It will also explore some primary religious impulses, including the ghost- and spirit-inhabited world of animism and ancestor worship in traditional African societies, to more clearly articulated and formalized practices in the early civilizations of Mesopotamia and Egypt.

In chapter Two the spotlight shifts to the remarkable philosophical and rationalist tradition pioneered in ancient Greece, further elaborated during the period of Roman authority, and foundational to Western thinking ever since. In particular, we will chart the emergence of naturalistic and materialist descriptions of human destiny, together with dualist views of body and soul – with the soul being liberated at death to experience at last the world of pure ideas. Appropriated and much amended by Christianity during the first century of the Common Era, the argument for the imperishable soul remained largely unchallenged throughout the Middle Ages and into the early stages of the Renaissance. Chapter Two will also trace the influence of the scientific revolution of the seventeenth century, the Enlightenment rationalism of the eighteenth century, and the empirical, positivist and physiological approaches to the body that gathered strong momentum in the nineteenth century. The leading experimental scientists of the late seventeenth century were eager to demonstrate the power and glory of God in His handiwork, but the collective fruits of their labours inadvertently undermined the biblical and canonical accounts of God's direct action in this world. Robert Boyle (1627–1691), one of the most distinguished experimental scientists of his day, was not alone in his concern over what he saw as the 'great and deplorable growth of irreligion, especially among those that aspired to pass for wits, and several of them too for philosophers'.[14]

During the eighteenth century the achievements of natural philosophy instilled confidence that both the natural environment and humanity's place in that environment could be understood and advanced without reference to transcendent narratives. The possibility of progress through the application of human reason to every area of inquiry led the *philosophes* to view traditional religion as a principal roadblock to the expansion of human freedom and happiness. The emergence of Marxist materialism, evolutionary biology and behaviourist psychology in the mid- to late nineteenth century rekindled interest in ancient atomism and undercut the interpretive monopoly previously enjoyed by those who deployed the biblical account of humankind's creation. Accounting for an immortal soul, externally imposed universal truths, the primacy of rationality in human culture and a life beyond the grave all suddenly became more problematic.

We next turn our attention to some of the major religious traditions that emerged during the so-called 'Axial Age' between approximately 600–200 BCE. In defining biological death as but a stage in life, a probationary or recurring condition prior to a much more significant, metaphysically speaking, afterlife, the great religions were committed to affirming a non-human taxonomy of meaning and purpose. Each posited a celestial order that the human mind could apprehend, and called for urgent moral reform, the pursuit of righteousness and alignment with a transcendent principle that was within the reach of everyone who pursued it. Chapter Three will briefly explore death and dying within those traditions that continue to shape much of modern religious culture: Confucianism, Hinduism, Buddhism, Judaism, Christianity and Islam. From Confucianism's humanistic emphasis on the Decree of Heaven, filial piety and respect for elders, to Judaism's notion of tribal covenant and obedience in return for collective special favour, to Hinduism's resolve concerning duty in every stage of multiple incarnations before the achievement of release and enlightenment, the major faith traditions located the afterlife firmly within the orbit of earthly teleology or purpose, making the work explicable to its adherents and re-enforcing a deeply conservative social order.

Chapter Three will also survey developments in post-Roman Western society, where the Catholic Church inherited the mantle of imperial authority, to the end of the sixteenth century, when religious explanations of death and dying were complicated by the fracturing of the Christian community during the Protestant Reformation and challenged by the rise of the natural sciences. Throughout this period, as before, the apparent randomness of mortal illness, helplessness in the face of disease and the physical pain that often accompanied dying, were simple yet brutal constants for women and men in every civilization. References to the fear of death were as much about the painful process of dying – something that has declined in the contemporary West thanks to advances in palliative medicine – as it was about the state of being dead. What strike us as inordinately high rates of infant, child and urban mortality were in the medieval and early modern world simply the common experiences of those fortunate enough to survive into old age. People of every social and economic station relied on established religious explanations of death and its sequel, and on a rich tapestry of symbol and ritual surrounding the experience, to marshal strength and courage in the face of death's arbitrary path.

Chapter Four considers how we have died over the centuries, both alterations in the leading causes of death and shifting attitudes towards premeditated actions whose outcome is the death of a fellow human. External violence, animal and human, brought most lives to a painful close before the advent of sedentary, agricultural societies. Indeed conflict appears to have been normative for most of prehistory, and in the absence of any neutral arbiter, the end result was usually fatal for one side or another. However, once humans began to live and work together in geographically compact communities – in villages, towns and cities – communicable disease became the outsized and totally mysterious killer. Civilized living may have offered amenities unavailable in hunter-gatherer communities, but the bonuses came at a very high price as unseen microscopic adversaries made their periodic and usually lethal rounds.

Still, premature death at the hands of other humans did not abate with the rise of civilization, as time-honoured patterns of cruelty continued apace. Infants were killed or left to die with little thought or remorse until fairly recently. Murder slowly evolved from a predilection of the elite to a common man's encounter. State-sanctioned killing or warfare became more destructive as new technologies were deployed, first against armed opponents and then increasingly against civilian non-combatants. And just as twentieth-century medicine began to win significant victories in the fight against communicable disease, increasing numbers of Westerners adopted unhealthy lifestyle habits that resulted in new leading causes of death. Civilized living in consumer-oriented, market-based economies, long the envy of developing states, began to pose its own silent threats to life and limb.

Increasingly in discussions concerning death, the conclusions of the natural sciences, together with tangible efforts on the part of industrial democracies to ameliorate conditions in the present life, facilitated a broader acceptance of the view that our point of reference must be terrestrial, our final allegiance solely to one another. This will be the focus of chapter Five. The experience of two horrific world wars, and the widespread deployment of new technologies to kill combatants and civilians alike on an unprecedented scale, shattered Enlightenment assumptions about the inevitability of human progress. The decline of institutional religion in Europe was paralleled by a redoubling of efforts to extend life, to equate longevity and consumer culture with a life well lived. In the aftermath of the Second World War, death began to take its place as a medical phenomenon first and a religious event second. Indeed a death-denying culture emerged where the institutionalization of the dying in hospital and nursing homes made conversations about mortality difficult, where a youth culture made cosmetic counter-offensives against ageing a massive – and massively expensive – service industry, and where the decedent, once the battle invariably was lost, was 'handled' by a multi-billion dollar funeral industry.

Perhaps most troubling of all was that no sooner had medical interventions and pharmacology achieved unprecedented levels of success in prolonging life than issues respecting the quality of one's final days and years, together with the nature of essential personhood, became highly contested terrain. Ironically, the universally welcome advancement of science and technology complicated the moment of biological death, allowing for situations where artificial ventilation, hydration and feeding could be undertaken indefinitely. Medical ethicists, philosophers, theologians and lawyers tussled over definitions: was life delimited by functional self-sufficiency, or was it fair to conclude that if a body exhibits many of the functions of a living organism, albeit artificially maintained, it too must enjoy the moral status of full personhood? Does identity cease at a particular moment, or is the distinction between life and death really an incremental matter, a question of faint degree? Can one be allowed to die at the moment of one's choosing, or is suicide to remain an essential taboo, indeed a criminal offence?

Meanwhile, outside the industrialized West, the relatively stronger influence of the major religious systems, together with a comparative lag in development and an arguably deeper family allegiance and respect for tradition, allowed for a more widespread affirmation of a view of biological death as a mere stage in life rather than its irrevocable conclusion. But even this can be described as a matter of degree, for in the West there remain many who, having once embraced the talisman of happiness through temporal goods, have ended that fanciful quest in disappointment. Theirs is an acknowledgement not only of the limits of consumer culture, but of the fundamental mysteriousness that surrounds the death experience, an undercurrent of longing for something more intrinsic, more substantial. This non-rational sense or feeling that death is not the final act in our search for meaning, that another type of reality exists beyond the veil, continues to engage serious thinkers around the globe irrespective of religious allegiance, or the material and medical conditions that so strongly influence popular thought. The emergence of psychical research in the late nineteenth century, the controversial work of parapsychologists, recent scholarly efforts to examine the power of prayer, and research into near-death and out-of-body experiences all bespeak an ongoing resistance to the materialist finale.

Our concern with death, then, is a perpetual focus in our lives – sometimes at the forefront of our attention and sometimes in the shadows – even as we recognize that definitive, empirically verifiable answers will forever elude us. No traveller returns from Hamlet's 'undiscover'd country', but we continue to ask questions about mortality for the same reason that we engage with issues of justice and the nature of the good, seek to define beauty and the groundwork of truth. These inquiries shape our self-awareness, our responses to our environment and to one another. They help us define our humanity, direct our personal and formal relationships and set us apart from other species. Whether it be the Buddha's prelude to something greater or the philosopher Bertrand Russell's radical non-being, whether as preparation for real life or completion of the only one we shall know, the invariably personal nature of death has the potential to call each individual to greater purpose, to encounter vital meaning even in the commonplace, to live more authentically amid the disruptions and the sadness.

ONE

Preliminary Patterns

The modern human species, *Homo sapiens sapiens*, is a relative newcomer on the earth when studied in the context of the archaeological pre-human past. Our small planet has been orbiting the sun for approximately 5.4 billion years, and while the biological family *Hominidae* (proto-human) to which human beings belong may have evolutionary roots extending back some 7 million years, *Homo sapiens* did not appear much before 200,000 years ago. Coming to grips with periods of life on earth covering thousands and millions of years underlines the human adventure as a rather attenuated affair, what one anthropologist has called 'a mere geological eye-blink'.[1] But human activities and innovations, while brief thus far, have had an unprecedented impact on the natural environment. And it is this impact, even if it belies the immodest self-ascription of *sapiens* or 'wise', which helps define an explicitly human species. Our capacity to learn, to think abstractly, to transmit culture through language, our fashioning of composite tools and weapons to increase provisions and fend off enemies, the domestication of fire and its deployment in food preparation, heating and lighting, the ability to coordinate action in small groups, and the intentional inhumation of the dead, all signal *Homo sapiens*'s nascent dominion over its environment.

Each of the uniquely human skills and learned behaviours were many millennia in the making, with change imperceptible over many centuries, much less during a lifetime. Indeed 99.5 per cent of the human experience has involved a severe hunter-gatherer way of life, where small communities of 40 to 60 individuals foraged and wandered in a relentless search for sustenance and shelter. The perambulating itself was no small feat as humankind spread to almost every continent and ecosystem in fairly short order, the triggers to relocation perhaps forever beyond our ability to reconstruct. One scholar estimates that between 40,000 and 10,000 BCE 'human hunting groups occupied all the main land masses of the earth, except for Antarctica.'[2] In our complicated and stressful modern age, there is a recurring sentiment that simple foragers must have lived a more environmentally balanced and worry-free existence, with ample leisure time due to life's minimal requirements, the absence of what we might call a competitive and consumerist mentality. Nothing could be further from the truth. For although their relationship to nature was certainly more passive than ours, hunger, pain, physical conflict and material want were normative in the prolonged hand-to-mouth stage of human development.[3]

So too was the prospect of an early death from disease, physical malformation, malnutrition, natural disaster, accident or sudden trauma at the claws, jaws or hands of hostile predators, an environmental condition that still exists for most animals. Indeed early peoples may have had little awareness of the inevitability of biological breakdown and personal death, so commonplace was the death event within the context of accident or violent encounter. Examples of inter-group conflict and personal hostility have been identified in a variety of hunter-gatherer cultures. Australian Aborigines, for example, numbered some 300,000 before the arrival of the first European settlers in 1788, but archaeologists have no doubt that there had been violent death on the continent for millennia. According to one recent scholar, 'fighting scenes with the whole range of armament are extensively depicted in Aboriginal rock art dating back at least 10,000 years.'[4] Among the Yanomamo peoples who inhabit the forests on the border of Brazil and Venezuela, 30 per cent of all deaths among adult males have been attributed to violence. Modern anthropological studies of the nomadic !Kung San peoples (formerly called Bushmen) of southern Africa serve to illustrate another type of sudden violent death. For the !Kung the necessity of carrying all one's possessions after food sources in a particular area had been exhausted had a direct impact on child-bearing patterns. A woman can carry one child along with her possessions, but not two, thus a second pregnancy is postponed until the first child can walk. If an infant is deformed at birth, it becomes the mother's duty to smother it, the act unrelated to infanticide as understood in modern sedentary society.[5] In this case ending another's life is viewed as an unfortunate but necessary social good, a requirement for the continued well-being of the able-bodied. To take an additional instance, it is widely recognized that in most hunter-gatherer societies the practice of female infanticide was similarly equated with overall survival strategy, as parents more readily dispensed with those who were less skilled at hunting and fighting, those less able to support the community.

Our modern luxury – or burden – of recognizing death as inescapable and having time to prepare for it in senescence was unavailable to most of our earliest predecessors. Today the majority of dying people in developed societies are to varying degrees attentive to their fate prior to the final stages of bodily decay. They make wills and sign advanced medical directives, dispose of their property in an orderly manner and conclude their remaining social obligations, all in full awareness of their impending demise.[6] Our earliest ancestors departed without any such formal closure. The now-famous Ötzi 'The Iceman', discovered by climbers in 1991 in the Tyrolean Alps bordering Italy and Austria, died alone from massive bleeding caused by a single flint-tipped arrow some 5,000 years ago.[7] There were additional wounds on his hands, head and chest, but it was the flint blade, clearly the result of some chance violent confrontation, that ended his life in the frozen landscape. The seventeenth-century English philosopher Thomas Hobbes famously described life prior to the advent of civil society as 'solitary, poor, nasty, brutish, and short'.[8] Making allowance for an element of smugness given the relative comfort of his own socio-economic setting, and removing 'solitary' from the mix, Hobbes could be speaking for the better part of the human experience over many millennia. Unhappily, we humans have always been rather adept at taking each other's lives.

Before History

What our earliest ancestors made of the death event is hard to conclude in any detail, for what the archaeological record provides is at best the physical remains and possible beliefs of a small and relatively privileged elite. At some point in human evolution, perhaps very early on, the individual drive to build alliances with others for mutual protection evolved into a deeper social behaviour, the need for emotional bonds with others across a range of human activities. The desire to be valued by those whom we value began to make its way into consciousness and gradually became a crucial factor in human flourishing. Once this band of emotional connection was in place, a subsequent step was taken, unique to humans, in striving for relationship beyond the temporal arena and into the realm of what we would describe as religious imagination or transcendent meaning-making. In a world filled with unknowns, with daily natural terrors and multiple threats to life and limb, the drive to control one's environment led to the need to feel prized at a level beyond immediate family and community. Relationships with the sacred, whether under the heading of non-physical beings or forces, met this need.[9]

Of course human beings are not alone in their awareness of mortality. The variety of defensive postures employed by other animals when threatened indicates a rudimentary recognition that life can be brought to a close very quickly by unfriendly forces. The dependent young among chimpanzees are known to become listless after the death of their mothers, while African elephants will stop before the carcass of one of their own and reach out to touch the body with their trunks.[10] And *Homo neanderthalensis*, a species contemporary with *Homo sapiens* until the former mysteriously vanished around 30,000 years ago, appear at least in some cases to have buried their dead with signs of honour. The construction and positioning of the body in the grave, the placing of artefacts and the arrangement of stones around the place of burial are all distinct.[11] What sets us apart, it seems, are the more sophisticated cognitive and linguistic abilities that allow us to anticipate, reflect on and ascribe some form of higher meaning to death.[12] This can be seen in Palaeolithic or Old Stone Age cultures (from approximately 90,000 to 10,000 BCE), where death could rarely be anticipated, but where funerary rites of some sort were not uncommon, indicating the initial emergence of what historian J. M. Roberts called 'one of the greatest and most enduring myths, that life is an illusion, that reality lies invisible elsewhere, that things are not what they seem'.[13]

Concern for the dignified internment of one's beloved, a practice archaeologists tell us began no more than 130,000 years ago, does not always afford us reliable evidence about early beliefs. Spectacular burial finds at Sunghir some 120 miles northwest of Moscow and from Dolni Vestonice in the Czech Republic dating back to approximately 28,000 BCE reveal human remains strategically placed and adorned with beads, pins, shells, pendants, daggers and other artefacts. At both locations there was great care taken in the disposal and provision of certain bodies, implying that the afterlife must be prepared for, but whether this reflects any deeper position on the nature of that afterlife remains unclear.[14] Indeed most archaeologists are quick to caution against inferring too many ideas from objects, especially when those objects are both few and perhaps unrepresentative of the wider material culture.[15]

Even with these important caveats, however, anthropological study can both enrich and complicate efforts to understand the billions who lived and died before the advent of writing. Recent investigations of hunter-gatherers in Africa, for example, suggest that in some cases burial practice is related to social custom and not to specific belief in an afterlife for the deceased. A 1990s study of the Hadza people of northern Tanzania found that death was accepted as a matter of course and burial rites were simple. There was no period of mourning in the aftermath of a death since the event had no supernatural consequences for the living. The spiritual existence of the person, it appears, ended with its biological demise.[16] Studies of some North American hunting tribes reveal a similar perspective on death as a normal part of life, to be faced without fear.[17] But even when our earliest ancestors did affirm that the deceased would remain in communion with the living and with the gods, as in the case of the Yombe of northern Zambia, we have no way of knowing whether the sequel to this temporal passage was thought to be qualitatively superior to the myriad pains and terrors, the repeated failures, of human existence.[18]

What we can say is that belief in continuity, whenever such belief began, was a demonstration of the growing power of the human mind to formulate anthropomorphic parables around a non-sensory reality, a discarnate state, a life beyond appearances that negates the finality of death. It was also testimony to the deep concern of those who remained behind for the fate of the deceased as they passed across death's threshold. As the Spanish academic Miguel de Unamuno cleverly remarked over 80 years ago: 'Stone was used for sepulchers before it was used for houses.'[19] And the placement of artefacts in some of those graves, including food, clothing and other personal belongings, suggests to some archaeologists and anthropologists that belief in an afterlife involved some type of journey analogous to our earthly one. A number of Palaeolithic cave paintings discovered in western Europe (the most famous at Lascaux in southwestern France) indicate a certain degree of trust in death as another form of existence, where the process of dying actually continues in an afterlife adventure or trial that can be assisted by those who are still alive and who remember their absent kin.[20] That assistance could come in the form of the art object itself, which may have been designed with the goal of influencing or manipulating magical or religious powers.

Modern anthropologists have inferred from figures wearing animal masks in some of the cave paintings that a shaman elite may have acted as intermediary between humans and the spirit world, with the latter located somewhere between the living and the larger divine forces. Indeed some scholars have attributed the origins of the whole religious enterprise to a concern for the fate of those who have died, a series of cults dedicated to the service of the departed. At the very least, cave art demonstrates the extraordinary ability of early humans to think symbolically and act beyond the observable world. Whether the overwhelming majority who died and whose physical remains have disappeared ever shared in the exercise of these budding intellectual powers cannot be determined. But it is apparent that theirs was a more egalitarian death overall, occurring within small communities that lacked the type of sharp social and economic stratification we associate with sedentary civilizations. And as those foraging communities journeyed from the place of death in their unending search of food, the dead were left behind, solitary at last, accompanied in their anonymity only by the sounds and echoes of nature.

The Proximate Dead: Agricultural Society

With the retreat of the last Ice Age around 13,000–10,000 BCE, the first great lifestyle change in human history took place. The domestication of plants and animal husbandry occurred just as a changing climate adversely affected the availability of big game animals favoured by hunter-gatherers. Made possible by the inventive and conceptualizing powers of the human brain, the agricultural revolution, which involved forcing nature to yield more in one place over an extended period of time, appears to have developed first in certain areas of Asia Minor and the Middle East, often called the 'Fertile Crescent', before spreading or emerging autonomously elsewhere around the globe. This so-called Neolithic or New Stone Age period ushered in a sedentary village lifestyle, complete with the introduction of personal property, the division of labour, permanent dwellings, pottery to store and cook agricultural produce, and more durable and sophisticated tools to cultivate the soil.

The transition from hunter-gatherer to agriculturalist took place over centuries (a process rather than an event) and involved a novel emphasis on the management of resources and shared labour, an understanding of social relations where the highly individualized skills of the hunter were replaced by the need for planning and collaboration on a wide scale. Tree felling, stone clearing, planting, cultivating and harvesting were labour-intensive group endeavours. The social structure included new distinctions between the producers of food, those engaged in specialized crafts and tool-making, and political and religious leaders who wielded control over the general population. By the mid-second millennium BCE changes in land tenure and agricultural practice, including the advent of field systems and boundaries, forwarded the notion of place-bound identity at the level of household and family. It also made possible a dramatic upsurge in human numbers and required the development of more complex social relationships and organizations. One historian estimates that the world's population stood at 5–8 million in the millennia preceding the adoption of agriculture.[21] By 4000 BCE the total had expanded to between 60 and 70 million – and most of these lived in agricultural settings where nomadic notions of freedom and equality had been exchanged (or forcibly withdrawn) in return for the promise of greater security and sustenance.

A village-based peasantry initially grouped into clans or extended families that believed they had a common ancestor, or tribes comprising a number of clans, soon emerged as one of the most important cultural types in the history of world civilizations, comprising between 80 and 90 per cent of the entire global population well into the modern era.[22] As they took shape, settled communities around the world began to adopt religious ideas involving reverence for ancestors and the forces of nature. They also began the construction of religious monuments and legitimized a core of religious experts who served as official intermediaries. Finally, they began to bury their loved ones nearby and experienced a strong presence of the dead among the living that probably involved the conviction that the deceased remained involved in community affairs.

The earliest known example of a settled community comes from people known as the Natufians, who lived in the area of modern Israel, Jordan and Syria about 15,000–11,500 years ago. They gathered and stored wild wheat and barley, employing stone sickles to harvest the cereal grasses. Burial locations indicate the emergence of a ruling elite as about 10 per cent of the known sites contain decorative shells and pendants. Bodies were adorned with necklaces, bracelets and shell headdresses. The Natufians also began a practice that would later become typical of Neolithic burials: the skulls of the deceased were separated from the body before burial, covered with plaster and kept in the homes of descendants.[23] This practice (and the emergence of a place-based ancestor cult) can again be seen at Jericho, dating from around 11,000 to 9300 BCE, where the skulls of the deceased, complete with new faces made of plaster and eyes of seashells, shared the domestic living space of their descendants over several generations.[24]

Sedentism led to the multiplication of certain plants and animals while others were displaced, thus reducing biological diversity within the village and local setting. In addition to new work routines associated with farming, constant vigilance was required to protect precious livestock and food supplies from human predators, whose lightning attacks would intensify during periods of shortage and famine.[25] Substituting animal for human power after the invention of the plough around 3000 BCE enhanced productivity in Europe and the Middle East, but sedentism also brought with it much higher levels of infectious and parasitic diseases as humans began living in close proximity to domesticated animals. Measles, malaria, diphtheria, tuberculosis and dysentery all emerged as significant threats to humans. Malnutrition was another great killer for peasants whose modest agricultural surplus and narrow diet was often expropriated by elites and/or invaders. So too was famine, the result of natural weather disasters, including drought and flood, adversely affecting the relatively smaller range of foodstuffs available. Together these new variables in mortality made it possible for people to anticipate death and prepare for their biological ending. Dying was no longer linked to a process that continued in the next world and instead became a major personal and social event in the present one. The dying person could to some extent arrange for death as an episode in the larger cycle of nature, in a world where material progress was neither anticipated nor experienced.[26]

In time the agricultural surpluses of small villages made possible the emergence of large urban centres, a stratified social system that led to greater inequalities and exploitation, and governing elites who exempted themselves from physical labour to concentrate on civil, military and religious matters. The latter tended to focus on the relationship between divine forces and the cycle of sowing and reaping. And with larger populations concentrated in more densely inhabited areas, the incidence of lethal disease and death, not to mention the vulnerability of sedentary people to external human predators, increased proportionally. Burial grounds gained increased prominence as urban life now made proximity between the living and the dead a lifelong possibility. In southern Britain between 3500 and 2000 BCE, for example, over 200 long barrows were constructed to house the remains of an estimated 1,500–3,000 individuals.[27] As suggested above, this physical proximity of the deceased to the living allowed for a deeper sense that one's ancestors remained somehow in touch with and concerned for the fate of the wider community.

One of the more complex of these early urban sites was at Çatalhöyük in central Turkey, first discovered by archaeologists in the late 1950s. During its peak between around 7400 BCE and 6000 BCE, this remarkable settlement spread over 30 acres and accommodated between 6,000 and 8,000 inhabitants. They grew wheat, barley, lentils and peas, and they were herdsmen. Architecturally independent mud-brick houses were clustered together and featured living quarters and storage spaces that were accessible solely by ladder from the rooftops. Of particular interest to us is the fact that most residences served a dual purpose, providing shelter for the living and a resting place for the departed. The bodies of the dead were wrapped in reed mats and interred beneath the hearths and beds of the main living space, strongly suggesting some form of belief in an ongoing connection across the generations. Archaeologists have identified the remains of as many as 62 people from the excavation of one house.

As in the earlier examples from Jericho, the proximity of the dead to the living in domestic quarters may have been related to labour-intensive seasonal planting and harvesting, where the living could call upon the assistance or good favour of the deceased. At any rate, the physical proximity of the corpse with the living community appears to have been a commonplace from the advent of the agricultural revolution up until the late nineteenth century. Also surviving at Çatalhöyük are a number of small figurines that may have been associated with formal religious beliefs, but as yet no evidence of temples or other communal worship buildings has been found. The proximity of the deceased to the living indicates that survivors may have had an important role to play in the quality of the otherworldly journey undertaken by the dead. What activities and rituals may have been associated with the work of assisting the dead in their journey is unknown, but final goodbyes, it appears, were rather extended affairs.[28]

Not every ancient village-based society felt the need to ensure physical proximity of the dead with the living. Rudimentary notions of the potential health risks of being adjacent to decaying corpses may have informed alternative practices. For example, in one area of pre-Roman Denmark (around 500 BCE), 160 settlements and 300 cemeteries have been excavated, yielding strong evidence of a cultural pattern more familiar to the modern experience. Here, in southern Jutland, inhabitants lived in wooden longhouses complete with separate areas for domesticated animals. The deceased were cremated and the ashes were placed in pots that were buried in cemeteries located between 300 and 900 metres from the settlements. In one-third of the burials, the cremated remains were buried within or adjacent to earlier burial mounds dating back to 1700–1200 BCE. Few grave goods accompanied the dead. Yet another pattern has been identified by archaeologists in Britain, where farming people near Haddenham in Cambridgeshire first buried and then periodically rearranged the larger bones of the deceased in a mound-type communal tomb. The bones had been separated from the corpses that perhaps had been exposed to scavengers before interment in the communal charnel house. What such burial practices meant to those who carried them out, and what it meant for notions of personal or collective identity after death, remains a mystery.[29]

One possible answer comes from the archaeologist Timothy Taylor who reminds us that whenever humans first formulated the idea that a person is composed of both material and spiritual elements, they believed that the animating force or soul remained active after death, struggling to reassert its earthly prerogatives, at least as long as flesh lay on the bones. This disembodied soul was viewed as dangerous by the living while the body remained intact, thus the incentive to accelerate its decomposition through exposure or burning. Proper disposal of the body and accompanying ritual practices kept the soul at bay, until such time as the bones were white and the spirit could make its final transition to the otherworld, the realm of the ancestors. Ancient burial practice, then, was as much about protection for the living as it was about respect for the deceased; proper procedure in handling the corpse deflected the power of malevolent spirits, unprovoked harm from unseen quarters. When the bones were placed and later rearranged in the communal burial mound at Haddenham, the culmination of the death experience – the departure of the souls – had been accomplished.[30]

Neolithic peoples reserved their greatest architectural talents for the benefit of the dead. In the community's efforts to maintain a connection with deceased family and tribal members, human remains were located in communal tombs adjacent to the agricultural land that was worked by the living. These chambered tombs or cairns, constructed of stone, turf, timber and earth, were important features of the landscape throughout the British Isles beginning as early as 4000 BCE.[31] Ireland hosts the greatest concentration of these tombs from the early Neolithic period (c. 4000–3200 BCE), followed by sites in Wales and southeast Scotland. In Ireland the tombs range widely from simple stone tripods with capstones called Dolmens to massive passage graves containing multiple burial chambers. The latter is in dramatic evidence along the Boyne river valley, north of present-day Dublin in County Meath. In this rather compact area a highly organized, if still largely rural, society emerged, its leadership capable of marshalling a very substantial labour force that was employed in the construction of megalithic (large stone) passage-graves like Newgrange, carbon dated to approximately 3200 BCE.[32]

Passage tombs were built in many parts of western Europe during the Neolithic age, but the Newgrange site undoubtedly is one of the most impressive. Here and at the nearby mausolea of Dowth and Knowth, a characteristic narrow passageway leads into a central chamber, the whole covered by a circular mound or cairn. Inside the main chamber sculptors were set to work enhancing the abode of the dead with geometric and non-representational figures that were most likely symbolic and magico-religious in purpose. The ancestors were thought to be essential to the success of the harvest and the security of the tribal community from hostile neighbours. Archaeologist Jacquetta Hawkes memorably compared the construction of Newgrange with the building of a great medieval cathedral. Whole communities were involved in the project at different times throughout the year and over many years. There would be gangs of unskilled labourers dragging megaliths from long distances, while others carried the smaller stones and timber that served as key building materials for the cairn. The skilled masons, sculptors and their apprentices may have been supervised in their work of cutting sacred motifs by social and religious leaders, the act of cutting the stone a sort of sacred operation not unlike the celebration of the Eucharist in the Roman Catholic tradition. The great burial chamber at Newgrange speaks of the extent of surplus energy available to this agricultural society, the high level of artistic skill practised by a select few, and the perennial human craving to make life meaningful by securing a lasting connection with the ancestors.

Transition to Civilization

Preceded by small groups of herders and tillers, then by farming villages that produced modest agricultural surpluses, the genuinely complex, resource-dependent and socially stratified urban societies that must qualify as the first civilizations emerged around 3500–3200 BCE along the Nile in middle and lower Egypt and between the Tigris and Euphrates in Mesopotamia, while comparable transitions took place in the Indus River Valley by 2500 BCE, in China's Yellow River basin by 2000–1500 BCE, and in Meso-America after 1500 BCE. In each of these settings, favoured by climate and an abundance of native species of plants and animals, ambitious societies organized large labour resources to build rural irrigation networks, develop urban environments with monumental (often funerary) architecture and free a minority elite of artists, scholars, priests and temporal rulers for the specialized work of organizing and protecting large populations.

This combination signalled a dramatic new stage in cultural evolution that continues to this day. Viewed in the context of what some scholars call 'big history' or the human experience during the multiple millennia prior to the advent of written records, civilization is a novel and perhaps futile experiment, the inaugural step in what has become an interminable effort to manipulate and master nature for human purposes, to bring to a close humankind's evolutionary adaptation to environment. The quest, or what one recent historian has called 'humanity's most radical act', continues today, but with the very real possibility of mastery resulting in irreversible ecological breakdown, a type of lengthy suicide as its unintended consequence.[33]

The Elusive Eternal in Mesopotamia

In some respects, the successful emergence of the first civilization in the area the Greeks called Mesopotamia, or land 'between rivers', is surprising. With little rainfall and few natural resources like stone, metal ores or wood, and subject to periodic invasion and migration across open frontiers, the region seems an unlikely candidate for civilized living. But the process of remodelling nature better to serve human purposes in Sumer, the southernmost area of present-day Iraq, was made possible by an abundance of rich soil deposited and renewed by the flooding of the Tigris and Euphrates rivers. Harvests were plentiful in this relatively flat alluvial plain as long as the rivers, prone to unpredictable flooding, were managed appropriately. Carefully constructed and diligently maintained irrigation networks enabled farmers to cultivate crops at significant distances from the rivers. Sailing vessels and wheeled vehicles facilitated long-range movement of food surpluses and supplies.

Not surprisingly, religious ideas centring on the forces of nature took shape just as efforts began to organize the physical environment for human comfort. Indeed the earliest Sumerian managerial elite may have consisted of experts in the supernatural, priests who interpreted the will of the gods and directed the population in pleasing – and appeasing – divine forces. By 2800 BCE, the southern region contained a number of cities, each with a stepped temple, or ziggurat, and its own local god who delegated day-to-day authority to the theocratic priest/ruler. We know this thanks in part to the invention of a system of writing called cuneiform that modern scholars can understand, providing rich new source materials that deepen our knowledge of the ancient peoples who inhabited the lower reaches of Mesopotamia.[34]

In these written remains the myriad gods of the indigenous people appear as personified aspects of nature, and as such often behave in a contrarian, hostile and capricious manner. The unpredictable and irregular flooding of the Tigris and Euphrates, for example, was interpreted as a direct manifestation of divine power, contributing to what some have interpreted as a generally gloomy, nihilistic outlook on life. Transmission of disease parasites in the warm and shallow water of irrigated land and the resultant sickness and death did not improve matters. The pre-eminent deity, Anu, or god of the sky, was thought to assemble the great gods annually to decide what would transpire in the year to follow, with Enlil, god of storm and thunder, serving as the chief executor of the majority will. Individual gods were thought of in anthropomorphic terms, living in a house or temple and inhabiting a cult statue much as a person's soul was located in the body. Priests, or *ensi*, were charged with interpreting signs and omens respecting the will of a particular god, and with supervising the formal rituals and festivals associated with the care of the deity. The Mesopotamian universe was therefore unpredictable but self-contained; every occurrence in nature, disaster as well as delight, was explicable in terms of divine, if rather unholy, action. For over 3,000 years this dynamic understanding of reality guided the lives of rich and poor alike, and the appeal of their cosmology reached well beyond the flat plain bordering the Persian Gulf to inform the outlook of their neighbours east and west.[35] The genocidal flood story which appears so prominently in the later Hebrew Bible, for example, has its roots in Mesopotamian religious writing.

The first Sumerian cities were largely autonomous, and disputes involving water rights and the need for coordinated defence against hostile outsiders were brokered by the priestly elite, most likely meeting at the host city's temple. In some of the private houses graves were located below the floors and contained the remains of inhabitants who were singled out for special treatment. Affirming the fact of social inequality, many of the dead were buried with abundant grave wares, including cloths, ornaments, tools and weapons that were probably designed to aid them in the other world. Royal burials affirmed the authority and dignity of the king, and in some cases servants and attendants were buried nearby in accompanying chambers. Each person had a soul, but at death it would leave the body and relocate to a dismal underworld. Early Sumerian texts describe the afterlife as a place of darkness bereft of pleasures, and while it is impossible to draw conclusions about the beliefs within wider society, for some, either informed by religious belief or enabled by affluence, it was deemed important to make the journey fully equipped.[36]

As the wealth of the cities increased, so too did rivalries and the need for security in a region where there were no naturally defensible borders. The rise of consolidated kingship after 2500 BCE may have been the result of the growing militarization of cities that found it increasingly difficult to defend their land and assets. The kingdom of Kush enjoyed supremacy before 2500 BCE; the dynasty of Sargon prevailed around 2350 BCE; and the empire of Hammurabi of Babylon emerged after 1800 BCE. All substantiated their authority through innovations like written laws and official bureaucracies that included regional judges, tax collectors and military officers, but in the end none of these states lasted for more than a century before succumbing to external attackers, internal corruption or a toxic combination of the two.[37]

One of the best-known rulers was the semi-legendary hero-king Gilgamesh, ruler of the city of Uruk around 2700 BCE, but known effectively through what is arguably the oldest story in the world, written down some time after 2000 BCE. In it the hero, who seems to be a rather oppressive ruler, loses his rival-turned-best-friend Enkidu, with whom he had shared many bold adventures, some in defiance of the gods. After choosing friendship with Enkidu over the love offered by the goddess Ishtar, Gilgamesh is punished by being made to watch helplessly as his friend dies from an illness sent by the gods. The shock of this death sets Gilgamesh on a lonely quest for eternal life. At one point in his journey he questions Utnapishtim, who was granted immortality because he saved a representative of all living creatures from a great flood. Utnapishtim will not divulge the secret of eternal life, but his wife tells Gilgamesh about a miraculous plant that restores youth to anyone who consumes it. He locates the plant, but a great snake steals it from him during the journey home. It is the barmaid Siduri who reminds the hero that his quest is futile:

> Gilgamesh, wherefore do you wander?
> The eternal life you are seeking you shall not find.
> When the gods created mankind,
> They established death for mankind,
> And withheld eternal life for themselves.[38]

In the end, a chastened but wiser Gilgamesh returns to his home city of Urek and takes some consolation in pointing to his accomplishments as a temporal king, a type of metaphorical immortality. The *Epic of Gilgamesh* details an all-too-recognizable world of misfortune, where once-confident people devolve into fearful supplicants, where selfish gods take little notice of humans except to demand from them altars abundantly stocked with offerings. *Gilgamesh* is representative of a culture that believed immortality was reserved for these self-important and unpleasant gods. For humans, unhappily, there was no reward in the afterlife for earthly deeds, even the most heroic ones. Enkidu dreams of a house:

> . . . whence none who enters comes forth,
> On the road from which there is no way back,
> To the house whose dwellers are deprived of light,
> Where dust is their fare and their food is clay.[39]

Enkidu's deathbed vision of the underworld outlines a shadowy netherworld where even kings and priests languish without hope, eating dust and clay. To what degree the Mesopotamian environ-ment – subject to sandstorms and flooding, intercity strife and assault by outsiders – contributed to this dour outlook is a matter of some debate in scholarly circles. The experience of physical insecurity, as we shall see elsewhere, could also engender a strong belief in the prospect of justice and reward in the next life. But whatever the combination of factors that shaped the outlook of humanity's first civilization on the subject of death and the afterlife, the final product seems to have been rather severe.[40]

Egypt: Death as a Stage in Life

As in Mesopotamia, geography was crucial to the remarkable polit-ical and cultural longevity of ancient Egypt. Sheltered from potential enemies by the Mediterranean to the north and by mountains and deserts on its flanks, Egypt enjoyed extraordinary wealth, peace and stability for more than three millennia. In a manner that runs counter to modern notions regarding the importance of inter-national engagement to national affluence, Egypt's relative insular-ity over many centuries was key to its economic and political prowess. To live and die in Egypt was the aspiration of every inhabit-ant, and there seems to have been a concern that those who died outside the kingdom were denied the possibility of an afterlife. The kingdom's plentiful agriculture, made possible by a favourable cli-mate and the rich alluvial soil of the Nile valley, and the regularity with which the river flooded and replenished that soil, contributed not only to multiple harvests of grains, fruits and vegetables each year, but also to a deep sense of permanence and divine favour within the culture.[41] So too did ease of transportation on the world's longest river, where southward travel was aided by prevailing winds from the north and passage north was driven by the river's normal current. From the first cataract in the south of the country to the Mediterranean this waterway was unimpeded, and with a fertile valley no more than 12 miles across at its widest, the river outlined a long green ribbon of civilization where 95 per cent of the population lived. So important was this sliver of arable land that the Egyptians buried their dead in the sandy deserts to the west, where the sun descended each evening after its journey through a cloudless sky.[42]

The Greek historian Herodotus, visiting Egypt in the fifth century BCE – some two millennia after the largest pyramids were constructed – appropriately described the land as 'the gift of the Nile'. This generally supportive environment may in part explain Egyptian culture's more sanguine outlook on life and hope for new life after death. It certainly makes understandable the Egyptian tendency to associate the gods with natural forces like earth, sky, air and water. The 'gift' of the Nile was not gratis, however. Although Egyptians had domesticated plants and animals as early as 5000 BCE, villages that relied on agricultural surpluses did not emerge until around 3500 BCE. Agricultural productivity required constant labour, especially as it related to the manipulation of nature with large and complicated irrigation networks. And coordinated labour in turn required strong leaders and constant appeasement of the gods who in the end were believed to control nature and provide justice. Hundreds of gods and goddesses existed in the Egyptian pantheon, many of them depicted as animals, humans or a hybrid of the two. Different places evolved different cults, nurtured and sustained by a hereditary priestly class.

The resident god on earth and chief lawgiver was the king or pharaoh (meaning 'great house'), who guaranteed order, or *ma'at*, through his monopoly over coercive power and his strict adherence to a ritualized and symbolic lifestyle.[43] It was not until about 3100 BCE that Menes, king of Upper Egypt, conquered the delta region and unified the country, but the dynastic system proved its durability over many centuries, interrupted only by brief periods of instability. Unlike the quarrelsome and distant gods of Mesopotamia, Egyptians were privileged with a god among them on earth who was committed to maintaining balance and order. So absolute was royal power that ancient Egypt never developed a written, impersonal code of laws. The will of pharaoh was deemed sufficient in every instance, while a large bureaucracy served in various capacities to oversee religious ceremonies, organize defences, maintain written records and supervise extensive public works projects.[44]

The monumental tombs of the pharaohs of the Old Kingdom (2700–2200 BCE) provide multiple examples of the close relationship between life and death in this culture. Identifying themselves with Ra, the sun god who travelled through the underworld at night fighting evil spirits, or with Horus, the sky god who was always depicted as having the head of a falcon, pharaohs carefully planned their resting places, and worshipful subjects carried out their arrangements with skill and deliberation. During the Middle Kingdom period (2052–1786 BCE), funerary rites for a pharaoh took upwards of 70 days to complete.[45]

Every aspect of life, it seems, was organized around the knowledge of death and confidence in an afterlife. The elaborate practice of mummification, where internal organs were removed and preserved in jars while the corpse was dried, bandaged and dipped in pitch before entombment, offered compelling evidence for a materially oriented view of the next life, albeit one in which the person is transformed. Egyptians held that the ka, or vital essence of a person, lived on only if the body was preserved.[46] The earliest pyramids (of around 2550 BCE) were used exclusively as royal tombs, but the process of construction involved thousands in the work of preparing pharaoh for an appropriate afterlife. Pyramid building was both the product of conscript labour and a collective act of fidelity to the god-king. Many of the pyramids include a spiral ascending staircase, whereby pharaoh 'stepped' into heaven. According to historian Alan Segal, 'The association of heaven with immortality is uniquely an Egyptian invention, occurring many millennia before it becomes part of Biblical or Greek tradition.'[47]

While the great majority of Egyptians lacked the fiscal resources for tombs and elaborate burial ceremonies, the practice of mummification extended widely and the prospect of immortality was not restricted to the elite.[48] The heart was considered to be the most important organ, the physical location of the soul and spirit, the essential core of individuality. In Egyptian mythology, it was believed that after death every person would receive judgement before Osiris, the great fertility god of the Nile who himself had experienced death and resurrection. Murdered by his evil brother Set, who cut the victim's body into pieces and scattered them around the kingdom, Osiris's widow Isis gathered them up and wrapped them in linen. Restored to life, Osiris became for Egyptians the god of the dead, who judged all persons at the time of death. Now the heart was weighed on a scale against the feather of *ma'at*. A balancing of the scales for a soul free of sin meant an afterlife of happiness and contentment, while a negative assessment resulted in abandonment to the god-destroyer Attim who was part crocodile, part hippopotamus. To be devoured by Attim meant total annihilation, a second death that was anathema to every Egyptian. Texts known as the *Book of the Dead*, containing prayers and incantations designed to assist the deceased in the journey and examination to come, have been discovered in numerous tombs. Communication with the dead was possible at the grave site and family members would assemble there to share a meal, to converse among themselves and to leave letters with the deceased.[49] Egyptian society may have been highly stratified, but death became the great equalizer as the future life was to be shared by nobles, priests and peasants alike.

Beyond the West

The Body and Death in South America

The Egyptians were not the first to practise mummification. As early as 5000 BCE the Chinchorro people, groups of sedentary fishers who lived along the coast of the arid desert region of northern Chile, were engaging in elaborate techniques whose goal was to maintain bodily integrity after death. Archaeological work began here in the early twentieth century, and extensive excavations in 1983 provided researchers with almost 100 mummies. These latter discoveries spurred a wave of intensive research into the meaning behind Chinchorro burial practice. Intentionally slowing the process of putrefaction seems to have been an exercise unrelated to social status in this culture, with infants, young children and even miscarried foetuses included. The work itself involved skilled labour, ample time and a detailed knowledge of anatomy. The process included the removal of skin, organs and soft tissue, the reinforcing of the bones with sticks and the stuffing of the body with animal hair and grass. Such complex treatment in what was an otherwise technologically simple society suggests that a very powerful belief system informed these efforts.[50]

But what were these beliefs? Did the practice of mummification involve the spiritual needs of the living, the dead, or both? Was the practice a way of healing the community after the chain of life had been broken or was it designed to leverage the assistance of the dead in the ongoing work of the family and the larger society? The remains of food and fishing materials alongside some of the mummified remains point towards belief in an afterlife journey, but without a written language, it is impossible to say with any certainty.[51]

Allied Notions in Sub-Saharan Africa

Egypt is but one, albeit the best known, of the ancient African cultures. Prominent in the northeast corner of the expansive continent, its dependence upon the Nile precluded easy export of its culture to the south. But it is to the south that most archaeologists turn to find the earliest evidence of the evolution and spread of humanity to other continents. Unlike their neighbours in the Near East and in the northwest corner of the continent, however, most African peoples continued to follow the rhythms of a hunter-gatherer lifestyle long after the Chinese, the Indians and the inhabitants of southwest Asia had transitioned to sedentary practices and created formal, territorial states. The reasons for the divergence are still debated, but there is little question that climate, or what some refer to as ecological determinism, had its role to play. Around the time that Egyptians were adopting agriculture (around 3000 BCE), the Saharan region still supported people who grazed cattle, sheep and goats. What was once a flourishing savannah region began its gradual conversion to forbidding desert in the following centuries, creating a geographical divide between north and south.[52] More than half the land mass south of the desert remained grassy plains known as savannah, while about one-tenth was equatorial jungle.

Here in the mineral-rich but soil-poor sub-Sahara a hunting and foraging lifestyle predominated, although pastoralism and agriculture did emerge in areas with sufficient rainfall.[53] With torrential rains causing erosion and scorching heat robbing the soil of nutrients, many farming communities practised a form of 'slash and burn' agriculture, which obliged them to move to a new location every few years. Despite the constant movement, the emergence of a wide range of socio-linguistic and ethnic groups, and the framing of a host of cosmological world views, it is possible to identify within this great diversity some shared cultural ideals and common threads in respect to death.

Written sources, of course, do not exist until the modern period, but the regionally based oral traditions, the stories and myths transmitted across the generations, all seem to recount some version of human transgression as the origin of mortality. The immediate cause of death can often be connected with an act of sorcery or witchcraft, retribution on the part of spirits who held a grudge against the victim, or the failure of the victim to fulfil an oath. The Fang people of modern Cameroon and Gabon, for instance, affirm that witches and ghost ancestors live among them and are apt to inflict great suffering.[54] Physical illness may appear as the proximate cause of death, but the underlying source more often involved indirect human or spiritual agency. In light of such beliefs, traditional African societies welcomed the services of diviners and medicine men who could expose the perpetrator and restore relations with the intermediate divinities and the high god.[55] The former were thought to be active in the affairs of the living and were situated to appeal before the supreme deity.

Most basic to ancient sub-Saharan African cultures was the widely accepted idea that all of life, human and non-human, was interdependent and commonly owned by a transcendent power. Maintaining the proper relationships between humankind and other created beings brought forward the prospect of a good death at the appropriate time. The Yoruba people of present-day Nigeria, for example, seek to return to the comfort of heaven after death because it is here alone that relationships can become permanent.

For the Yoruba, three criteria must be met before entry into heaven can be secured: the deceased must be at least 40 years of age, as longevity was associated with a moral life; burial must take place in the earthen floor of the ancestral home; and the death must be natural and accompanied by the appropriate rites.[56] Irrespective of regional variations like this one, most sub-Saharan Africans took care to develop funeral and mortuary rites that would ease one's safe passage into what virtually all accepted was the reality of a dynamic afterlife.

Successful passage assured community contact with the 'living dead', a world of identity with one's remembered ancestors. Lacking this safe passage, the deceased was relegated to 'an invisible world of lost beings and spirits without individual identity and recognition'.[57] Festivals, most religious rituals and rites of passage all constituted the nexus between the living, ancestors and the lost spirits. Carefully planned and carried out, rituals affirmed the community's ongoing need for the assistance of the deceased. Once the living dead passed beyond the memory of a new generation, the process of dying was complete. At this point the living dead became part of a collective immortality, a community of spirits without personal communication with living families. Here was their final status, their designated function in a more comprehensive cosmology.[58]

A distinctive view of death as a twice-occurring progression through life comes to us from a contemporary anthropological study of the Mende people of Sierra Leone in west Africa. Rice-growing villagers, they believe in the existence of a high god, numerous minor spirits and the continuity of their ancestors. The first death for the Mende is a social construction and occurs when male and female initiates into the culture's secret associations are taken from their families to enter the realm of the spirits. Social personhood takes place after separation from the community for several months and rigorous training in the skills of adulthood. During this period the youngster is considered to be dead, swallowed by the spirit of the secret association. Rebirth occurs when the initiate is reunited with his or her community. The second, or biological death, signals the transition to the familiar ancestor status where the deceased re-engages with dead relatives and continues his or her concern for and engagement with the living.[59] The transition is facilitated by observance of the proper burial or death rituals, the neglect of which can lead to an afterlife in which the departed becomes a wandering ghost, disgruntled and eager to visit misfortune on the living.

The Ancestral Way in Early China

The agricultural revolution began in China during the fifth millennium BCE along the Yellow River, where the climate was much milder than it is today. The earliest villages were located in isolated clearings along the slopes of the river valley.[60] Some of the best archaeological evidence of early sedentary life in China comes from Yangshao in Henan Province. First excavated in the 1920s, Yangshao culture dates from around 5000–3000 BCE. The inhabitants lived in wattle and daub pit dwellings, cultivated millet, wheat and rice and domesticated pigs, dogs and goats. A defensive earthen wall and moat surrounds the residential part of the village where grain was stored in a series of underground pits, suggesting that communal defence was a priority.

With respect to mortuary practice, the Neolithic Chinese appear to have treated their dead with exceptional care. Burial remains from as early as 4000 BCE indicate that attention was placed on the posture and orientation of the corpse, while the presence of grave goods tell us that an economically and politically stratified society had emerged in certain areas.[61] In Yangshao, the bodies of children were placed in urns buried within the residential perimeter, while adults were interred in a separate cemetery north of the village. Another Neolithic culture to the northeast of Yangshao known as Longshan probably emerged somewhat later. Here the village graves were dug under residences and some funeral urns were cemented into foundation walls, but unfortunately the archaeological remains uncovered thus far tell us little about the belief systems of the residents.[62]

The consolidation of Chinese political authority seems to have taken place around 1700 BCE under the dominant tribe of the north called the Shang. Over the course of the next 700 years the Shang court occupied a number of walled capitals in succession, with the greatest of these discovered by archaeologists in the 1920s near present-day Anyang. Among the ruins of this cult centre that housed ancestral temples and royal tombs were the archives of a department of divination of the Shang court, with thousands of 'oracle bones' or fragments of animal bones (generally the shoulder bones of oxen or lower shells of tortoises) containing archaic Chinese writing. Most of the inscribed oracle bones were used to determine the outcome of future actions and events. These records indicate the existence of a complex social order under the rulership of warlike kings and aristocrats who commanded enormous military and labour resources. The Shang evolved a theory of governance that combined secular with religious power, and a sophisticated pictographic writing system to transmit their directives over wide geographical areas.[63]

The oracle bones also confirm belief in an impersonal supreme being typically referred to as Di, but it was the ancestors who played a pivotal role in the affairs of state.[64] The veneration of ancestors can be found in many ancient religions, of course, but in China the practice seems to have been central to the ruling elite's images of life after death. Divination, or the consultation of the living with the dead, permeated daily life at court. Instead of the continuity of the individual in some form after death, the Shang rulers embraced the idea of persistence through their descendants, for whom they had laboured and sacrificed much. It was a view of life consistent with an emerging non-dualistic understanding of reality. The entire cosmos was thought to be a single entity, with humans charged with maintaining harmony between heaven and earth through virtuous living, ritual sacrifice and obedience to a wise ruler. Dutiful offspring would themselves work hard, conscientiously fulfil the appropriate rites and practices towards the dead and live in a manner that reflected well on their ancestors. Ancestral intervention in earthly affairs was possible, thus reciprocal obligations were stressed, including the duty of the living to honour their ancestors through proper conduct. The ethical component in this set of beliefs was subordinate to the main goal of achieving a plentiful harvest and physical security through proper ritual practice.

At the highest political level, the king was responsible to the supreme deity Di, with lesser deities – the sun, moon, rain, earth and wind – in charge of different aspects of nature. Excavated royal graves at the Anyang contained ample symbols of wealth and power, including lacquerware, bronze weapons, decorative chariots and, most importantly for archaeologists, the inscribed oracle bones accumulated during the reign. The reigning monarch maintained a direct link with the spirit world and was expected to advocate with his ancestors on behalf of his subjects. The living sovereign was assisted in his work by a corps of priest-astrologers who performed the divination rights. In the words of one recent scholar, 'Shang kings derived their authority from the powers they could command through the mediation of their deified ancestors.'[65] In a very real sense the Shang believed that ancestors ruled through the king, with death only augmenting their temporal power.

Evidence of widespread human sacrifice in Shang society is strong, with royal tombs including the remains of hundreds of slaves, prisoners of war and courtiers. Offerings to the ancestors also solidified their influence with a supreme god who remained generally inaccessible and indifferent to human concerns. Slavery seems to have been widespread, with most victims coming again from the ranks of war captives. Along with the majority of common people, slaves had no recorded ancestors and thus no opportunity existed for connections across the generations. Most laboured as cultivators on lands controlled by their social superiors. The Shang elite deliberately reserved the divine realm for themselves, and Shang gods 'never became gods of the masses, nor of the community as a whole'.[66] We know almost nothing about the burial practices of the non-elite under the Shang, but it is believed that the cosmological outlook of the ruling dynasty was diffused throughout the wider culture, strengthening the practice of ancestor worship that was officially limited to aristocratic circles.

Conflict, Ideology and Early Death

The inclination to dominate others played out at many levels throughout prehistory, in sibling rivalries, blood feuds, clan disputes and revenge attacks. And occasions for conflict were many. In the words of Nicholas Wade, 'Warfare between pre-state societies was incessant, merciless, and conducted with the general purpose, often achieved, of annihilating the opponent.'[67] The hunter-gatherer existence, constituting 99 per cent of human evolutionary history, required that personal property, the usual prey of aggressors, be kept to a minimum.[68] There was not much that predators could claim in victory beyond what had been taken in the most recent hunt – and the 'sell by' date on the spoils was always imminent – but the prospect of reprisal was one of the main reasons that attackers sought to exterminate whole communities under siege.

The advent of agriculture and the domestication of animals undoubtedly enhanced the quality and quantity of food for growing populations over the long term, but as noted above sedentary agriculturalists initially found themselves in a vulnerable position with respect to hostile outsiders for whom it was easier to plunder than to grow their own foodstuffs. Organized violence was of course not a by-product of civilized living. But attacks against agriculturalists, together with inter-village raiding, greatly expanded the range, frequency and calculated precision of unnatural death. Still, the type of planned combat associated with war came rather late in our existence as a species. Weapons 'are among man's oldest and most significant artifacts', but most of the earliest weapons were designed for sustenance, not the destruction of fellow humans.[69]

In part, we can trace the origin of formal states (as opposed to loose-knit family or tribal units) and the priority assigned to military security to the need for common defence against outside marauders. As we have seen, Neolithic villagers in north China isolated themselves in walled towns as early as 4000 BCE in an effort to rebuff aggressive bands of nomads who lived in the foothills and plains. Chronic threat from these invading groups, and high per capita death rates when defensive mechanisms failed, contributed mightily to the formation of the first unified Chinese state. In the earliest known Indian civilization located along the Indus River Valley (c. 3000–1600 BCE), on the other hand, the absence of signs of violence and warfare as depicted in Indus art suggests that conflict may have been limited.[70] But once Ayran invaders from the north penetrated the region after around 1600 BCE, the complex Indus Valley civilization disappeared. In those lands where state structures did emerge, the security imperative led to the growth of social inequality, the division and specialization of labour, and the emergence of hereditary kingship. There were steep social costs involved in adopting a settled lifestyle.

Whether aggressive instincts are a constituent element of human nature, or whether they are culturally conditioned, the fact remains that humans are the only creatures who intentionally kill their own kind over socially constructed economic, religious and political ideologies.[71] And these ideologies are most often composed by the increasingly lethal state and its principal officers. Once early states consolidated power, their potential for reversing the relationship between sedentary and hunter-gatherer populations was enormous. Stone tools and weapons were replaced by bronze after approximately 3500 BCE, and again by iron after 1500 BCE. Armour, helmets and axes magnified fighting capacity, while wheeled chariots increased mobility. Autocratic rulers now had at their disposal the administrative and supply structures capable of sustaining large armies over wide areas and long distances. Aggression against one's neighbours at ever more deadly levels was legitimized by new communal ideologies framed and advanced by the ruling elite. Allegiance to the state – and to the king as personal embodiment of the state – took the place of duty to family, tribe and clan. Formerly undisciplined and unreliable warriors who engaged in clan feuds and ambushes evolved into a permanent military class. The state endowed these forces with political and religious legitimacy, and provided the tools and the leadership to carry out unprecedented levels of killing.

Death in such an environment became systematic, dehumanized and brutal. Once 'the enemy' was identified, the full power of the state turned armies into ruthless offensive assets. The Late Assyrian Empire (c. 1100–612 BCE) stands as one of the more extreme illustrations of this new posture, for here the principal occupation of the state was warfare and imperial expansion. From their base in northern Mesopotamia, Assyrian armies wrested control of lands from Egypt through Palestine, Syria, Asia Minor and Mesopotamia. Armed with iron weapons, the highly trained Assyrian army engaged in calculated atrocities designed to terrorize its enemies. In some cases, most memorably involving the people of the kingdom of Israel, whole populations were removed to break up pockets of resistance. Rebellions were not infrequent, but the consequences of failure were dire. Across the Atlantic in Cerro Sechín, Peru, the remains of an urban culture from around 1500 BCE signal a comparable use of official violence. Walls at Cerro Sechín are covered with scenes of warfare and the beheading of victims.[72] The role of the state in unnatural death through orchestrated violence, together with the elevation of this type of behaviour to the status of noble social function, has only intensified over the last two millennia, with lethal consequences for ever-larger numbers of combatants and non-combatants alike. We will return to this difficult topic in chapter Four.

Human sacrifice is another form of state-sponsored violence that, while rarely highlighted in textbooks, was global in its reach. The Sumerians, the Maya, the Aztecs, the Shang, the early Egyptians and the inhabitants of the Indus valley – all embraced it as acceptable practice.[73] Although some scholars interpret the ritual as a strategy for channelling humankind's inveterate penchant for violence into discrete cultural corridors, human sacrifice was almost always connected with religious belief and practice, and its purpose was most often to placate, appease or appeal to a god who might otherwise visit misfortune or natural disaster on the living. Both the perpetrator and the victim understood, rather ironically, that the goal of human sacrifice was to save lives through a pious act.[74] In agricultural societies where the forces of nature were identified with particular gods, human sacrifice could mean the assurance of a change of season, a bountiful harvest, the warmth of the sun. The hereditary divine ruler of the Incan state, to take only one of the more chilling cases, commanded that war victims and sometimes children be sacrificed to the sun. In order to confirm the divinity of the emperor, later burial practice called for mummification and entombment, with the dead ruler accompanied to the grave by multiple servants, concubines, wives and priests.

Still, the line between religion and politics was often blurred. The high incidence of sacrificial victims for the funerals of autocratic rulers has been correlated directly with the state-building enterprise. Egyptian First Dynasty tombs (c. 3100–2890 BCE), Mesopotamian royal tombs at Ur (c. 2500 BCE) and Shang dynasty tombs at Anyang (c. 1500 BCE) were all amply provisioned with servants, soldiers, courtiers and animals, presumably on the assumption that the security of the kingdom hinged on the fate of the deceased ruler in the afterlife. For the victims there was the assurance of renewed life in return for a selfless act, but one can only wonder over the emotional state of those whose lives were about to be taken. One suspects that war captives and foreigners destined for sacrifice on the bloodied pyramid temples of Tlaloc and Huitzilopochtli in the Aztec capital of Tenochtitlan may have been less assured of their fate, having no connection to the afterlife belief system of their enemies. Ritual killing was a common practice in the ancient world, but the element of coercion that undoubtedly accompanied the practice when victims did not embrace the practitioner's world view cannot be discounted.

From the fossil record it also appears that cannibalism was widespread in the ancient world, mirroring practices that can be observed in other biological systems. The post-Second World War academic community was disinclined to acknowledge this behaviour in humans, not least because of the way that accusations of cannibalism were associated with nineteenth-century Western racist and imperialist agendas.[75] But the evidence is compelling and recent scholarship now reflects this unsettling fact. Cannibalism is known to have taken place in Central and South America, the American Southwest, Fiji, New Zealand and Africa – in fact the practice was globally inclusive. More troubling perhaps is that for most animals cannibalism is solely the result of nutritional and survival needs, but in humans it evolved as accepted practice for putative spiritual and medicinal reasons. For example, in some cultures consuming the flesh of defeated enemies was thought to be an effective means of extracting the latter's spiritual power or an efficacious means of warding off evil. For others, the practice ensured that the spirit of a beloved companion or community member lived on in another's body. In the world view of the practitioners, consuming the body of the recently departed was more respectful, more reverential, than allowing it to rot in the ground. Standards of funerary practice obviously differed dramatically in cannibal and non-cannibal cultures, but the motives were not always mutually exclusive.[76]

Primeval Aspirations

Whether or not our Palaeolithic ancestors reflected on the deeper meaning of death remains an open question, and it is unlikely that the archaeological record will ever be robust enough to afford us solid inferences, much less empirically based answers. However, the known frequency of sudden death from a wide range of non-natural causes makes it possible for us to assume that most early peoples could have viewed death exclusively as the product of misfortune or magic, and believed that if these could somehow be avoided life would continue on indefinitely. Millennia later the Christian story of death as the consequence of one couple's transgression in a garden would offer a not dissimilar reading of the external source of death.

The position of Palaeolithic humans on bodily expiration, then, was not entirely unlike our modern efforts to treat death as a disease, as something to be overcome through techno-scientific innovation. Today of course we understand that life is constrained by organic processes that conclude in degeneration and decomposition; the quest to arrest that process is quite different from an assumption that all will remain well if malevolence on the part of gods or demons is avoided. Still, it would be difficult to fault our predecessors for their misperception given that most of them died at what today would be considered the years of peak human performance. Unanticipated death, viewed within the context of lives taken up with the relentless search for food in a world of conflict and violence, left little opportunity for sustained reflection on the possibility of something beyond direct appearances.

But on the basis of the scant material remains that have been gathered and examined by archaeologists, it does appear that some of our earliest predecessors (those who were afforded the opportunity to consider their own deaths), did not think in terms of inevitable finality. When the unfortunate event did occur, most cultures maintained that the individual transitioned into a state where the need for food, drink and earthly accessories still existed. Instead of being a radical alteration, the end of biological life became the passageway to another dwelling place whose quality was in part contingent upon the way in which one's body was handled and rites performed by the living. Perhaps most significant is the fact that the majority of ancient peoples seem to have thought in terms of personal, highly individualized post-mortem experiences. Whether these were physical or spiritual in nature, whether consisting of a shadowy underworld, an abode of pleasure or an interactive stage from which the ancestors influence the world of the living, the deceased retained their unique individual identity and moral agency through some level of consciousness.

There were important exceptions, of course. Chinese cosmology rejected the idea of transcendence and the other, emphasizing instead the imminence and harmony of nature, together with the connection between cosmic balance and social order. But even in the evolving Chinese model of ancestor worship one can perceive a need to think in terms of individual personality beyond the grave. Irrespective of the unique and myriad features within every global culture, then, it was difficult for most early peoples to equate the end of life with non-existence, with the irrevocable cessation of personal thoughts, emotions and intentions. With their embrace of continuity after death they sought to affirm the meaningfulness, the essential value of life. They saw themselves as 'in the world' in ways that were different from other living beings, for they believed that their journey into an afterlife form was essential to the larger architecture of the cosmos. As humans they viewed themselves as unique, empirically non-replicable, and claimed their relationship with the living as essential to the well-being of the social world from which they had departed. Their general indifference to what preceded life, and paramount concern with what succeeds it, testified to the value of the interregnum, the chain of belongingness that early humans yearned for, fought and sacrificed over. It was a sombre and disquieting start to civilization.

TWO

Thinking Things Through

The number of people in the world today who believe in some form of afterlife is enormous, and a significant number of those who do not believe genuinely wish they could. Reasons for the widespread and deeply held belief in continuity are diverse, but among the strongest is the feeling that in order for the world to be morally significant there must be a larger reality and rule of law into which humans enter upon death. A much smaller aggregate have concluded that life ends with the running out of the biological organism, that just as we did not exist before our birth we shall not exist again after our last breath. We live in the moment, the specious present, and must make our mark in the instant that is allotted to us. Although continuity is denied us, most contemporary non-believers are adamant that a world without design need not be meaningless, that in fact humans are uniquely advantaged to be meaning-makers, to courageously shape their own destiny in the face of an otherwise indifferent universe. When Thomas Jefferson spoke of 'the laws of nature and nature's God' in the Declaration of Independence, for example, his eighteenth-century contemporaries assumed that a divine architect had indeed fashioned immutable laws for humankind. Many twenty-first-century thinkers question that assumption, but Jefferson's words are no less significant to our lives and actions for being the product of an eighteenth-century secular faith tradition.

Faith traditions aside, what is the nature of the evidence for and against an afterlife, and what is the logical standing of each position?

These are questions that have engaged and often confounded philosophers across the centuries and continue to inform debate today.[1] At one level the philosophical arguments can seem a bit abstract and wearying, clever hypotheses resting on suspect evidence since no philosopher – or even non-philosopher for that matter – has experiential data from the tomb. None of us can report on the full experience of death. But certain of the hypotheses have enjoyed a wider currency across the centuries thanks to the contributions of scientists, mathematicians, prose writers and poets, and it is here that the practice of thinking things through is most matured, even offering provisional guidance into the realm of the great unknown.

A Greek Project

If at its core philosophy can be defined as the description and critical analysis of assumptions about reality, knowledge and values, then the philosophical approach to death must be distinguished from other modes of inquiry that rest on supernatural revelation, inspired texts or the privileged claims of human authority. The latter are totalizing and inclusive, they provide – and sometimes impose – ready-made explanations. The philosopher, on the other hand, begins by insisting that all questions are open and all positions contestable. Today there is general consensus that it was the ancient Greeks who pioneered the philosophical approach in the West, although they too enjoyed some cosy presuppositions, more often than not framing their experiences of the world in terms of overarching archetypal principles, primordial essences that supposedly underlay the multiplicity of our sensory encounters.[2] As observers of human nature the Greeks tackled the big questions with vigour and discernment. They explained the nature and structure of reality along a continuum that ranged from abstract idealism to severe materialism, but always with the goal of discovering explicatory unity, a logical order amid the apparent strangeness and general untidiness of the universe.

Some 60 years ago the historian Crane Brinton observed, 'We cannot know ourselves if we know the Greeks not at all.'[3] Medieval

Christian writers from Augustine to Aquinas certainly knew and admired the pagan Greeks, especially the Greek view that objective truth was within reach, clouded though the mind was by the imperfect senses. Greek assumptions about the essential meaningfulness of the universe were shared wholeheartedly by early Christians as they articulated the message of salvation through the mediation of the Church. Ironically the same was true for critics of that church, from the sixteenth-century Protestant reformers to the eighteenth-century *philosophes* of the Enlightenment. Until very recently Western thinkers by and large accepted the Greek ontology (theory of being) that everyday reality was derivative of something larger but also simpler, giving form and meaning to the phenomena of nature and the sprawling universe. Only during the past two centuries has this big picture been called into question, the victim of the very type of critical analysis pioneered in Athens and other Hellenic city-states.

The Greeks bequeathed two primary but divergent views of death and its sequel to later ages. The first view assumed a polarity between physical matter and non-extended soul where the latter, although not accessible to the senses, constituted the enduring feature of personhood even after the expiration of the body. Advocates for this abstract and idealist approach were distrustful of the sensory world, the world of sight, smell, touch, unremitting change – and death. The senses were, after all, notoriously fallible, leading us into miscalculation and mirage on a regular basis. On the other hand, unhurried rational reflection and the careful use of logic would bring us to an accurate understanding of a non-material reality that ascribed immanent value to the human project. Under this reading, personal identity inhered in changeless, non-material and immortal substance. And reality beyond the world of shifting appearances was the only field of truth and eternal life.

The second view embraced the material world and held to the position that what was not subject to observable, empirical investigation and rigorous analysis simply was not real. Functions typically associated with the soul, including thought, desire, emotion and moral calculation were better understood as attributes of the biological organism – in particular cerebral activity – in a world of constant modification and decay. A stronger version of this materialist view maintained that since human intellection ceases at the moment of one's biological demise, death was simply a non-event for the subject, something we do not live through. According to this reading of the situation there is no stage of greater fulfilment, no orderly sequel that will redress the inadequacies of current experience, no provision for things desired. All living beings – including humans – move ineluctably towards expiration in the universe, our abandonment a cause for existential sadness perhaps, but no reason to forego the relationships and opportunities for happiness, albeit brief, that exist for individuals and species alike. Between these two analyses hinged all subsequent Western views of human nature and essential personhood.

Practising for Death: The Immortal Soul

The sense that something of the human personality distinct from the physical body endured, if not eternally, then at least for some period after death, emerged in Greece as early as the ninth century BCE. The poet Homer (b. c. 800 BCE) was one of the first to refer to a life principle or *psyche* that departs the body once its biological processes have ceased to function, but did not attribute immortality or essential activity to the soul after death; the shadowy soul, in other words, is not the essence of personhood. Most pre-Socratic Greek writers agreed that whatever survives death, typically understood as a shade or shadow localized in the chest area during life, continues an unappealing existence beneath the earth, most immediately within the tomb of the decedent. The Homeric era texts do suggest a post-mortem reward for the select few who have led a heroic life: Hesiod in his *Works and Days* (c. 730 BCE) refers to the Isles of the Blessed, while in the *Odyssey* Homer opens the Elysian Fields to the good and the great.

But for the vast majority of persons, the post-mortem existence is a pitiable reflection of earthly life, with little sense of reward or improvement in evidence. The dead were most often associated with the underground kingdom of the god Hades, where there is neither punishment nor recompense. Communication between the living and the dead shades was possible through propitiatory gifts (food and drink) and the relationship was set on its proper path by funeral rites that were pleasing to the gods, but the advice of Achilles to the mournful father Priam at the end of the *Iliad* remains in force: Priam's son Hector has been killed, he shall not return, and one can accomplish nothing by grieving.[4] As for Achilles' own experience of Hades, he despondently observes in the *Odyssey* that he would rather be the lowliest mortal on earth than king of the underworld.

The ancient Greeks wrestled regularly with the question of personal identity, for it was central to all conceptions of the afterlife. What is it, exactly, that persists over a lifetime in spite of bodily changes and even survives death? An immaterial essence of the whole person complete with consciousness, an astral (non-physical) body, or a semi-conscious sub-person? There was much discussion among the Greeks about the fact of change in the observable world; nature alters constantly, with humans transformed most visibly through the process of ageing. But the early Greeks also were aware that some ideal objects such as geometrical shapes appear not to change at all. Perhaps after all there did exist a separate, immaterial realm of changelessness that involved humans, an undying reality as opposed to an ever-changing one.

One of the earliest-known Greek philosophers, the mathematician, geometer and possible shaman Pythagoras (c. 570–490 BCE), believed firmly in a non-material or spiritual side to personhood and expounded the doctrine of transmigration, the controversial notion that at death a person's immaterial, unchanging soul or *psyche* might be transferred to another animal. The Greeks called the theory metempsychosis and for Pythagoras the process continued across a number of lifetimes until the soul, now considered to be an indispensable feature of personhood, was reincarnated in another human being and lastly into the impersonal world soul, the divine creative mind of the universe.[5] The sixth-century geometer and physicist Thales, while wary of metempsychosis, similarly argued for the immortality of the permanent soul even as he maintained that the fundamental principle of nature could be reduced to one impersonal substance. And the Ionian philosopher Heraclitus (*fl. c.* 500 BCE) also distinguished a 'psyche' from the body and endowed the former with a 'logos' or rational plan that was common to all humanity. For each of these pre-Socratic thinkers, an immaterial substance or soul was the seat of an individual's feelings, emotions, thoughts and prompts to action. It also served as the bearer of moral qualities and the location of ethical decision making. These important claims, if difficult to demonstrate, would enjoy a long and varied history down to our own time.

Plato's Precedent

The truly innovative feature of Greek thought on the nature of death and the afterlife begins with Plato's conception of a radical dualism between the physical body and an immaterial substrate soul which temporarily inhabits the body. In his *Phaedo*, one of the best-known and compelling dramatic dialogues of the Western tradition, Plato brings the reader up close with a heroic Socrates as the great teacher faces imminent death on the trumped-up charge of impiety and the corruption of youth. The hero faces his end with supreme composure, anchored in the firm belief that while his body may be destroyed his immortal soul will live on, freed from the shackles of this earthly vessel.[6] 'Other people may well be unaware', Socrates reminds his students who have gathered at his jail cell to converse with him on his final day, 'that all who actually engage in philosophy aright are practising nothing other than dying and being dead.' The true philosopher seeks to stand aside from the body and its myriad wants and agitations. Only with the nonextended intellect 'by itself and unsullied' can a person approach eternal truths or Forms, the fundamental life goal of the philosopher.[7]

Plato's mature world view is on full display in the *Phaedo*, including his theory of non-material Forms and his belief in knowledge as recollection. For Plato personal identity was synonymous with the pre-existent incorporeal soul, and the soul 'is most similar to what is divine, immortal, intelligible, uniform, indissoluble, unvarying, and constant in relation to itself'. The multiform and dissoluble body, on the other hand, is 'never constant in relation to itself'. In the *Phaedo* we learn that after the death of the body the soul of the good person, the one who has meticulously avoided the agitations of the flesh and the call of the emotions, will enjoy the company of the gods forever. The impure soul, on the other hand, the one that has spent a lifetime 'bewitched' by bodily appetites and sensory diversions, will roam among tombs and graves until, 'owing to the desire of the corporeal element attendant upon them, they are once more imprisoned in whatever types of character they may have cultivated in their lifetime.' The gluttonous and the lecherous, for example, will find themselves reincarnated as donkeys, while the unjust and tyrannical may be re-embodied as wolves or hawks.[8] Even those who practise goodness, justice and temperance in their lives, if they have not 'practised philosophy and departed in absolute purity' are not admitted into the company of the gods; they must return again in bodily form, most likely as kind and decent humans, to complete their disentanglement from the realm of sensory illusion.[9]

Socrates' death is thus a mere inconvenience, the troublesome preamble to the great liberation where the burdensome body is at last cast aside and the soul, self, or person which pre-existed our earthly tenure is restored to the realm of wisdom, the abode of the Forms. For Plato, immortality is no longer the preserve of the select few who are rewarded by the gods for their heroic acts. Physicality is replaced by reasoning, the triumph of the body supplanted by the victory of intellect. In the *Republic*, Plato even drew an analogy between the proper functioning of the soul and the ideal state. The soul is tripartite, he argued, consisting of a lower appetitive element, a middle spirit-like element, and a higher rational element, each corresponding to the lowest class, the military class and the ruling class respectively in a well-ordered society.[10] The rational element of the soul always transcends the particular and is manifest in the human intellect, with its distinctive power to know eternal archetypes or universals. Reality is within us, Plato taught, the product of the soul's awareness of changeless truth, and while not everyone may enthuse over an eternity of intellection without the body, the Platonic theory at least had the advantage of uncomplicated clarity.

Matter and Form

Plato's most illustrious student was Aristotle (384–322 BCE), a member of Plato's academy who later established his own school, the Lyceum, in Athens. Aristotle was disquieted by Plato's dismissal of the physical body as a sort of detention centre for the soul and sought to restore a monistic theory of personal identity. In *De Anima*, a major work devoted to investigating whether psychological states are also material states of the body, Aristotle developed the philosophical concept of hylomorphism – a compound word for the Greek concepts of matter and shape – where substance is understood as a synthesis of matter and form. For example, bricks and mortar are potentially a house, but a form must be added to the materials before the particular configuration known as a house is realized.

Aristotle held that a soul is a substantial form, a changeless dimension within living bodies that makes these bodies, or primary matter in this case, truly alive. Thus matter is a potential principle of a natural body and soul is the animating principle, inherent in all animate beings – plants, animals and humans. According to Aristotle, plants have nutritive souls or life principles, animals have in addition sensitive souls (feelings and emotions), while the human soul is a tripartite combination of nutritive, sensitive and rational principles. The last quality is very special indeed, empowering humans to engage in activities like mathematical reasoning and abstract reflection. Most importantly for Aristotle, body and soul exist as composite substance, not separate Platonic substances. He denied that the soul pre-exists in the transcendent realm of the Forms and functions in an independent manner, a central tenet of Plato's metaphysical theory. And while Aristotle was willing to speculate that one aspect of rationality (*nous*) was separable from the body and survives death, this did not amount to Plato's personal immortality since *nous* is a general rational faculty.[11]

The Bequest

Early leaders of the Christian Church were deeply influenced by Greek philosophical thought on the nature of the person, not least because they found it useful in validating Christian doctrine concerning post-mortem resurrection. Tertullian of Carthage (c. 160–220) believed that the soul was generated with the body and consisted of corporeal elements, but his was very much a minority outlook. Origen of Alexandria (185–254) embraced the Platonic view that the soul is incorporeal and eternal, preceding the formation of the particular body, while St Jerome (c. 347–420), perhaps best known for his translation of the Bible into Latin, maintained that the immaterial and eternal soul was created at the time of conception, a perspective that would later come to have enormous currency within the Catholic Church and still informs its position on abortion. St Augustine of Hippo (354–430), whose influence on subsequent Church teaching was unparalleled, similarly advanced a Platonic view where an immortal, although not eternal, soul used the body for the cultivation of its higher powers, an essential prerequisite to salvation.[12] But for each of these influential leaders, as we shall see in the next chapter, so much blending of Greek philosophical thought into Church teaching was a helpful but not sufficient path to truth in these matters. In the end one had to rise above fragile reason and accept a dramatic narrative bordered by miracle.

St Thomas Aquinas (1225–1274), the most influential of the scholastic theologians of the High Middle Ages, made full use of the re-introduction of Aristotle's thought into western Europe during the thirteenth century. Aquinas single-handedly raised Aristotelian hylomorphism into the official doctrine of the Catholic Church. Following Aristotle, Aquinas affirmed that the powers of the soul were arranged hierarchically, with nutritive and reproductive powers at the foundation. Humans shared sensitive faculties, including sight, smell, locomotion, touch and emotion, with animals, but the rational faculties were reserved for God's special creation alone, and these included the power of speech, abstract thought and a will whose object is the good or the vision of God.

Morality for Aquinas was a function of our attraction to the good combined with our rational judging of actions that advance the good. Like Aristotle, Aquinas claimed that the form or soul gives each thing its operative power and directs its development.[13] Every living thing is programmed to pursue its natural end, the acorn into an oak, the caterpillar into the butterfly, and the human into communion with divine truth or God. This model of a purposeful universe striving across a great chain of being privileged humans as never before, making them 'ensouled' actors in a uniquely divine drama of life, death and final resolution. And that drama was acted out on a relatively small stage, one first identified by an Egyptian astronomer, mathematician and geographer of Greek descent named Ptolemy (c. 85–c. 165). His geocentric, or earth-centred, world picture was finite, closed and hierarchically ordered, a natural complement to the anthropomorphism of early Christianity.

Thus the main outlines of ancient natural science blended nicely with Christianity's picture of humankind's location in God's material handiwork. But perhaps the greatest appeal of Aristotelian theory for medieval Christians was in its affirmation of the essential function of the material body. Christians were taught to celebrate the goodness of physical creation as the outcome of divine action. If, as Aristotle maintained, the body is a necessary vehicle for the soul to perform its functions, then in order for humans to fulfil their purpose, both constituents are essential and complementary. The soul, according to Aquinas, causes the body to act and thus precedes it. It therefore can exist without the body, but only in an incomplete manner. Completion for Aquinas, and for medieval Christians more generally, had to await the resurrection when the two would be united again in glorious communion with the God the Father.

Material Matters

For individuals who believe firmly in the reality of an afterlife, even one of chastisement and pain for those who abuse the gift of life, the threat of annihilation is the ultimate penalty. The twentieth-century philosopher Martin Heidegger perceptively observed that while most of us understand the statement 'all men are mortal' we are hard-pressed to admit its significance for ourselves, especially if annihilation is involved. But one of Aristotle's near contemporaries, the Greek philosopher Epicurus (c. 341–270 BCE), argued this was the wrong approach to life and its conclusion. Most often associated with hedonism (from the Greek *hedone* or pleasure), Epicurus was interested mainly in how humans can secure happiness through the removal of mental and physical pain in this life. Despite modern caricatures, he and his followers were emphatically opposed to a life of self-indulgence. In fact, convinced that much of our unhappiness was the result of irrational fears and misplaced desires, Epicurus placed luxury and personal immoderation squarely in the latter category. His overarching goal was freedom from bodily hurt and a troubled mind, and he was convinced that mental equilibrium would never be achieved so long as humans held to a false understanding of death. His ethical project was to eradicate that fear.[14]

The solution for Epicurus was first to secure a firm grasp of natural phenomena. 'A man cannot dispel his fear about the most important matters', he wrote, 'if he does not know what is the nature of the universe but suspects the truth of some mythical story.'[15] And for Epicurus, the materialist atomism of Democritus (b. c. 460 BCE) provided the most plausible understanding of the natural world. Everything is an aggregate of tiny indivisible particles or atoms, Democritus claimed, and all appearance of change in the sensory world can be attributed to minute alterations in the rela-tionship of atoms one to another. Death is one such change, the coming apart of a particular arrangement of atoms, and from a subjective stand-point the end of life is the end of the world. 'Get used to believing that death is nothing to us. For all good and bad consists in sense experience, and death is the privation of sense experience.'[16]

The non-existence of death is not to be feared, just as none of us feared pre-natal non-existence as we lacked conscious being. On the strength of his atomistic theory, Epicurus insisted that our fear of death, indeed even our engagement with the subject, is misplaced because 'so long as we exist, death is not with us; but when death comes, then we do not exist. It does not then concern either the living or the dead, since for the former it is not, and the latter are no more.'[17] Life after death becomes merely the return of immutable atoms to another state, to be realigned and manifest in another form. The reasonable person comes to understand that 'infinite time contains no greater pleasure than limited time' and accepts the pleasures of a quiet life, a life without fear of a non-existent sequel. For an ancient culture where the dreary shades of Hades still framed most discussions of the afterlife, the Epicurean alternative was not without its attractiveness to his Greek contemporaries. The modern philosopher Geoffrey Scarre has described this Epicurean view of death succinctly as 'a condition without a subject'.[18]

The Roman poet Lucretius (94–55 BCE) gave wider currency to the psychology and physics of Epicureanism with his *On the Nature of the Universe* (*De rerum natura*). Praising Epicurus for being the first to 'raise mortal eyes in defiance' of superstition, Lucretius insisted that the 'dread and darkness of the mind' can only be removed 'by an understanding of the outward form and inner workings of nature'.[19] Adhering solely to the evidence of the senses, he challenged the whole notion of temperamental and meddling deities who threaten humans at every turn and instead set out to demonstrate that the world and its operations are the product of natural causes.

Since mind and spirit are for Lucretius both composed of matter, death is no more than the dissolution of a material entity soon to be reduced to its essential atomic parts. 'As the eye uprooted and separated from the body cannot see, so we perceive that spirit and mind by themselves are powerless.' Those atomic parts may for all we know have combined once before across 'the immeasurable extent of time', the eternal process of aggregation and dissolution, but we cannot bring this to remembrance. Fear of death, Lucretius argues, is an extrapolation of the terrors and ills of this life into a state where no such sensations or consciousness are possible. Once the union of body and spirit has ended, 'nothing by any hazard will happen any more at all' and 'one who no longer is cannot suffer'.[20] Happiness and sorrow, love and disdain, pleasure and pain, memory and desire – none of these shall intrude again.

Lucretius took time to consider the regrets of those who confront imminent death and the grief and lamentations of loved ones left behind, but even here he offers a brighter balance sheet. 'If something returns to sleep and peace, what reason is that for inconsolable grief?' Our worries and oppressions are at an end, pain and sorrow are banished for ever. And for the pain of good-byes with those we have loved, Lucretius allows Nature to offer a parental rebuke:

> What is your grievance, mortal, that you give yourself up to this whining and repining? Why do you weep and wail over death? If the life you have lived has been a pleasant thing . . . why then, you silly creature, do you not retire as a guest who has had his fill of life and take your care-free rest with a quiet mind?[21]

The pleasures of this world will never satiate us, 'no one knowing what he really wants and everyone forever trying to get away from where he is, as though mere locomotion could throw off the load'. In words that anticipate Stoicism, Lucretius asks us to diagnose the essential source of our melancholy as 'this deplorable lust of life' and fruitless quest to dodge death through distractions and pleasures that will always, in the end, fail to satisfy.[22]

Stoic Acquiescence

If Greek philosophy delivered an abundance of options for anyone interested in the significance of death, Roman belief systems by contrast offered little in the way of addressing life's most perplexing questions. The official state religion was concerned largely with carrying out the ceremonies thought necessary to secure the protection – and avoid the wrath – of the gods. It was left to philosophers to engage with moral and metaphysical matters. What is the nature of the universe and humanity's place in it? Do the gods, if they exist, take an interest in our affairs? What, if any, are our obligations to one another and what is our ultimate destiny beyond the tomb? For many members of Rome's educated elite, Stoicism became the leading source for direction on these and other essential questions.

Founded by Zeno of Citium (334–262 BCE) in early fourth-century BCE Greece and evolving under his followers Cleanthes (c. 331–232 BCE) and Chrysippus (280–206 BCE) as a system of ethics, Stoicism counselled a life in conformity with nature and informed by rigorous self-discipline and virtue. Like the Epicureans, the Stoics were metaphysical materialists. They reduced everything, even thought, to material substance and believed the universe to be the handiwork of a single unifying principle which was God. Despite being equated with a form of matter, the Stoic God was also synonymous with absolute reason, which in turn meant that God's handiwork, humanity included, is informed by reason. The rational person accepts that body and soul are one and the same substance, the body producing thoughts derived from sense in the soul, and the soul producing movement in the body.[23]

The Roman statesman and philosopher Seneca (c. 3 BCE–65 CE) offered what was perhaps the most recognizable Stoic position on death. In his disquisition *On the Shortness of Life*, he cautioned against inappropriate use of our allotted days and rejected the arguments of those who equated the brevity of life with universal evil. For this former tutor and adviser to the Emperor Nero who was forced by his erstwhile student to take his own life, each person is accorded an appropriate portion by nature. Our mistake is in our preoccupations, our distractions, our compulsive misuse of time. 'Life is long enough, and a sufficiently generous amount has been given to us for the highest achievements if it were all well invested.'[24] But for those whose lives are frittered away by distractions, old age is a time of regrets. And when at last an illness reminds them of their mortality, 'how terrified do they die, as if they were not just passing out of life but being dragged out of it'. The wise man who has so ordered his life that its meaning is clear 'will not hesitate to meet death with a firm step'. Only he is really alive, having kept a close watch over his own lifetime.[25] In a letter to his friend Lucilius, Seneca insisted that suicide was a legitimate and rational option not just for those in distress, but also for those 'who think of life in terms of quality, not quantity'. When one dies is of no consequence to the wise man. 'To die well', he wrote, 'is to escape the danger of living ill.'[26]

For Seneca, the key to extending mortal into everlasting life involved engagement with the past, annexing every age to one's own experiences. If we are able to transcend the fleeting present with its multiple diversions then we can cultivate lasting friendships and partner 'with better men than we'. Unlike present acquaintances, none of the great minds from the past 'will be too busy to see you' or allow one to depart empty-handed. We can take from them whatever we wish, and they will add their years to ours. Seneca accepted the common saying that we cannot choose our parents, but he reminded his readers that they could choose whose children they would like to be. The right adoptive parents 'will offer you a path to immortality and raise you to a point from which no one is cast down'.[27]

The last in the long line of important Stoic philosophers who addressed the question of mortality was the second-century Roman emperor Marcus Aurelius. His own death of an infectious disease at the age of 59 in the year 180 followed thirteen years of lonely military command at the head of legions fighting on the Danube frontier. The last of the so-called 'good emperors', Aurelius composed a series of short reflections which he called 'to himself' but which we know as his *Meditations*. The work assumes that nature will, at its appointed time, dissolve each material body and use its components for other purposes. Death should be understood not only as a process of nature but as 'a positive contribution to nature's well-being'. The rational person waits 'with a good grace for death, as no more than a simple dissolving of the elements whereof each living thing is composed'. As for the sequel, there are but two possibilities, neither unpleasant; if one disembarks this life for another, then there are gods everywhere, 'even yonder'; if, on the other hand, one enters into final insensibility, 'then you will be out of the grip of pains and pleasures, and thrall no longer to this earthen vessel'.[28] Either way, death is a good in itself, an acceptable closure to a life of adherence to duty.

A New View of Nature

During the High Middle Ages a furious debate raged among philosophers and theologians over the relationship between particular objects and their alleged eternal archetypes. The Platonic tradition in philosophical thought held that particulars, which were the object of sense perception, were less real than their eternal forms which were known by reason. There were, for example, particular trees and the archetypal tree, just as there were particular humans and the ideal human. Realists claimed that particulars were less real than universals, while their opponents, known as nominalists, insisted that universals were nothing more than wishful thinking, generalized mental constructs from particular instances that had no reality beyond the mind of the proposer.

At one level this specialized academic debate hardly seemed relevant to views about death and the afterlife. But a wide range of important Church teachings concerning life and death assumed the validity of the realist position. For example, the sinfulness of each person and the absolute need for Christ's redeeming sacrifice was predicated on the assumption that all had inherited the taint of original sin from Adam, the universal man. Similarly, the relative unimportance of the earthly city and the primacy of the heavenly city, magisterially set forward in St Augustine's *City of God*, verified the limits of this world and the supreme importance of focusing one's attention on the eternal domain of heaven. Theological study was at the core of the university curriculum – the queen of the sciences – because it dealt with unchanging, universal truths and the reality behind appearances. Any suggestion that particular things, the object of sensory engagement, constituted the whole of reality would threaten the entire edifice of the Church's hierarchical and static world picture.

Peter Abelard (1079–1142) and Thomas Aquinas sought to establish a middle ground in this debate by claiming that universals were contingent, existing as ideas in the mind of God prior to particular things in the sensory world. When humans think in terms of universals, at a minimal level they are sharing in the mind of God.

But William of Ockham (c. 1285–1347), perhaps the foremost critic of this compromise position, warned against any suggestion that God was limited by supposed eternal ideas or the dictates of reason. For Ockham and other nominalists, God's creation is a function of choice or divine will that cannot be captured by formulas or pre-determined patterns. And God's omnipotence meant that our effort to understand reality beyond appearances was a futile quest. Nominalists like Ockham insisted that revelation was the sole source of celestial truths; conclusions reached through philosophy and reason had to do with this world, the world of change and decay, not the world of permanence and actuality.[29]

Together with the recovery and translation into Latin of the works of Aristotle during the thirteenth century, the nominalist perspective inadvertently advanced the separation of religious and scientific approaches to truth. No longer understood in purely symbolic terms where physical phenomena were mysteriously linked to some higher reality, the investigation of nature could now begin to proceed in an independent manner. Interest in the world of nature for its own sake, and for the amelioration of the human condition, began to affect every facet of experience – even the experience of death. Perhaps it too was to be considered a natural event, something unrelated to theological concerns about the first sin of the first man. Perhaps there was no archetypal man whose progeny was burdened evermore with the consequences of the Fall.

Control Over Physical Nature

It was a common assumption of late medieval thought, when the works of Greek and Roman antiquity were rediscovered and restored, that much more new knowledge could be added to the common store. An essentially rational God who created and sustains the universe could now be known through his works as well as his words.[30] The period of the Renaissance and Reformation (the fifteenth and sixteenth centuries) in many ways represented a return to the intellectual and spiritual roots of European civilization. But in the realm of natural philosophy, or what we refer to as natural science, a major revolution shattered centuries of Aristotelian physics and cosmology, buffeting and then collapsing a view of humanity's place in the universe that had been promulgated by the Church since the early Middle Ages. The results would have a major impact on thinking about the nature of death.

As we have seen, Aristotelian science held that substantial forms combine with matter to help make things what they are destined to be. This notion of teleology or purpose, of things striving to realize their natural end, presented the entire universe as a sort of conscious mind seeking to attain a greater goal.[31] For upwards of 2,000 years most thinkers understood this universe as limited in scale, hierarchical in nature and monarchical in governance. Animated by angels, spirits and the workings of divine grace, God's creation was alive with energy and activity. The sun, moon and planets all revolved around the earth, the definite centre of the cosmos, in perfect concentric circles, their movement regularly influencing daily lives. In the end, the whole of creation was micro-managed by a prime mover who was constantly and intimately involved in his handiwork, solicitous of human welfare and quick to punish those who rejected his sovereignty.[32]

From the middle of the sixteenth century until the end of the seventeenth, a new picture of nature gradually emerged. In the work of Nicolaus Copernicus (1473–1543), Tycho Brahe (1546–1601), Johannes Kepler (1571–1630), Galileo Galilei (1564–1642) and Isaac Newton (1642–1727), matter and mathematics usurped the role of teleology and final causes as the key to understanding the physical world. One no longer sought divine correspondences, connections between microcosm and macrocosm, the alleged interrelationships of all things. A starkly mechanistic book of nature, written in the language of mathematics and studied solely in terms of inert matter, presented objects with no ends to achieve. There ceased to be any room for non-material essences in the scientific quest to study observable properties, while secondary qualities like taste and colour were relegated to functions of the subjective brain. Suddenly the ancient Greek and Roman atomists were relevant again, their abandonment of non-material substance the rediscovered road forward in the effort to build a rational science of nature and humanity. In this new intellectual environment, as philosophers struggled to probe the relationship between consciousness and mechanized nature, the Aristotelian consensus gave way before an updated version of Platonic dualism.[33]

Descartes' Mind–Body Problem

In the winter of 1650 the French ambassador to Sweden, Hector-Pierre Chanut (1601–1662), found himself tending to his friend and mentor, René Descartes, who lay dying in the ambassador's residence in Stockholm. Descartes was not quite 54 years old, his reputation as a revolutionary thinker already well established. This great mathematician and founder of analytical geometry was driven by the prospect of formulating a general method for scientific inquiry and was largely responsible for restoring to prominence the ancient Platonic quandary over metaphysical dualism. Simply put, Descartes believed that the incorporeal mind and its thoughts exist independently of the inanimate material world, that mind and matter are fundamentally different and that while one may question the reality of the latter, the authenticity of the mind is proved in the very process of questioning its existence. If I doubt the existence of thinking substance, after all, then who is doing all the doubting?

Descartes had travelled to Sweden at the invitation of Queen Christina (1628–1689), a young and ambitious monarch who was seeking to surround herself with recognized thinkers and scholars. He took up residence with his protégé Chanut but was soon struck down by a fever that developed into pneumonia. The queen sent her personal physician to attend to Descartes, but the patient refused to undergo the standard treatment of phlebotomy (bloodletting). Having long before called into question the whole system of medicine pioneered by the ancient Greek physician Galen, a system that viewed all illness as an imbalance in the humours – the body's blood, phlegm, black bile and yellow bile – it is no surprise that the dying man angrily ordered the court physician out of his presence.[34] In his major philosophical (and partly autobiographical) statement,

Discourse on the Method of Rightly Conducting One's Reason and of Seeking Truth in the Sciences (1637), Descartes called for the interrogation of all received opinions and doctrines, recalling the approach of Socrates almost two millennia earlier. Descartes committed himself 'never to accept anything as true that I did not incontrovertibly know to be so ... and to include nothing in my judgements other than that which presented itself to my mind so clearly and distinctly, that I would have no occasion to doubt it'.[35] The serious enquirer after truth must start afresh with a step-by-step, incremental approach to knowledge where clear and distinct ideas form the building blocks of more complex principles.

Our modern habit of conflating the soul with the mind, and mind with human self-identity, began with Descartes. Breaking with Plato and Aristotle, Descartes saw no reason to concede that non-human animals have souls and regarded them merely as complex automata. His approach was audacious and had the advantage of being in alignment with the Christian picture of the soul. But there was one problem for Descartes, and it was no small matter: how can a thinking, non-extended indivisible substance like the human mind interact with and cause a change in a non-thinking, extended but divisible thing like the human body? How, for example, can my desire to slow my bicycle on a steep descent cause a change in my brain and muscles to apply the bicycle's brakes? Conversely, how can physical senses have an impact on the incorporeal mind? How does the pain of falling from my bicycle translate into the idea of embarrassment at having been inattentive while riding?

This conundrum has engaged philosophers for four centuries, since the issue was first brought to the foreground by Descartes. His solution, reached in the wake of his own dissecting experiments, was to claim that the nexus between the real René Descartes, a thinking being or thing, and its material body is located in the pineal gland, a tiny organ at the base of the brain. Descartes' critics immediately pounced, indicting the philosopher for offering what amounted to an assertion rather than a proof. The challenge continues today, as evidence from the sciences mounts against the dualist hypothesis. The impact of serious brain injuries on reasoning

functions, the deleterious effect of alcohol on foetal brain development and executive capacity, the eviscerating power of Alzheimer's
on thought and memory over time – each of these organic mis-
fortunes erode our identity and have an ugly effect on the world of
ideas, and the presumably autonomous mind or soul.

Despite this theoretical messiness, Descartes was convinced
that not only the existence but the immortality of the soul was open
to rational demonstration. He never provided the requisite demonstration as he confessed it would 'depend on an account of the
whole of physics' but in a letter to an unknown correspondent,
Descartes claimed that corruptibility requires an entity composed
of parts that can be separated. The soul's unitary nature led him to
conclude that 'while the body can very easily perish, the mind is
immortal by its very nature.' There was only one qualification. In a
letter dated December 1640 to his lifelong friend Marin Mersenne
(1588–1648), Descartes acknowledged that he could not prove that
God could not annihilate the immortal soul. 'This [immortality] is
all that is required as a foundation for religion, and is all that I had
any intention of proving.'[36] In the end, the declaration of faith in a
loving God made the possibility of annihilation unthinkable.

The Debate Engaged

A number of Descartes' contemporaries weighed in on what quickly
became the philosophical problem of the day. Pierre Gassendi (1592–
1665) argued that humans have both immaterial and corporeal
souls. The latter produces corporeal effects like sensation and
reproduction, while the former allows for self-reflection and the
knowledge of universals. The Englishman Thomas Hobbes (1588–
1679) would have none of this, insisting that human bodies, like all
bodies in nature, are animated by matter in motion, forces that have
no prevision of their ends. Not only human souls, but angels and
even God were sorts of material beings. When the philosopher John
Locke (1632–1704) suggested in his Essay Concerning Human Understanding (1689) that matter might think, he was immediately accused
by his orthodox critics of accepting Hobbes's stark materialism.

Locke countered with the claim that he was simply affirming God's omnipotence.[37] Few were convinced. Half a century later the great French philosopher Voltaire was still serving as a witness for the defence, insisting that Locke 'did not say that matter thought; but he said that we do not know enough to demonstrate that it is impossible for God to add the gift of thought to the unknown being called "matter" after granting to it those of gravitation and of motion, which are equally incomprehensible'.[38]

The Dutch philosopher Baruch Spinoza (1632–1677) sought to resolve the controversy between dualist and materialists in his major work, *Ethics* (1677). According to Spinoza, Descartes was correct to distinguish between mental and physical properties, but where he erred was in assuming that each was an attribute of distinct substances. Spinoza did away with causal relations by insisting that mental and physical phenomena, while appearing distinct to humans, were in reality attributes of a single substance which was God. According to this audacious theory, mental events appear to cause bodily actions but in fact are part of a single unified reality. The French Catholic priest Nicolas Malebranche (1638–1715) offered a comparable model called Occasionalism where God arranges the appearance of causation between mental and physical events. While it may seem that my mind commands me to withdraw my hand from a hot surface, the physical move is actually the occasion for God to order the action, producing the perception that the mind acted autonomously. And the German mathematician and philosopher Gottfried Wilhelm Leibniz (1646–1716) offered yet another interpretation known as psychophysical parallelism, where the appearance of causality is in fact a perfect harmony between mind and body that was pre-established by God. Mind and body are the same thing, non-extended, infinitesimal monads that give the appearance of interaction from the imperfect perspective of humans.[39]

The French scientist and mathematician Blaise Pascal (1623–1662), perhaps recognizing the difficulty in coming to any conclusion over the issue of mind–matter causality, famously advanced the so-called 'wager' argument for a personal God who took special interest in humanity and created nature as a stage where we act out our hopes and fears. In his celebrated *Pensées*, Pascal asserted that life is bereft of meaning without a spiritual dimension to sustain it, and that humans demand a God who will lift them out of dread and uncertainty. He compared the human journey to a voyage over an expanse of ocean, each person 'a Nothing in comparison with the Infinite, an All in comparison with the Nothing, a mean between nothing and everything'.[40] Each of us longs for stability, security and answers to the deepest questions about the purpose of existence, yet the rational person sees little in physical nature to convince him of a benevolent providence.

> This is what I see and what troubles me. I look on all sides, and I see only darkness everywhere. Nature presents to me nothing which is not matter of doubt and concern. If I saw nothing there which revealed a Divinity, I would come to a negative conclusion; if I saw everywhere the signs of a Creator, I would remain peacefully in faith. But, seeing too much to deny and too little to be sure, I am in a state to be pitied.[41]

According to Pascal, the rational person who understands that the nature of our existence hides us from both knowledge of first beginnings and the infinite, must take the wager in favour of God's existence. The believer, after all, loses nothing after death if their belief is mistaken and annihilation becomes our fate. But they would be rewarded with eternal bliss if correct in assuming God's existence and his promises to humankind. The unbeliever, on the other hand, loses nothing if his or her hypothesis ends up being the correct one, but risks an eternity of damnation if proven wrong. A simple risk–benefit analysis should be enough to command rational assent to the proposition that God is real and his promise of immortality genuine.[42]

Enlightenment Scepticism

Rarely had an imminent departure garnered such popular interest. One month after the American colonists declared their independence from Great Britain, the influential Scottish philosopher and historian David Hume, aged 65, lay dying at his home in Edinburgh. Crowds gathered outside in anticipation that the great man would at the last moment forsake his infamous views regarding the implausibility of miracles and, more importantly, the mortality of the human soul. The latter position had first been brought to the public's attention in 1755, when a few pre-publication copies of an essay, 'Of the Immortality of the Soul', were circulated despite having been pulled by the publisher from a work entitled Four Dissertations. Finally in 1783, the year when the United States of America signed its peace treaty with George III's government ending the successful War of Independence, the essay on immortality, together with another controversial essay on suicide, appeared in print under the late author's name.

For those who had gathered for the death watch outside Hume's home, the result would prove unsatisfactory. The famous economist and fellow Scotsman Adam Smith (1723–1790), a close friend of many years, wrote that Hume's cheerfulness, 'and the most perfect complacency and resignation', remained with him until the end. Smith recounted one rather humorous scene where Hume's physician told the patient that he would inform a mutual friend that Hume was doing a bit better. Hume would have none of it, telling the doctor, 'As I believe you would not choose to tell anything but the truth, you had better tell him that I am dying as fast as my enemies, if I have any, could wish, and as easily and cheerfully as my best friends could desire.'[43] Soon thereafter he was gone, and gone unreservedly if his views were at all accurate.

In his essay Hume, ever the empiricist who insisted that sense experience is our only source of knowledge, disputed the argument for immortality on metaphysical, moral and physical grounds. By reason alone, Hume argued, we are incapable of demonstrating the immortality of the soul. Since the notion of underlying substance is 'wholly confused and imperfect' it is impossible for us to be definitive about the specific qualities or powers that inhere in matter and spirit. If we draw an analogy between the known fate of the body, where experience tells us that death brings dissolution and eventual reabsorption into nature, and the fate of the immaterial soul, the indications are on the side of mortalism. As an illustration Hume asked his readers to consider the position of the ancient Stoics, who believed that a spiritual substance or ethereal fire was dispersed throughout the universe. Just as individual bodies are dispersed at death only to compose successively elements of new animal life, so too individual soul consciousness is dissolved at death and is reallocated to new life. But new life does not discern this reconstitution of matter or spirit, nor is it aware of a previous identity. 'The soul therefore if immortal, existed before our birth; and if the former existence no ways concerned us, neither will the latter.'[44]

Moral arguments for the immortality of the soul were equally problematic for Hume. For example, the widespread claim that God is interested in the reward of the just and the punishment of evildoers ascribes to the Creator anthropomorphic qualities that are not reflected in the universe he has created. ''Tis very safe for us to affirm, that whatever we know the Deity to have actually done, is best; but 'tis very dangerous to affirm, that he must always do what to us seems best.' Accounts of heaven and hell assume two distinct types of person, the good and the bad, 'but the greatest part of mankind float between vice and virtue'. How could a just God assign such inconstant beings to 'punishments eternal and infinite?' Even the idea of earthly life as a probationary estate seemed misplaced in light of high rates of infant mortality, the half of humankind that die 'before they are rational creatures'.[45]

Hume then pointed to the fact that with all closely related objects, alterations in one are observed to have a proportional impact on the other. The weakness of body and mind in infancy, the observed influence of advanced age and bodily illness on mental clarity, and the apparent absence of consciousness in deep sleep all point in the direction of total dissolution in death. Even as trees perish in water and fishes perish in air, 'What reason then to imagine, that an immense alteration, such as is made on the soul by the dissolution of its body and all its organs of thought and sensation, can be effected without the dissolution of the whole?' For David Hume, as for Pascal, reason cannot carry us to the threshold of immortality. Only faith in the veracity of divine revelation can bring us such news, 'since we find that no other medium could ascertain this great and important truth'.[46] Where Hume and many other leading figures of the eighteenth-century Enlightenment departed from Pascal was in their unwillingness to employ the wager. Given the complete absence of any empirical evidence, they elected for agnosticism as the only rational choice.

Science, Body and Culture

Pioneering work in the geological and biological sciences during the nineteenth century resulted in what was perhaps the strongest critique of both the uniqueness of humans and their alleged status as necessary 'ensouled' creatures. Geologists and palaeontologists vigorously contested the meaning of fossil remains and a physical record that suggested some species had died out. Those known as 'catastrophists' upheld the biblical account of a world once engulfed in ocean waters while others dubbed 'uniformitarians' pointed to the power of natural forces over periods of time that could not be reconciled with a literal reading of the Christian Old Testament. Charles Darwin's (1809–1882) ground-breaking theory of evolution was as significant to biology and our conception of time as Newton's work had been to physics and our conception of space. By stressing continuities between humans and other animals while contesting the biblical account of humankind's creation, Darwin's *On the Origin of Species by Means of Natural Selection* (1859) linked humanity with a process unfolding aimlessly over many millennia rather than a solitary act some 6,000 years ago. And in *The Descent of Man* (1871), Darwin explicitly included humans in the evolutionary paradigm, our alleged exceptionalism nothing more than hubris; our current status and skills emerging unhurriedly out of the non-human past.[47]

Now closer to the apes than the angels, Darwin's naturalistic picture of humanity shocked many laypeople, not to mention members of the religious establishment. Gone was the great chain of being and its static hierarchy of life forms from lowest to highest; in its place were species transformed slowly over great sweeps of time, the result of mere accident and impersonal forces. A furious argument ensued, one that in many ways continues into the present day, with opponents, secular and well as religious, charging Darwin and his protagonists with bad faith and flawed science. It was undeniable that Darwin's early Christian beliefs were forever undermined by his own scientific inquiries. But while he seems to have held fast to an undogmatic theism, the cruelty and chance of a natural environment that resembled a battlefield pointed in the direction of a designer who was far removed from the benevolent watchmaker deity of Darwin's youth.[48]

Subsequent work on heredity by Gregor Mendel (1822–1884) and Hugo de Vries (1848–1935) highlighted the role of sudden genetic mutations and the importance of biochemical factors in heredity. Gradually the wider culture began to incorporate this new view of the natural world into its collective consciousness. The supernatural and the mysterious, including the drama of salvation, was confronted with a picture of morally neutral processes that covered millions of years and offered no evidence of transcendent significance for a 'best adapted' human species whose appearance was too difficult to pinpoint. Perhaps the mind of man was itself a product of a very long evolutionary process, ideas – including moral ideas – simply survival strategies unique to one's time and place. Perhaps human reason, instead of being a neutral, God-given investigative tool, was itself a product of the very nature it purported to understand.

These were thoughts bound to unsettle adherents of traditional faith narratives. Westerners had grown accustomed to seeing themselves as superior to other life forms, as just below the angels and God in the great chain of being.[49] The psalmist had asked 'What is man that you are mindful of him, the son of man that you care for him? You made him a little lower than the heavenly beings and crowned him with glory and honour.'[50] After Darwin the question took on new meaning, while the declaratory sentence now seemed hard to justify. Evolutionary theory may have aligned with ideas of progress current in the nineteenth century, but progress by means of natural selection, which might be equated with accident and blind chance, was little comfort to those who conceived of the world as a static hierarchy, a loving plan emanating once and for all from the mind of God.

Death as Emancipation

Arthur Schopenhauer (1788–1860) died of heart failure at the age of 72 in his apartment in Frankfurt. Although active as an author into old age, he had composed his major philosophical work, *The World as Will and Representation*, while still in his mid-twenties. Published in 1819 but largely ignored by contemporaries until much later, Schopenhauer comforted himself in the face of the book's early obscurity by observing, rather immodestly, that 'whoever has accomplished an immortal work will be as little hurt by its reception from the public or the opinions of critics, as a sane man in a mad-house is affected by the upbraidings of the insane.'[51] Convinced that his novel ideas would eventually command the attention of serious philosophers, Schopenhauer regarded the relationship between life and death as one of the key problems of human nature.

The World as Will and Representation adopted an introspective approach to truth that was deployed by idealist philosophers reaching back to Plato. If one looks deeply and intently enough into oneself, Schopenhauer claimed, one will find not only individual but general essence, the essence of total reality. The structure of one's inner being contains an element of the eternal and can speak to the supreme organizing principle of the universe. Plato, we recall, identified this principle with rational consciousness and intellection. Schopenhauer, in a radical shift, identified it with what he called the 'Will', a non-rational, fierce and directionless urge at the heart of reality. This Will is unitary and manifests itself in all natural forces as the impulse to survive, affecting everything from inanimate objects to animals to humans.[52]

Trained in the western philosophical tradition but familiar with the Hindu Upanishads, Schopenhauer associated the individual Will with an unceasing striving to avoid pain, secure happiness and live. The goal is futile, however, at least so long as endless worldly desire is our compass and death our inexorable destiny. Our clinging to life 'is blind and irrational, explicable only by the fact that we are in our whole nature the will to live'. And in the end our desire produces nothing but aggressiveness, self-centredness and destruction. If reason truly guided our approach to death, we would step back and consider how we never lament the fact of our non-being for millennia prior to our birth. 'We do not grieve at all that an eternity has gone by during which we did not yet exist. After this momentary and ephemeral interlude, an eternity will again go by; but this we find hard, indeed unbearable.'[53] Life at its best for Schopenhauer was merely delayed dying, 'the fleeting duration of life as its one redeeming virtue in eventually ending the suffering of the individual will-to-live'.[54] While individuality ceases with death, the impersonal essence of being, the Will, is indestructible. Short of the complete eradication of the individual Will, Schopenhauer counselled an approach to our single lives through the cultivation of artistic, aesthetic and moral awareness. Only with less individuation and a greater concern with universal principles could the sufferer find some recompense, some solace, in life.

Emerging Social Sciences

Questions about human identity and greater purpose traditionally had been the preserve of fields like philosophy, religion, literature, history and the arts, but in the wake of fossil studies and the Darwinian revolution the natural and social sciences came to play an increasingly outsized role in the discussions. The academic study of social phenomena (later labelled sociology) emerged out of efforts to understand humans partly as the product of their cultural and physical environments. And arguably the most important social theorist of the nineteenth century was Karl Marx (1818–1883), who dispensed with theories of humankind's essential nature and in its place associated the contours of human thought, values and institutions with underlying social and economic relations.

Marx was deeply influenced by the ideas of Ludwig Feuerbach (1804–1872), whose *Essence of Christianity* (1841) maintained that every personal aspect attributed to God as a separate being is actually a reflection, a projection, of man's idealized self. In *Thoughts on Death and Immortality* (1830), Feuerbach argued that Christian belief in individual immortality distracted humans from their more important duties to each other, impoverishing this life by calling our attention to an illusory next venue.[55] God is made in man's image, Feuerbach insisted, not the other way around. Once this was widely understood, humans could commit to the present life not as an indicator of one's worthiness for heaven but for the purpose of mutual well-being. He hoped through his writings 'to turn men from theologians into anthropologists . . . from religious and political lackeys of the heavenly and earthly monarchy into free, self-confident citizens of the world'.[56] Denying immortality, Feuerbach believed, was an essential part of the effort to advance human dignity and freedom.

For Marx, all of human history followed scientific laws every bit as demonstrable as the laws of Newtonian physics or evolutionary biology. He ridiculed the idea of fixed human nature, insisting that humans had no essence, were always in formation, and forged their world view on the uneven foundation of dominant social and economic relations. Moral codes, metaphysical systems, religious frames of understanding all flow from basic material conditions and reflect the priorities of the dominant class. Human happiness was not to be found in an imaginary future life; indeed for Marx the religious view of life with its codes of obedience, resignation in the face of suffering and the equating of misfortune with personal sinfulness was nothing more than an imposition foisted upon the majority by the class wielding economic power.[57] Throughout history the class that controlled material production also controlled mental production, first crafting and then imposing the dominant ideas of society. The compensatory afterlife was one of the most powerful of these impositions and Marx fought to replace it with a new form of worldly salvation, a stateless, communitarian norm built around a transformed humanity where genuine equality in this world (since there was no other) marked all social relations.

A New Illness

The controversial philosopher Friedrich Nietzsche (1844–1900), whose works had a deep impact on artists and intellectuals at the end of the nineteenth century, was inspired partly by the writings of Darwin and Schopenhauer. Nietzsche renovated the latter's pessimistic assessment of life as pointless into a call for embracing the absurdity of existence by jettisoning conventional morality, politics and culture for a more authentic standard. Christianity was for Nietzsche, as it was for Marx, the religion of the crowd, the chief buttress of slave morality. 'Belief is always most desired, most pressingly needed, where there is a lack of will: for the will, as emotion of command, is the distinguishing characteristic of sovereignty and power.'[58] All talk of another life was a cynical distraction, preventing humans from taking hold of their own destiny, creating their own values, and demonstrating a powerful will to live undistracted by either faith or sterile reason.

Nietzsche knew something of the dark irrational forces that lurk in the recesses of the unconscious long before a more intentional study of these forces was undertaken by the Viennese physician Sigmund Freud (1856–1939). While a student at the University of Vienna, Freud had moved away from the theism of his youth and embraced the radical idea that God was simply a construction built on basic human longings and emotions.

In his early professional career Freud did not focus much attention on the meaning of death, but in mid-life, after recovering from a serious illness and in the wake of his father's death, he began to reflect more intently on the subject. Now claiming that religion and its promise of a new beginning after the trials of this world was a fantasy fitted for the neurotic personality, Freud's psychoanalytic theories had a profound influence on his contemporaries.[59]

In *Totem and Taboo* (1913) Freud traced early humanity's response to death and concluded that the primitive man's 'persisting memory of the dead became the basis for assuming other forms of existence and gave him the conception of a life continuing after apparent death'. Later, in *The Future of an Illusion* (1928) he maintained that religious claims do not admit of proof and that the contradiction which they offer to reason is enough for us to dismiss them in the interest of mental health. And in his essay 'Thoughts for the Times on War and Death' (1915) he reaffirmed that 'what came into existence beside the dead body of a loved one was . . . the doctrine of the soul and the belief in immortality'.[60]

The anthropomorphism at the centre of the human world view, where creator and cosmos exist to allay human anxiety, is understandable inasmuch as humans cannot conceive of reality without using the conceptual tools available to them. But for Freud, these wish-fulfilments can neither be proved nor refuted; they reflect an infantile stage in the life of the human race. Belief in an afterlife was a psychological defence against the great fear of annihilation, a perspective that has powerfully informed the outlook of modern psychology and psychiatry. Reflecting on Freud's influence on twentieth-century thought, the Anglo-American poet and essayist W. H. Auden (1907–1973) described the great psychoanalyst as 'not a person, but a whole climate of opinion'.[61]

The Appeal of Materialism

The powerful censure of religious views of life contained in the works of Marx, Nietzsche and Freud hinged on their claims to a level of scientific certainty comparable to what had been achieved by Newton in physics and by Darwin in biology. Socioeconomic and psychological factors explained the origin of belief in the afterlife much as the universal law of gravitation explained the movement of planets and natural selection explained the rise and fall of species. Over the course of the twentieth century, the fields of genetics, the cognitive neurosciences, and even biotechnology served, in the main, to strengthen the naturalistic understanding of the person.

Research in these areas led to a shift away from more traditional notions of a fixed human nature and introduced instead the more synthetic idea of constructed identity.

Some of this work converged at mid-century with the advent of existentialist philosophy. Jean-Paul Sartre (1905–1980), one of the leading voices in the movement, called for a rejection of universal theories of human nature and instead held up the ideal of autonomous identity formation. That autonomy, Sartre believed, must be cultivated in the face of hard facts about death as a conclusive ending, not just for humans, but for an entire universe that is destined for extinction too. The novelist Albert Camus (1913–1960) wrote about the implications of our living with a silent God, if such a being exists. In The Outsider and The Myth of Sisyphus (both 1942), Camus captured both the spirit of individual despair in the midst of the Second World War and the much larger alienation occasioned by the absence of God. As unplanned and unloved parts of the larger order of things, homeless and adrift in a temporary place where anything goes because there is no arbiter of right and wrong, existentialist philosophy called for steely resolution. It was distressing advice for many, but leading existentialists found the prospect truly liberating, humanity free at last to choose its own destiny, individuals stamping life with meaning instead of receiving it pre-packaged by a personal yet strangely aloof grand architect.[62]

An increasing number of twentieth-century intellectuals were in basic agreement with this finale. Sartre's near contemporary, the British philosopher and social critic Bertrand Russell (1872–1970) reclaimed David Hume's argument that God's existence and the prospect of immortality for humans were not subject to rational proof. His personal position on the matter was categorical: 'I believe that when I die I shall rot, and nothing of my ego will survive.' Unlike Hume's last days, however, no one stood outside Russell's home in anticipation of a deathbed recantation, for by the mid-twentieth century the annihilationist standpoint no longer seemed so strange or atypical. For Russell, the fact that one could neither prove nor disprove God's existence made scepticism the only intellectually defensible position. 'The Christian God may exist,' he wrote in 1925, 'so may the Gods of Olympus, or of ancient Egypt, or of Babylon. But no one of these hypotheses is more probable than any other; they lie outside the region of even probable knowledge, and therefore there is no reason to consider any of them.'[63] Contemporary analytic philosophers have concurred with this recommendation, insisting that death does not constitute a relevant theme in philosophy.

From the mid-twentieth century and into the third millennium the materialist or physicalist position continued its slow but sure advance into the general culture. The zoologist and defender of evolutionary theory Richard Dawkins (b. 1941) has produced a number of influential books that have reached a popular readership, each book using evolutionary theory to assault religious explanations of reality as false and oppressive. And the highly regarded American biologist Stephen Jay Gould (1941–2002) joined the debate with his own forceful arguments presented in a manner that was easily accessible to a wider reading public. But unlike Dawkins, Gould questioned the claims of those who insisted that the scientific method necessarily led one off the plank into an atheistic ocean of nothingness. And even if we did live in an indifferent universe, Gould called for an existential-like response; each person must proclaim their autonomy and freedom, define and enact a world of decency.[64]

Again to Athens

There were, of course, alternate readings of the significance of evolutionary theory and psychological inquiry. Some early twentieth-century thinkers forcefully renewed the case for distinguishing between mind and body within the same organism. This organic or self-psychology perspective, while acknowledging that the soul is immanent and not transcendent, nevertheless asserted that this immanent soul is capable of surviving death. Psychologist Carl Jung (1875–1961), an early apostate from Freudian orthodoxy, wrote about the limits of organic medicine in treating various forms of neuroses and championed the curative role of psychic methods. For

Jung 'modern man can no longer refrain from acknowledging the might of the psyche, despite the most strenuous and dogged efforts at self-defence. This distinguishes our time from all others.'[65] In a 1934 essay titled 'The Soul and Death', Jung maintained that the psyche transcended the space–time continuum and deserved further research. 'The fact that we are totally unable to imagine a form of existence without space and time by no means proves that such an existence is in itself impossible.'[66] The philosopher George Santayana (1863–1952), although a metaphysical materialist who accepted that all religion was a work of human imagination, reminded those who would disparage religion that poetry, prose fiction and dramatic art were similarly imaginative works. And just as the latter three served to enrich our lives by deepening empathy and understanding, Santayana claimed that religion possesses value by virtue of its ability to lift us beyond the mundane, beyond material matters. 'The vistas it opens and the mysteries it propounds are another world to live in; and another world to live in – whether we expect ever to pass wholly into it or no – is what we mean by having a religion.'[67]

A Dome of Many-coloured Glass

The American physician, psychologist and philosopher William James (1842–1910) shared this awareness of the potential power of aesthetic and emotional forces on human well-being. A man of broad cultural and intellectual interests, James began his academic career as an instructor in physiology at Harvard and moved to the department of philosophy as senior faculty member (where one of his students was George Santayana). He was an admirer of the scientific method but grew wary of its unilateral approach to truth. Modern science, James observed, follows an unduly prescriptive set of rules, demanding that phenomena must be predictable, testable, replicable and confirmable. Identifying with a countermovement known as spiritualism, the product of growing interest in late nineteenth-century Europe and America in incidences of clair-voyance and ghostly visitations, James offered a more nuanced view of the brain's activity and purview.[68] In a lecture delivered at his home institution in 1898, he maintained that the consensus of scientifically minded observers and educated laypeople regarding the absolute dependence of one's inner life upon the brain is misplaced and denies us the possibility of considering alternative approaches to reality. While the orthodox position of anatomists, physiologists and pathologists was that all thought is a function of a brain that perishes, James wondered whether this convention, even if true, necessarily compelled us to disbelieve in immortality.

James's dissent was based on a distinction between what he termed productive and transmissive power.[69] The modern physiologist who insists that thought is a function of the brain is like the observer who claims that steam is a function of the tea kettle, light the function of an electric circuit, or power the function of the moving waterfall. Here material objects have a function of inwardly creating or producing certain effects. But in the world of physical nature productive function is but one of a number of observable functions. For example, James pointed to the trigger of a crossbow as exhibiting a permissive function when it is released; similarly when a hammer falls upon a detonating compound it permits the explosion to occur. More immediate to the problem at hand, James pointed to a transmissive function that is observable when, for example, a prism or refracting lens sifts and limits the energy of light, creating a distinctive path and shape. The keys of an organ are also transmissive, opening various pipes and thereby allowing the wind in the air chest to escape in different ways.[70]

In considering the activity of the brain, James insisted that it was appropriate to consider both functional and transmissive roles, especially in light of the fact that our view of natural phenomena may be obscured by our finite faculties of observation and analysis. What we experience on the street and in the laboratory, in other words, might in fact be mere epiphenomena of a much deeper reality. In the words of the poet Shelley: 'Life, like a dome of many-coloured glass / Stains the white radiance of eternity'.[71] James asked his audience to consider that the brain may be transmitting finite rays of consciousness that penetrate the dome from their source of origin in the absolute life of the universe. As the white radiance comes through the dome 'with all sorts of staining and distortion imprinted on it . . . even so the genuine reality of matter, the life of souls as it is in its fullness, will break through our several brains into this world in all sorts of restricted forms, and with all the imperfections and queernesses that characterize our finite individualities here below'. Even if the brain decays (witness our culture's current focus on Alzheimer's disease) and eventually dies, James held that the source of pure consciousness may continue still in the world behind the veil.[72]

To his many critics who held such a theory to be too complex and fantastical, James asserted that the functional explanation of the materialists is no less so. Indeed the production of consciousness in the brain 'is the absolute world-enigma'. All that science (even sophisticated modern neuroscience) can unveil is the concomitance of events in the brain, as 'when the currents pour through the occipital lobes, consciousness sees things'.[73] James insisted that we have no more understanding of the scientific details of function than we have of transmission. We cannot explain how material brain matter produces non-material thought – the old Cartesian dilemma – but modern science privileges (rather arbitrarily) this explanation over all others.

A Desirable State?

Self-preservation is a basic human instinct operating at a very high level irrespective of one's social and economic status. From the foragers and food gatherers of ancient times, to peasant agriculturalists of the pre-industrial age, to the more recent pioneers of medical research and practice, those engaged most directly in sustaining and prolonging life are key to individual and community well-being and in the case of the latter are accorded special recognition and appreciation. Only a tiny percentage of humans choose to end their own lives, and society persists in viewing these individuals as either unfortunates or sinners, and sometimes both. But while it is often assumed that humans naturally seek a long mortal life and immortality after death, the value of eternal consciousness or personhood has been investigated critically by some writers who foresee eternity as something less than the desirable condition that is so often assumed, something that actually diminishes the value of life, however brief it may be.

In his *Dialogues of the Dead*, the Syrian satirist Lucian of Samosata (c. 125–180) has the centaur Chiron relinquish his immortality out of boredom, now finding pleasure 'not in always having the same thing, but also in doing quite without it'.[74] Desire, it seems, the pursuit of a goal in a world of constant change, stands as a human good even if the goal is never attained. Would linear or even timeless immortality offer anything to satisfy us? In *Gulliver's Travels*, Jonathan Swift (1667–1725) introduced the immortals of Luggnagg, called Struldbrugs, who are initially admired and envied by Gulliver. But in Luggnagg the prospect of immortality was held to be a fate worse than death, as the immortals were subject to all of the infirmities of old age, including loss of memory and the onset of senility. Death will never free them from their debility.[75] The twentieth-century philosopher Bernard Williams (1929–2003) reprised Lucian's dour interpretation of immortality, suggesting that the experience would be meaningless inasmuch as closure is important to appreciating the value of an individual life. Even personal relationships with loved ones, the eternal extension of which is often cited as reason enough for immortal longings, are made more vital by their very transience. Death, in other words, gives meaning to life by virtue of the fact that we are allotted a limited time in which to make a difference both for ourselves and for others.[76]

Even Platonic disembodied immortality strikes some observers as unattractive. While for Plato the enduring soul is the real self, how would a person without a body enjoy perceptual experiences if the organs of sense have been jettisoned at death? The theologian H. D. Lewis (1910–1992) compared non-bodily eternity to the experience of dreaming or living with thoughts alone. Bernard Williams countered that while a select few of us might welcome such a disembodied state, would it satisfy 'a jolly, good-hearted fun-loving sensual character from the seaside?' To such a person the prospect of a disembodied existence might appear as the worst form of imprisonment.[77]

In a remarkable end-of-life memoir composed by a 43-year old stroke victim who awoke from a coma with full cognitive powers but having lost all physical control except for the ability to move his left eyelid, the prospect of intellection without a physical anchor is explored. The author, Jean-Dominique Bauby (1952–1997), painstakingly dictated his words letter-by-letter to an amanuensis who recited a frequency-ordered alphabet until the author acknowledged the correct letter by blinking his left eyelid. The memoir is titled The Diving Bell and the Butterfly, denoting the heavy disability of the body and the simultaneous persistence of the author's spirit and integrity. Left with virtually no means of interacting with the physical world (Bauby could see and hear), and fully aware that the medical science that saved his life has in fact prolonged his agony, Bauby imagines himself engaged in once pleasurable, everyday activities that have suddenly become part of a sensory world from which he is now forever exiled. Written with grace and without self-pity, the memoir cannot but serve to remind the reader that anything approaching disembodied personhood is a difficult concept to accept.[78]

Some writers have found comfort in the impersonal immortality associated with their progeny, while others are content with the faith that their individual identity will become one with the great over-soul of creation. Many have found reassurance in the thought of living on in the memory of family members, friends and colleagues, in what can be described as social immortality. If we are fortunate, our immediate successors – and perhaps even complete strangers – may be moved to action by the influence of our ideas, beliefs and engagements. Writing about the deism of the leading figures in the Enlightenment, the historian Carl Becker observed that 'the thought of posterity was apt to elicit from eighteenth-century philosophers and revolutionary leaders a highly emotional, an essentially religious, response.'[79] While distinction as democratic revolutionaries may elude most of us, we will certainly enjoy some measure of immortality through loved ones, and, if we are fortunate, through the memories of those who knew us. The novelist George Eliot

(1819–1880) captured this outlook at the end of her novel *Middlemarch*, where the narrator says of the story's heroine:

> the effect of her being on those around her was incalculably diffusive: for the growing good of the world is partly dependent on unhistoric acts; and that things are not so ill with you and me as they might have been, is half owing to the number who lived faithfully a hidden life, and rest in unvisited tombs.[80]

But Eliot understood that memory, individual or collective, is usually of very short duration. She would concur with Marcus Aurelius who reminded us that 'life is a little thing, and little, too, is the longest fame to come – dependent as it is on a succession of fast-perishing little men who have no knowledge even of their own selves, much less of one long dead and gone.'[81]

Two Transitions

Before the age of 50, and at the midpoint of an enormously successful professional life, the Russian author Leo Tolstoy (1828–1910) experienced a deep intellectual crisis, one that is perhaps not uncommon for even the less famous among us. Outwardly Tolstoy's personal circumstances were enviable: huge literary fame, a comfortable income and favourable domestic circumstances surrounded by a loving family. But beneath the veneer of happiness and success, the author began to experience recurring 'moments of perplexity, or a stoppage, as it were, of life, as if I did not know how I was to live, what I was to do'. What on the surface seemed like childish questions became for Tolstoy 'the deepest problems of life' that had to be answered. Why oversee his estate, educate his children and continue to write books when he knew in the end that none of these activities and accomplishments would bring satisfaction? His children, after all, were living (though unaware at the moment) in the same cruel and absurd situation. Even art (including his writing) lost its significance since it merely reflects life, and much-vaunted science offered only empirical descriptions, not meaning. A philosopher is quick to describe a principle of life and call it an idea, substance, spirit or will, 'but why this is so he does not know'.

Life, it appeared, was without meaning; death meant annihilation, and Tolstoy 'was brought to feel that I could live no longer, that an irresistible force was dragging me down into the grave'. Any residual images of a creator God were reduced to a malevolent being who must take perverse pleasure in our wretched situation. 'Illness and death would come (indeed they had come), if not today, then tomorrow, to those whom I loved, to myself, and nothing would remain but stench and worms.'[82] The only absolute knowledge available to humanity was the recognition of eternal nothingness.

These oppressive thoughts led Tolstoy to consider suicide, a means of escape 'through strength and energy of character'. But in the end he was unable to act as his reason, which confirmed the absurdity of life, dictated. Another type of 'unreasoning' knowledge offered an escape, although it had earlier been rejected by Tolstoy. It was the mainstay of the ignorant common person, those who lived and died in circumstances immeasurably more difficult than anything men of Tolstoy's social standing had ever experienced. He began to realize that for the meaning of life to be understood, 'it was first necessary that life should be something more than an evil and unmeaning thing discovered by the light of reason'. Guided not by reason but instead by a feeling that there was a cause of his being which could be accessed through the simple faith of his childhood, Tolstoy returned to the religion of his youth, outside of which he had found 'nothing but ruin'.[83]

This view was subsequently affirmed by the Spanish philosopher Miguel de Unamuno (1864–1936) in his *Tragic Sense of Life*, where he wrote that even if God and immortality are myths, we must attach ourselves to them to fend off feelings of desperation in an otherwise absurd universe. 'If consciousness is, as some inhuman thinker has said, nothing more than a flash of light between two eternalities of darkness, then there is nothing more execrable than existence.'[84] We must have assurance that our lives and work have meaning in some larger context.

But what type of afterlife? If our destiny is more than mere resuscitation, if we can be allowed to anticipate a future life that is in character fundamentally different from the one we now lead, what can we say about the connection between our imperfect present and an unrevealed sequel? Can we secure an understanding of final things, what the theologians call an eschatology?

The mathematical physicist and Anglican theologian John Polkinghorne (b. 1930) has observed how the old Platonic conception of an eternal soul temporarily confined in the fleshy body, where essential personhood is independent of the biological organism, seems increasingly untenable today. Evolutionary biology links humans with a fairly recent primate history and a much older – on the order of two billion years – history of very simple life forms. The impact of severe brain injuries, not to mention (sadly) more common drug addiction and alcohol abuse, on cognitive ability and personality are well documented and lend support to the position that essential personhood (if such a thing exists) cannot be separated from an animated body.[85] At least in the cases mentioned here, the continuity of personhood appears to rupture as brain states alter.

On the other hand, Polkinghorne reminds us that the physical atoms at the core of our bodies are continuously replaced, that we have very few atoms in our present bodies that were there as recently as two years ago. Yet for the vast majority of humans, personal identity carries seamlessly across the years and decades of our lives from childhood to old age. What seems to be the 'carrier of continuity', to use Polkinghorne's term, is an information-bearing pattern in which matter is organized in specific, highly complex ways. The pattern is never static but instead modifies as we undergo new experiences, acquire new knowledge and preserve memories during the course of our lives. For Polkinghorne, the pattern is nothing less than the enduring soul, and it is preserved beyond death by divine faithfulness. Theologians like Polkinghorne celebrate the work of scientific inquiry, but are quick to add that the economy and beauty behind the laws of nature point to something more than blind accident; they point to agency, an intelligent power at work in the universe and solicitous of human well-being. For Polkinghorne and many others who have wrestled with this question, the afterlife principle is supported by a type of evidence that is every bit as compelling as the conclusions of natural science, and offers a degree of emotional satisfaction that science cannot pretend to match. The religious understanding of life – and a possible afterlife – continues to stand its ground against the competing signals of the unlikelihood of survival after death.[86] Ancient Athenian principles retain their warrant even in the wake of a turbulent intellectual journey over the past two millennia.

THREE

Extraordinary Narratives

At its core, religion is about approaches to the transcendent from the standpoint of the temporal, observations on the infinite through the lens of the finite, and belief in the reality of an unseen order and in the rightness of action consistent with that order.[1] Religious systems engage all three of the main branches of formal philosophy: metaphysics, epistemology and ethics. The first asks about the nature of reality beyond mere appearances, the meaning of life in its deepest sense. In this context most religions assuage the great human terror that with death consciousness comes to an end, our fear that our feelings, creative impulses, personal values and hopes for reunion with loved ones will end in annihilation. Epistemology investigates what we know and how we know it, especially as this relates to establishing truth, while ethics encompasses the study of morality, the standards by which we guide our lives, how we understand right and wrong.[2] Under the latter category, religions entail a set of beliefs about a supernatural agent or agents, personal or impersonal, and a series of practices enjoined by those beliefs. Practice is typically organized in response to the demands or wishes of the supernatural power and is taken as the basic measure of religious commitment.

The religious world view has enjoyed unrivalled influence throughout history, informing systems of ethics, law, social organization and politics. Indeed despite recent philosophical challenges, the overwhelming majority of people, in every age and on every continent, have embraced a religious understanding of reality and have struggled to make that understanding manifest through doctrines, rituals and the wider lived experience. The origin and expansion of the world's major living religions is testimony to humanity's cognitive and emotional need for ordered narratives to guide us in this life, and to the strength of the human urge to live again, to secure some measure of continuity after death. The confidence that an ineffable power governs both sensory and non-sensory reality, serving as a directive force in history and providing each life with existential meaning, has translated over the centuries into a wide variety of formal belief systems.[3] Each of these systems has confidently mapped the afterlife for its adherents and provided detailed instructions on how one must complete the journey.

Since we possess no empirical knowledge of life after death, no conceptual tools to penetrate the veil, religious systems old and new tend to speak of the next world as an extrapolation of current conditions. The good afterlife, whether marked by personal consciousness or not, is simply better. At the dissolution of the biological organism all problems evaporate, illness and anguish depart, the limits of the physical are eclipsed, joy replaces sadness, peace and communion are normative.

In those religious traditions that adhere to a twofold picture of time without end, where the abode of the good stands opposite the dwelling of the damned, the residents of the latter encounter pains that seem quite physical and even barbaric. Personal deities, both in poly- and later monotheistic religions, tend to exhibit characteristics that are very human too. They can be loving and solicitous of human welfare, but just as often they can be indifferent, quick to anger and downright capricious. In most Western monotheistic religions, the relationship between the adherent and the deity is modelled after the social structure of an absolute monarchy. The deity must be praised, supplicated, feared, obeyed and loved – all unconditionally – while the votary can hope for (no guarantees here) reward in another life.[4] The late critic and famous atheist Christopher Hitchens (1949–2011) once described, in typically acerbic style, the monotheistic faiths as 'celestial North Koreas' complete with an eternal president and an earthly 'dear leader' whose cult of personality is sustained with the full range of disciplinary options associated with unlimited autocracy.[5]

A Moment of Alignment

As we saw in chapter One, the process of religious formation has prehistoric roots, but the work was never as intense as during the so-called 'Axial Age' in human history. The term was first advanced by the philosopher and psychiatrist Karl Jaspers (1883–1969) in *The Origin and Goal of History* (1949), where the author maintained that one could identify the key religious and philosophical ideas of all subsequent civilizations in formation during the pivotal centuries between approximately 800 and 200 BCE. Impressed by the appearance of major intellectual and spiritual figures around the world during these centuries, including Confucius, Laozi, Buddha, the unknown authors of the Upanishads, Zarathustra, along with the Jewish prophets and Greek philosophers, Jaspers argued that their independent explorations of the big questions – the purpose of life, the meaning of suffering, the nature of good and evil, and human destiny – were meant for a universal audience and for all time.

The ideas emanating from this era transformed culture and even collective consciousness, spurred the rise of individualism and self-awareness, and deepened the individual's relationship with larger transcendent forces. Today those who embrace a religious view of the world point to the Axial Age as a period when divinely ordained moral laws were revealed, while for secular thinkers it represents an extraordinary period of social and political crisis worldwide that gave rise to seminal teachers of great moral insight and reformist passion.[6]

A broad constellation of afterlife narratives came into view during these centuries, with each extrapolating from biological, historical and contemporary socio-cultural experience to depict the hereafter. The major religions of South and East Asia set the scene in highly figurative, even abstract terms. Bodily continuity was of less importance than conscious reunion with an overarching order of being, and while interventionist gods and spiritualized ancestors were abundant, true divinity or the final principle of creation was intangible and impersonal. Overall the tendency to anthropomorphize was absent in South and East Asian religions, with much greater attention devoted to the unitary nature of reality and its actualization in human experience.

The Abrahamic religions of the West, on the other hand, posited a dynamic relationship between God and humankind that was deeply personal and of great moral consequence. Very ancient religions generally held to the notion of a single cosmic reality, with gods inhabiting inaccessible regions of the same physical space as humans. Mountaintops, sacred groves, regions of the sky, underground dwellings – these were home to deities of every variety. Their actions determined natural phenomena, while subject humans attempted to influence the course of these divine proceedings through prayer, sacrifice and other ritual acts. The more recent religions of Christianity and Islam, on the other hand, adhere to a dualist view, with a personal God separate from the profane earth, inhabiting a region outside time and space but still active in the affairs of His subjects.[7]

According to the affiliated Western belief systems, humanity had been in chronic rebellion since the narcissistic act of Adam and Eve, and a jealous and judgemental God was serious and severe, quick to rebuke but in the end truly solicitous of the well-being of his creation. Judaism, Christianity and Islam all embraced Abraham as the first prophet and together adopted the language of secular politics (God as king), patriarchal family (God as father), and commerce (covenant with God) to describe humanity's relationship with the divine. In their mature forms all three religions hypothesized a bifurcated afterlife where very physical pains and blessings awaited the recalcitrant and the faithful respectively. For Christianity in particular, the death event was at the core of the faith, inasmuch as formal remembrance of the judicial murder of Jesus – together with his subsequent bodily resurrection – became the elemental confessional tenet for believers in community.

One of the defining features of the Axial Age was that for the first time in the history of the afterlife, the focus of attention turned decisively to the fate of the individual rather than the group or clan, where adherence to a specific life course and obedience to an ethical code functioned as a prologue to the everlasting. The significance of this shift can be seen in contrast with ancient Roman religion, the main purpose of which was to promote social cohesion and the stability of the state through civic ceremonies of prayer and sacrifice to gods associated with the public weal. It was not a personal faith centred on the relationship between the individual and his maker, but rather a collective dealing with gods who exercised power over key aspects of communal life. When early Christians refused to honour the Roman gods through the prescribed public ceremonies, they placed the state in jeopardy of losing the goodwill of the divine forces. It was this recalcitrance more than anything else that prompted the intermittent persecution of Christians by Roman authorities.

The explication of sacred written texts also moved to the fore-front of religious dialogue during the Axial Age, with important thinkers de-emphasizing the older reliance on ritual and animal sacrifice and stressing in its place the primacy of spiritual discipline and compassionate behaviour. To take just one example among many, the major religions opposed unnatural deaths like infanticide and suicide. It was the practice of empathy, the benevolent passage or Golden Rule, that enabled one to glimpse the root of creation in this life and participate in it fully after death. This ethical turn in religion emerged within the context of brutal Iron Age warfare and growing social inequality spurred by urbanization and market eco-nomics. Recoiling from the violence and persecution of their world, Axial Age thinkers strove to articulate a new religious sensibility.

For the first time, action in this life appeared to demarcate the critical attributes of the eternal journey. Distorted, abused and misappropriated by later generations to justify myriad acts of self-centred inhumanity that continue into our own day, the highly original thinkers of this period provided a touchstone for followers who sought to rise above the merely selfish and mundane. They offered guidance to those who would anchor the quest for the eternal in behaviour rather than belief, in a more expansive understanding of the human community and its needs.

Western religious perspectives on death will be our main focus here, but it is useful to gain some sense of the wider global context first, not least because non-Western traditions have enjoyed a significant level of interest in the modern, post-industrial West. This engagement with global faith pathways is especially true for those who have forsaken the traditions of their birth but who still yearn for a compelling picture of the transcendent, the wisdom of an ancient narrative that provides a larger and deeper meaning to life, even if that meaning lacks any measure of individual uniqueness or personal consciousness.

Beyond the West

Popular and Official Belief in China

Chinese civilization developed more or less independent of outside influences, and as we saw in chapter One, religion under the Shang was the product of what scholars call 'diffused' or substrate lay practice as opposed to any institutional, clerical or text-based framework. Popular beliefs, folklore, myths and values evolved gradually from within Chinese culture and were shared by the majority of the population, while later court-inspired and directed practice built upon these earlier folk ideas. Popular views of death and dying were learned originally within the context of family and village, not through a formal doctrinal religion.

In lay belief the idea of a discrete self (kuei) continuing after death was much less important that the generational and ancestral implications of the death experience. Even so, the immaterial soul was to be respected by the living. Each person was thought to be divided into two souls, an upper, intellectual soul (hun) which becomes spirit and ascends to the spiritual realm after death, and a lower or more material soul (po) which descends with the body into the grave and may function as a malevolent ghost or demon.[8] At death or in death-like experiences like sleep or coma, the hun soul left the body in the breath and wandered about; dreams were often understood as the extracorporeal wanderings of the soul while the body slept.[9]

In early Chinese culture what we might call a weak sense of survival, where one passes on one's genes or the influence of one's ideas and actions, was more significant than notions of personal continuity. For most Chinese, the prospect of moving into the ancestral spiritual realm after death, however that space was conceived, was the culmination of personal labour and sacrifices on earth. Concern with the afterlife as a permanent link with the living, then, was always an integral part of the most ancient of world civilizations, a way to acquire eternity through right action in the temporal arena. Belief in organic continuity or eternity through one's descendants, whose well-being and preparation for success in life was understood as the product of parental care and self-sacrifice, was for centuries the key principle in Chinese popular religion. Each person lived beyond the grave in the lives of their progeny, not in a personal heavenly abode.

Dutiful offspring, in return, were expected to maintain their physical bodies and conduct themselves always in a manner that reflected well on their predecessors. They were also obliged to care for aged family members and practise filial esteem. An essential facet of this communal world view was painstaking afterlife protection of the deceased – including funerals, proper burial of the corpse near the ancestral village and ongoing ritual offerings of food and gifts. The dead were to be consulted before any major undertaking, such as war, relocation or agricultural policy, since they remained a crucial part of the familial substance. Souls that were ignored or left untended not only demonstrated the unworthiness of the living descendants, but could become forces for evil in this world and wreak havoc on the social and familial well-being of the living descendants.[10]

These ancient family and clan practices were guided by belief in the essential unity and regularity of nature. Doctrines, codified articles of faith, and denominational sects, so familiar to the Western religious experience, have no counterpart in the popular Chinese tradition, where religion emerged from a particular world view and was embedded into the fabric of family and social life. Instead of formal doctrine shaping a world view, then, the Chinese world view found one of its expressions in popular religion. Under a supreme ruler, the Ti (or Di), that world view included the cyclical nature of days and seasons; the principle of growth and decline; the interaction of the living with the dead; and the bipolarity of creation – the principle of complementary and evolving opposites (yin and yang).[11] Under-pinning the authority of Ti and ancestors alike was the abstract and impersonal Tao that afforded all phenomena purpose and being. Identification with the metaphysical Tao, not with a personal god above or outside nature, was the critical Chinese quest.

Confucianism

Refinements on this basic outlook occurred during the period of the Eastern Zhou dynasty (771–256 BCE) under the guidance of a series of influential philosophical and spiritual thinkers. Often referred to as the period of 'one hundred schools', it was an age when a large number of Chinese philosophers offered their guidance in the search for an integrated reality of Tao beyond the sensory-laden experience of passive (yin) and active (yang) forces. And the advice came at a pivotal juncture for China, for by the sixth century BCE the country was afflicted by widespread political breakdown and violent civil conflict. Larger states waged relentless warfare on their smaller neighbours, internal usurpers threatened traditional leaders and the resulting social disintegration undermined respect for elders and ancestors alike. Many feared that such widespread disregard for the will of Heaven would result in cosmic upheaval, the beginning of the end time.

Into this troubled environment, around the year 551 BCE, was born the man later known in the West as Confucius. Raised in modest circumstances, he received a formal education and was employed in a series of minor official government posts before setting himself up as an itinerant tutor, offering unsolicited advice to ruling elites wherever he travelled and attracting to himself a small circle of dedicated followers. It would be these disciples who committed the main teachings of the man they called Kong Fuzi, 'Master Kong', to writing in the form of the *Analects*, short aphorisms and practical wisdom that on the surface lack much speculative content. Confucius died in 479 BCE, never having secured the influential political office that he felt would alone enable him to influence the wider culture.[12] In this he was to be proved quite wrong.

Although Confucianism is often interpreted as a secular ethical philosophy dealing solely with right (moral) behaviour and social order, when considered within the context of the overarching Chinese view of order in the cosmos, its essential religious character is brought into sharper relief. During the period of the Eastern Zhou, the worship of deities and spirits began to include a new emphasis on moral criteria in judgement. A person's moral behaviour became the key reference by which the spirits responded to supplications.[13] With heaven and earth as part of a continuum where one's ancestors inhabit the former, the living could be assured of joining those who have preceded them so long as right relationships were maintained on earth.

The specifics of that ultimate coming together were of little interest to Confucius. When questioned directly about death and the afterlife, Confucius responded that since humans know so little about life they should not presume to understand or speak about its sequel. As long as the living cannot serve each other, how can they expect to serve the ancestors? Confucius was a traditionalist; he looked back to the early Zhou as an age of peace and unity and he affirmed the priorities embedded in popular religion. But in addition to honouring one's ancestors through ritual observance, Confucius added that it was equally important to ensure that one's living neighbours be treated with generosity and respect.

By privileging humane service to others over the performance of sacrifice and ritual, Confucius made right behaviour the key prerequisite to a genuine religious sensibility or alignment with the Tao of the universe. Just as the early Zhou emperors formulated the concept of the 'will' or 'mandate of heaven' (Tianming) to legitimize their ouster of the Shang, the Confucians internalized the mandate and privileged desirable action over ritual. For 'Master Kong', the life of virtue always took priority over the most observant ritual; doing the right thing mattered more than doing things right. The fourth-century BCE thinker Mencius defended the Confucian approach to religion by highlighting the other-regarding and bene-volent (Ren) side of human nature, innate qualities that were to be cultivated through example and education.[14]

Taoism

Like Confucius and Mencius, the authors of the Tao-Te-Ching (Classic of the Way) and Zhuangzi, if in fact such wise men ever existed, lived through the early stages of the Warring States period (c. 475–221 BCE). Very little is known of the mystic Laozi, the supposed author of the Tao-Te-ching. Tradition places him as an older contemporary of Confucius who briefly served as court archivist under the Chou, but contemporary scholarship tends to identify him with a later period. Zhuang Zhou's historicity is equally uncertain, with some scholars maintaining that the book that bears his name may have been authored by multiple philoso-phers. Both men (or the works that bear their names) rejected the activist and engaged profile of Confucianism, advising instead an intensely esoteric, personal and inward reform, a release from conventional views of the world and the cultivation of spiritual self-determination.[15]

It is difficult to define or capture the essence of Taoism since the word applies broadly to both the mundane realm of proper conduct and to an anonymous divine will, the limitless order of creation. Early adherents were secretive and preferred to speak of Taoism's philosophical positions in riddles. The famous opening of the Tao-Te-Ching avers that 'The Way [Tao] that can be spoken of, is not the constant Way', suggesting the unchanging but indeterminate (for humans) first principle behind all sensory reality. The Tao is imper-sonal but requires a particular approach to life, reflected in the term wu-wei, or inactive action, a sort of doing without endeavouring. In Taoism, the human challenge is to act in the world without personal attachment to the act, to be in the world but not of it, living modestly and in alignment not with the standards of artificial civilization but with nature or the transcendent Way.[16]

Zhuang Zhou illustrated this unique approach to life by insisting that liberation was not simply freedom from restraint as conventionally understood, but freedom from the imperfections of consciousness, the preferences of one's inclinations.[17] Freedom also involves acceptance of biological death as a law of nature, for the truly wise person is prepared to move beyond the troubles of this world to embrace whatever state obtains after the end of life. Zhuang Zhou emphasizes the point by quoting the words of a disabled person – 'I received life because the time had come; I will lose it because the order of things passes on.' In another passage a wise man named Master Lai reflects on his impending death:

> Now, having had the audacity to take on human form once,
> if I should say, 'I don't want to be anything but a Man!
> Nothing but a man!' the Creator would surely regard me as
> a most inauspicious sort of person. So now I think heaven
> and earth as a great furnace, and the Creator as a skilled
> smith. Where could he send me that would not be all right?[18]

Life and death were but two aspects of the Tao, with death as transformation into non-being, from the active yang to the passive yin. Like the Tao itself, whatever comes after death is unknowable and every effort to articulate its contours only takes one further from the truth. The achievement of wisdom, the forgetting of self, includes the complete elimination of the distinction between life and death and acceptance of the natural order.

Taoism eventually reached the status of a formally organized religion with its own temples, monasteries and a strong emphasis on salvation, guiding adherents in the practice of right living in preparation for an eternal state. Belief in the value of alchemy, in the existence of heavenly immortals who reside in celestial regions, earthly immortals who inhabit sacred forests and mountains, and in human beings who appear to die but merely shed themselves of the body all became part of the Taoist picture of the afterlife. The individual who reached the state of perfection was assumed to be beyond ordinary feeling and perception, at one with the rhythm of being. He appears in the world to guide others, work wonders and otherwise help humanity move beyond its existential predicament. Consisting of a spirit essence and spontaneous intuitions, the Taoist sage is removed from the material world but accessible to those who make the right effort.[19]

Death and Life in South Asia

Our knowledge of the indigenous peoples of India is limited to the archaeological remains along the Indus river valley in the northwest. Here, beginning around 2500 BCE, a sophisticated urban civilization first emerged and flourished for over 1,000 years before a combination of natural disasters and outside incursions led to its collapse. Spanning hundreds of miles from the upper alluvial plain called the Punjab into the lower reaches of the Indus river called Sind, Neolithic farmers supported cities such as Mohenjo-Daro and Harappa that were home to as many as 40,000 inhabitants.

What the inhabitants of these highly organized towns and cities believed about death and the afterlife is unknown. Archaeological excavations have failed to identify the sorts of temples or monumental sculpture that were characteristic of the ancient Near East. In addition, the pictographic script used by this civilization has yet to be deciphered by modern scholars, and the meaning of many terracotta artefacts that have been uncovered, including what appear to be mother-goddess figurines, remains highly contested. The dead were buried with their heads to the north and grave goods included pottery and weapons, but nothing can be said regarding the significance of these early mortuary practices.[20]

What is more certain is that by 1500 BCE warring, light-skinned semi-barbaric migrants who called themselves Ayrans, or 'noble' people, entered the region from the north via the Hindu Kush passes and, with their superior weapons and horse-drawn chariots, proceeded to oppress the darker-skinned natives. The Ayrans referred to the indigenous population as *Dasas*, or savages, and treated them accordingly. It was the beginning of a system of formal social segregation that would result in the intractable caste system in India.

By 1000 BCE, four distinct classes were identifiable: Brahmins (priests), Kshatriyas (nobles and warriors), Vaishyas (artisans and landholding commoners) and Shudras (workers or servants). These basic social divisions, with their corresponding attitudes towards hierarchy and deference, would survive into the twentieth century.

Early Ayran religious beliefs, perhaps an amalgam of the two cultures, are known to us through over a thousand sacred devotional hymns and rituals recognized collectively as the Vedas. Believed to have been composed by divinely inspired priestly elites over a thousand years, from around 1500 to 500 BCE, the Vedas were memorized and transmitted orally for hundreds of years and became the touchstone of the most ancient of contemporary world religions. Written down in Sanskrit around 1000 BCE, they emphasize ritual observance and dutiful sacrifice to deceased ancestors and gods as the essential elements of religious practice.[21]

The Vedas introduced a pantheon of gods and goddesses that had to be propitiated under the careful guidance of the Brahmins. The god Yama, for instance, was the Lord of the Dead and in one version is represented as the first human to achieve immortality by triumphing over selfishness and maintaining steadfast loyalty to the gods. The god Agni was associated with fire and cremation rituals; he was believed to carry offerings up to the other gods and to safeguard the passage of the deceased into the world of the dead. The relationship between the gods and humans in these early texts highlights proper observance rather than right or moral action. But even with their multiple deities, these texts also anticipate the emergence of a spiritual reality transcending individual gods to present an abstract, pantheistic principle of absolute being, or Brahman. Indeed the multiple deities in the Hindu tradition, including Brahma the creator, Vishnu the benevolent preserver and Shiva the destroyer are introduced as official expressions or manifestations of an all-inclusive Brahman.

Vedic Brahmins originally followed the pattern of other Indo-European peoples in holding that individuals live only once and that the contours of the hereafter are determined by one's temporal behaviour. They conceived of life after death as a non-individualistic world of the fathers in the company of the sky-gods. Through ritual and offering the living seek to enlist the aid of this august collective. In these earliest texts the path of dutiful action, or karma marga, served as a prerequisite to an afterlife with the fathers, a state that is the ideal continuation of earthly existence.[22] But centuries after the first transmission of the Vedas, around 600 BCE, a series of poetic and prose commentaries known as the Upanishads helped to reframe the nature of the post-mortem experience.

Authored by a minority of Brahmins who came to reject what they viewed as the stultifying rigidity and complexity of ritualistic faith, the Upanishads and the two great Hindu epics from approximately the same period, the Mahabharata and the Ramayana, asserted that each person possesses within themselves an element of eternal Brahman, called Atman, which seeks to be released from the body and returned to its origin. That longed-for reabsorption, or moksha, was a quest that carried over through multiple cycles of death and rebirth where the soul transmigrated, a process known as samsara, until it achieved complete enlightenment through ascetic renunciation of the material. With meditation and asceticism one came to realize that the heterogeneous sensory world was maya or illusion; the true essence of life was unity and oneness with the total scheme of things, and one's actions, or karma, played a determinative role in setting one's path towards moksha.[23]

In this deeply anti-personal but ethically driven reality the fact of death is not to be lamented but rather seen as an ending to one incarnation among many, a stage in an extended journey towards true enlightenment and knowledge of the nature of being. Handling of the dead body reflected this outlook, with cremation occurring as quickly as possible in order to hasten the release of the spirit (athuna) for its next journey. For most ordinary Indians, following personal duty (dharma) meant accepting the responsibilities appropriate to one's caste, sex and stage in life. The fulfilment of dharma in our present station, the principal message of the Bhagavadgita (one of the books that make up the larger Mahabharata), is the only legitimate intersection between the activities of the transmigrated soul and the temporal world. For the exceptional follower, however, abandonment of the world, renunciation of action in it and the elimination of ego prepare one for moksha. Only genuine liberation can bring a close to life and the afterlife, a cyclical process in which one death is part of an elongated series.

In the view of the Upanishads, the enlightened soul is in the world but not of it, sees through conventional earthly ambitions and divorces itself from the illusion of beings and things. By the late Vedic period (c. 500 BCE) groups of ascetics began to claim greater religious authority throughout India, marginalizing orthodox Brahmin priests and practising a form of mystical exercise called *yoga* that stood in stark contrast to the externalities of brahminic sacrifice. In time the Upanishads became an integral part of the Hindu perspective, not abolishing the older focus on ritual and sacrifice but adding a newer ethical and non-material perspective. Death consisted of a series of changes through which the individual soul passed, while the permanent afterlife emerged as the soul's escape from all existence, from heaven and hell, from gods and goddesses, from the tiresome trials of temporal place.

Buddhism

Like later Christianity and Islam, Buddhism finds its roots in the words and actions of a historical founding figure who wrote nothing himself but nonetheless wields extraordinary influence over the faith community. Born around 563 BCE and raised in comfortable circumstances near the border of modern Nepal, at age 29 Siddartha Gautama abandoned home and family to pursue an answer to the problems associated with sickness, old age, death – and rebirth. His initial efforts, including study under respected teachers and self-mortification, proved unhelpful. Finally through yogic meditation, and without the assistance of ritual or devotion to a particular god, he was able to grasp the cycle of existence and discovered a means of securing full enlightenment in one lifetime.[24] From that point forward, teaching the 'four noble truths' to others became the mission of the Buddha or 'enlightened one'. These included the realization that (1) all life involves suffering, or dukkha; (2) the root cause of suffering is desire; (3) the elimination of desire brings a close to suffering; (4) and the appropriate path to this selfless end is eight-fold and includes both thought and behaviour. Without a strict theology or ritual practice, without an official priestly class or sacred texts, without caste or hierarchy, Buddhism's simple yet powerful message was that only through compassion and the complete elimination of selfish desire could one escape karmic bondage, the cycle of bodily existence.[25]

At the heart of Buddhism's understanding of death and the afterlife was its denial of the reality of the individual fixed self. Although an outgrowth of India's majority Hindu culture that stressed the underlying unity of self and Atman, Buddhism claimed that the impermanence of sensory reality included the personal 'I' and that once this was understood all fear of death would vanish. Nibbana, or Nirvana, is a state where the illusion of self is unmasked and peacefulness attained in a state beyond death, a state without striving or desire and thus without the accumulation of karma that leads to death and rebirth.[26]

The Buddha realized that eradicating all desires while still alive and committing to a life of selfless compassion towards all creatures was a path that only the spiritually mature could achieve; most humans would continue the cycle of death and rebirth for many life-times as they learned to temper and finally snuff out their earthly desires. In the narratives describing the Buddha's death, or Parinib-bana (Parinirvana), the 80-year-old teacher chose the place of his final departure, lay down on his right side, entered a process of desireless meditation – and breathed his last. The component elements of his identity as a person (the skandhas) dispersed and the earthly Buddha was eclipsed.

Buddhism, like Christianity, was to have its greatest impact in lands far distant from its point of origin. Introduced into China during the Han dynasty, it found some appeal among Taoists who shared Buddhism's approach to meditative practice. With the col-lapse of the Han in the early third century, a long period of political unrest and civil disorder undermined the influence of Confucianism and Taoism and provided an opportunity for the Buddhist monks, translators, teachers and missionaries who made their way from south and central Asia to China via a network of roads known collectively as the great Silk Route. The growth took place roughly at the same time Christianity was expanding out of Palestine into the western Roman Empire. And just as the patronage of the Roman Empire facilitated the diffusion of Christian teaching during the fourth century, the northern Wei dynasty of the fifth century oversaw translations and the building of Buddhist monasteries. During the Tang dynasty (618–907) additional royal support for the imported religion resulted in the capital of Chang'an becoming a major centre of Buddhist thought, home to Chinese Buddhists who had travelled to India and fostered additional cultural exchanges. It was during the Tang period that Buddhism began to make inroads into Korea and Japan.[27]

Jewish, Christian and Muslim Personalism

Early Judaism

The Jews of ancient Palestine felt no call to emphasize the integrity of the person after biological death, but envisioned instead a fate similar to the Hades of ancient Greece or the bleak underworld of the Mesopotamians. Life itself, not some future existence, was humanity's ultimate reward. Simply put, there is no theology of death and a personal afterlife in ancient Judaism because there was no significance attached to the expiration of the individual. 'The dead know nothing,' wrote the author of Ecclesiastes, 'they have no more reward; but the memory of them is forgotten.'[28] The Book of Genesis focused on the cause of death – human pride and disobedience – not on its sequel, and punishment involved expulsion, physical labour and the myriad pains of mortality.

In early Jewish culture each person was viewed as an animated body rather than an incarnate soul, as a part of the natural order instead of a special creation distinct from that order. At birth the impersonal breath of life quickens a material body for thought and action, but at the moment of death, when the breath returns to God, what had once appeared as a single personality in this life reverts to nothingness. All will follow Job into Sheol, 'to the land of darkness and of gloom, to a land as dark as midnight, utter chaos, with no light but the shades of death'.[29]

With the deceased continuing on in Sheol, an unattractive, non-moral shadow-world devoid of contact either with kinsman or God, the Hebrews shared a basic pessimism with the pre-Socratics in Greece. Homer's Elysian Fields, after all, were reserved for the select few, while the shades of Erebus offered at best a sort of half-consciousness for its inhabitants. Achilles' memorable rebuke of Odysseus after being offered the prospect of great power within the realm of the dead, where the hero 'would rather be ploughman to a yeoman farmer on small holding than lord paramount in the kingdom of the dead' sums up the gloomy prospect.[30] The ancient Jewish God was unmistakably a God of the living, and the integrity and continuity of the community through time took firm precedence over the eternal well-being of the constituent members of the nation.[31] Just as the Hindu strove to extinguish the self in the drive for the union of Atman with Brahman, ancient Judaism deprecated the centrality of the individual in discussions of the afterlife.

Still, the Jewish picture of the hereafter was never static, moving haltingly in the later, post-exilic centuries towards a focus on the self separate from the fate of the community. The influence of Zoroastrian and Egyptian ideas on the emergence of this evolving outlook should not be discounted. But of even greater significance was the tragic experience of political exile and national calamity in the centuries preceding the birth of Christ. Changes in analysis of the end time, in other words, were closely related to changes in Jewish society, culture and politics.[32] And while references to the resurrection of the third day in the Book of Hosea and talk of the reanimation of dried-up bones in Ezekiel are more properly metaphors for the national restoration of Israel, by the second century BCE the first unambiguous reference to the restoration of the dead occurs in the Book of Daniel. No longer solely concerned with the glorious re-establishment of the state and the inauguration of the temporal golden age, we now find a more particular comfort where 'many of those who sleep in the dusk of the earth shall awake, some to everlasting life, and some to everlasting shame and contempt.'[33]

Unfortunately, the Hebrew Bible, or Tanakh, does not detail the precise form this afterlife will take, but clearly the covenant has shifted from the fate of the people to the portion awaiting the individual, a momentous conceptual change that gave expression to the principle that Yahweh's love for the individual ego was supreme over death. This transition was doubtless strengthened by the influence of Hellenic thought after the region came under Greek rule in the late fourth century BCE.[34] Platonism, with its sharply dualistic picture of an immortal soul temporarily imprisoned in a finite and distracting body, where death is accepted, indeed anticipated with equanimity in the expectation that true knowledge awaits the liberated soul, captured the imagination of the Pharisaic community in Palestine.

During the mid-second century BCE, as Jews were singled out for punishment by their Greek overlords for refusing to give up their faith, rabbis began to claim that those who remained faithful to the Torah would rise again to enjoy eternal life. For the first time it was possible to conceive of death as a friend, a welcome albeit mysterious passage into an enormously more satisfying reality, one where temporal time-consciousness is abandoned for a static, changeless eternity. The fully liberated soul can then comprehend the overall order of the cosmos from nothing less than a God's-eye perspective.[35]

Another feature of this transition, championed by writers known as Pharisees, involved the exceptional Jewish idea of a Messiah or saviour who not only would emancipate individuals from their oppressors but establish the entire Jewish people in a restored land of the living. The Sadducees, or members of the upper-class clergy, tended to disparage these new ideas, but by the second century CE the Pharisee position, embodied later in texts called Talmud, had achieved canonical status. More than a Platonic oneness concept whereby what is essential is liberated at death and reunited with a supra-mundane reality or principle of eternity, resurrection entailed righteous victory of body and soul over one's oppressors and

the restoration of the Jewish people in community. It was a momentous reinterpretation of death and its aftermath that singled out a small
community for extraordinary treatment in a terrestrial locale. In the
nineteenth century, Reform Jews downplayed resurrection of the
body and again stressed the immortality of the soul, but conservative
Jews continued to accept the idea of bodily resurrection.[36]

The Christian Initiative

Historic Christianity is anchored firmly in the conviction that our
transient earthly journey is but a preface to eternal life made possible
by the God-man Christ's death and resurrection. The hardships,
suffering and injustices of this unfriendly world are to be borne with
patience and compassion in the expectation of a great reward, a
beatific vision of God where, according to the apostle John, 'We
shall be like him because we will see him as he really is.'[37] For now,
according to St Paul, 'We see through a glass, darkly; but then face
to face: now I know in part; but then shall I know even as also I am
known.'[38] Without Christ's supreme sacrifice on the cross, however,
without a painful and humiliating death as an alleged criminal at
the hands of Roman authorities, and without the miracle of a
resurrection, the entire framework of the Christian promise comes
to naught. Fideism, an attitude of mind which denies that unaided
reason, using logical arguments and intellectual speculation, can
reach certitude on these matters, is at the hub of the promise; one
must implicitly trust in the veracity of an extraordinary event.

As far as one can tell by relying on the Gospel narratives written
some four decades after the crucifixion, Jesus accepted the Pharisaic
emphasis on bodily resurrection and an afterlife for the individual.
But sharing with many of his contemporaries in an expectation of
the imminent close of human history, Jesus had nothing specific to
say about the condition of the faithful departed beyond the assurance that the new life would be spiritual and immortal, devoid of
both family ties and the marriage bond. It was a view not without
precedent in the Tanakh.[39] In fact, the only detailed picture of the
afterlife in Jesus's teachings concerns the lot of sinners, all of whom

will 'weep and gnash their teeth' in a place where 'their worm does not die, and the fire is not quenched' and where 'the smoke of their torment goes up forever and ever, and they have no rest, day or night.'[40] The Christian approach to death would until very recent times maintain this strong emphasis on the negative prospects for errant humanity. The shaping of a radically dualist system where extremes of serenity and torment, light and darkness, functioned as the transcendent reference points for those living in what is essentially a transfer station, defined the nature of human purpose within the divine order.[41]

But while confidently assuming the reality of a conscious soul substance in the afterlife, Jesus did not share in the Platonic conviction that this soul was immortal by nature. In a lecture at Harvard University in 1955, the German theologian Oscar Cullman dramatically illustrated the central difference between the Platonists and the nascent Christian view of immortality in his description of the deaths of Socrates and Jesus. Cullman juxtaposed the equanimity and composure of Plato's teacher when facing a death which would result in the liberation of the enduring soul with the anguish and fear which seizes Jesus the man who recognizes that immortality is a gift from the Father not lightly bestowed upon undeserving humanity, and if withheld would result in the annihilation of the self-conscious being.[42]

The indivisible and non-spatial human soul was immortal not by virtue of its defining qualities, as Socrates would have it, but by divine preference alone. In the words of the seventeenth-century English divine John Donne (1572–1631), 'It is Safelier said to be immortall, by preservation, then immortall by nature; that God keeps it from dying, then, that it cannot dye.'[43] Each human soul was fashioned anew, ex nihilo, sometime between conception and birth. Resurrection was nothing less than a reversal of death brought about by an all-powerful God who is master of the great creationist drama.[44] Indeed the intense concern which Jesus expressed over the need for men and women to bring their lives into conformity with the divine mandate was the product of his understanding of the contingent nature of eternal life.

The immaterial, indivisible, non-spatial soul substance of Christianity, while situated in the animated body, could not be localized to any particular part of the physical frame such as the head or heart. It was, nevertheless, linked with the life history of a unique person and as such would be subject to some form of conscious experience after the death of the body and before the general resurrection, end time or eschaton. The precise nature of this attenuated post-mortem experience would depend entirely on the conduct of one's life while the soul inhabited the flesh. Thus while the individual personality consisted of body and soul (metaphysical dualism), the soul would be the first to face the consequences of sinful conduct after death; it alone would taste the first fruits of divine justice while the body returned to ashes pending the great assize on the last day.[45]

In a manner strikingly similar to Confucius, Jesus cautioned that speculation about the particulars of a post-resurrection existence only served to distract from the important business of preparation. More than anything else, it was his concern with issues of life, with the way people behaved towards one another and before God, that led Jesus to enjoin men to follow him 'and leave the dead to bury the dead'.[46] The message of the synoptic Gospels was that God would provide all that is necessary for those who embrace the path of righteousness, that death had no power over those who believed. The biological death that has signified the demise of the entire psychophysical being in early Judaism can no longer destroy life as long as God wills otherwise. Christ's unprecedented sacrifice on behalf of sinful humanity had ensured the survival of the immaterial substance and made possible the reunion of spirit and matter at the resurrection.

Christian Anthropology

In light of the fact that the 27 writings that make up the New Testament are the product of two cultures, one Semitic and the other Hellenistic, and that new issues arose as the faith spread westward, it is not surprising that there is no clearly stated doctrine of death and the afterlife in the text, no unity of thought transcending a particular historical context.[47] In fact it was a Greek-speaking Jew from Tarsus in Asia Minor who was the first to address the topic of death in a direct manner. St Paul joined the community of early Christians well after the execution of Jesus, and his writings focus not on the life of Christ or on his role as judge at the close of historic time, but rather on the significance of his death and return for humankind, emphasizing the spiritualized nature of the resurrected body. This was in opposition to a competing theory calling for the restoration of an earthly kingdom and a reanimated physical body where the deceased would return to enjoy the fruits of a new Israel.[48]

This rival theory, as we have seen, was the product of Jewish apocalyptic thinking and the expectation of a renewed state under divine auspices. The Pauline dissent was part of a broader design, also endorsed by John in the later Book of Revelation, to appeal to a gentile audience by reorienting Christian thinking in the direction of a heavenly kingdom outside the petty concerns of national rehabilitation. For St Paul, who was probably unfamiliar with the empty tomb reports, bodily expiration was viewed not as a friend or stage of development, but as the last and greatest enemy, an enemy defeated solely by Christ's sacrifice.[49] In his precedent-setting letters to the Romans, Paul describes death as a punishment for the sin of Adam, something utterly alien to the classical point of view. As a consequence the entire death experience was redefined as something unnatural, something outside of God's initial promise to humankind, an evil which ought never to have been experienced. Under this new analysis, the first man had been created in the image of God and had he not sinned, he would not have merited the curse that now filled his descendants with fear and dread.[50]

In the early fifth century the influential North African bishop St Augustine would affirm Paul's verdict on the origin of death and extend its implications by remarking that Adam and Eve, 'having become sinners, they were so punished with death, that whatsoever sprang from their stock should also be punished with the same death'. Sin was pressing down on the immortal soul while the earthly city of man distracted Adam's offspring from the goal of rebirth in Christ. 'Hence the whole mass of the human race is condemned' unless delivered by undeserved grace of God.[51]

Critics of the Christian story across the centuries have insisted that on the popular level at least, fear of the pains of hell has been a more potent factor in shaping the conduct of men and women than any positive description or promise of salvation.[52] Certainly one can find substantial evidence in support of this view in the homiletic literature of the medieval and early modern periods. The sixteenth-century Catholic martyr Thomas More, to give just one example, in an unfinished treatise entitled 'The Four Last Things' thought that sin could be best avoided through 'the deep imagination of the dreadful doom of God, and bitter pains of purgatory or hell, of which every one passeth and exceedeth many deaths'.[53] Subsequent Church leaders embraced this harsh perspective and incorporated it into an action plan for the pastoral rehabilitation of the faithful.

The Islamic Derivative

As the youngest and fastest growing of the world's major monotheistic faith traditions, Islam first emerged in the Arabian Desert, its few cities a crossroads for merchants and traders whose caravan enterprises linked Mesopotamia and Egypt with the Indus Valley. In their travels many of these Arab merchants were exposed to Jewish, Zoroastrian and Christian thought; some even formed small communities in desert enclaves. Pre-Islamic Arabia was a physically harsh land of nomadic Bedouins organized by tribes who for the most part lived at subsistence level. Archaeological evidence indicates that the population adopted a polytheistic set of beliefs, organized around celestial and meteorological deities. Together with the rise of local gods associated with place and weather was an animistic belief in spirits and demons, or jinn, active in all aspects of life. The dead were buried with great care, with grave goods provided to assist those whose nomadic wanderings had come to a close, but there is no indication of belief in a distinct post-mortem existence.[54]

The man who would become the prophet Muhammad (c. 570–632) was a native of the city of Mecca, an orphan who was raised by an extended family in the Quraysh clan. By Muhammad's youth Mecca had emerged as a commercial caravan junction and, more importantly, as a pilgrim centre for those who came to venerate a black meteoric stone, the Kaaba. Tradition held that the Hebrew patriarch Abraham had built a temple around the stone during an extended visit with his son Ishmael. Muhammad began work in the commercial sector and in his twenties married his wealthy employer, a widow whose caravan business doubtless brought its employees into contact with a wide range of social and religious ideas that were unfamiliar to traditional pastoralists.

Tradition describes Muhammad as an introspective man who spent considerable time in nearby mountain caves engaged in solitary prayer and reflection. At the age of 40 this contemplative man of affairs suddenly heard a voice calling him to recite messages from the one God, Allah, through the mediation of Jibreel, the Archangel Gabriel. This Muhammad did, intermittently, over the next two decades. Taken down by his early followers and committed to writing in Arabic after his death, the sacred text of Islam known as the Qur'an is considered to be inerrant, with Muhammad serving as the mouthpiece of Allah and the last of the great prophets in a long line extending from Moses to Abraham to Jesus. The religious texts of Judaism and Christianity, rich with dramatic narrative and compelling characters, are viewed as important to Muslims, but secondary to the final and most sacred revelation of Allah – his direct words – in the Qur'an.[55]

With its firm foundation in monotheism and connections to the earlier Jewish and Christian traditions, the subject of death and the afterlife in the Qur'an and in later accounts of the sayings and habits of the Prophet, known as the Hadith, is treated in significant detail. The origin of death is traced back to the offence of Adam and Eve, and while expelled permanently from the Garden, their descendants are given a respite for the duration of their natural lives to return to the straight path and affirm their submission to God through orthopraxy.[56] For the prophet Muhammad, life is an extended preparation for death, and true believers are required to test each of their daily actions and decisions in light of their ultimate destinies. In particular, descriptions of paradise have an unusually physical and sensual quality combined with an exclusive focus on male enjoyment. Lush gardens (in sharp contrast to the desert environs where Islam was born), an abundance of nutritious food and the companionship of beautiful virgins are the main pleasures. In addition to sensory delight, the faithful will be rewarded with an eternity in the presence of Allah, a spiritual reward not dissimilar to the medieval Christian vision of God. The mystical Sufi branch of Islam accords special prominence to blissful union as a state incomparably more satisfying than sensual reward. Hell, on the other hand, is characterized by unending fire (an image familiar to Christians) and the use of boiling water to torment unrepentant sinners. The latter succumbed in life to the blandishments of evil jinn, the chief of whom, Iblis, is the equivalent of the Judaeo-Christian Satan.[57]

Given the emphasis in the Qur'an on the physical aspects of the afterlife, a strong affirmation of bodily resurrection after the final judgement stands at the core of the faith. Cremation was never an option within this faith community. Upon death the body was to be buried quickly, in a plain coffin and with modest cemetery markings, all in keeping with the equality of souls that is emphasized in the Qur'an. An intermediary state or Barzakh is the temporary fate of the majority, but as with Christianity the central text has nothing to say about its precise nature. The Hadith literature and subsequent commentary forged a composite picture where sinners and saved alike have a foretaste of their eternal fate, but the interregnum itself is often pictured as a dreamless state, one where there is no possibility of communication between the living and the dead. None of this applied to heroic martyrs in the faith who, like the Christian saints, enter directly into paradise upon completion of their difficult temporal mission.

Islam forecasts a dramatic end time, with the close of the temporal human story marked by the coming of a person named the Mahdi. Charged with destroying oppression and defeating the enemies of true religion, Sunnis associate the Mahdi with a member of the tribe of the Prophet while Shi'ites identify him with the Twelfth Imam, Muhammad al-Mahdi.[58] Both of the major branches of Islam believe that the rule of the Mahdi will restore peace and justice on earth in preparation for the return of Christ to Jerusalem, an event that will mark the close of history and signal the day of resurrection and divine judgement. The Qur'an describes that day in dramatic detail, with bodies swarming out of their graves like locusts, the heavens split open and mountains levelled. Books will be opened detailing every word and action, to be followed by a precise reckoning. Islam is a religion of salvation by works made possible through the mercy of God.

The Catholic Way and the Protestant Amendment

The Christian view of human nature was at once both deeply depressing and engaging, an outlook without peer in terms of its potential to promote, often simultaneously, concerted reform and insidious despair. Both responses were amply displayed during Europe's central and later Middle Ages, when an entire culture – clerical and lay, young and old, affluent and impoverished – seemed obsessed with death. Concern with the fate of one's soul, especially with the apparent postponement of the end time that had been eagerly anticipated by early Christians, led to the invention of a provisional post-mortem waypoint for sinners. This middle place or purgatory became a critical category, informing the thought, organization and even the architecture of the medieval Catholic Church.[59]

During the period between death and the final assize, Church authorities proposed that the soul experienced a life of its own outside the body. In the thirteenth century St Thomas Aquinas described how merit and fault 'are fitted only to the body through the soul', thereby making it reasonable to expect that 'since the souls had priority in the fault or merit, they have priority also in being punished or rewarded'. The soul, as historian Jacques Le Goff observed, was 'endowed with a materiality *sui generis*' in purgatory, the expiatory punishment inflicted there described in terms of physical experience.[60]

While certain of ultimate salvation, the inhabitants of purgatory were believed to suffer pains every bit as intense as those awaiting the damned after the final judgement. And in order for these cleansing pains to make sense to the unlettered faithful, a sort of analogue to the physical body was put forward by Church authorities. In the *Purgatorio*, the second part of Dante's *Divine Comedy*, the author fears that he has been abandoned by his guide because he sees only Virgil's own shadow before him. But Virgil is with Dante, just in a different body, one that is appropriate to a person who is neither damned nor prepared for eternal bliss. This purgatorial body is ordered by divine omnipotence

> To suffer torments, both of cold and heat,
> Bodies like this that Power provides, which wills
> That how it works be not unveiled to us.[61]

The majority of humans must be prepared to experience the pains of this locale, of course, for only those who have loved God for his own sake, who reject sin not out of fear of hell but for the greater glory of their Creator, would escape the violence of a cleansing fire where the punishment always fit the crime. A growing belief in the efficacy of the Catholic Mass to abbreviate the pains of the souls assigned to purgatory led to a robust expansion in the numbers of ordained priests during the High Middle Ages. Indeed a whole new category of 'chantry' priests who dedicated themselves exclusively to prayer on behalf of a deceased patron became a 'must have' for the ranks of the elite. For those less fortunate, recourse was naturally to the prayers of loved ones, neighbours and fellow members of guilds and fraternities, all of whom could play a critical role in abbreviating the time in which the faithful were assigned to purgatory.

Serving not only as a comfort for the dying, this constellation of beliefs made the loss of a loved one less final for survivors who could begin participating in a wide range of rites, perpetuity masses, anniversary services and memorial building, all designed to maintain the connection between the living and the dead.[62] One of the most popular and affordable rituals designed to extend the interaction between the living and the dead was the trental of St Gregory, a celebration consisting of three masses on consecutive days after burial. To take just one example, it is estimated that 28 per cent of all testators in the English town of Bury St Edmunds paid the required 10 shillings for these masses during the second half of the fifteenth century, testimony to the power of Church teaching on the subject of death.[63] The Feast of All Souls, bringing members of the parish together for a procession around the churchyard and the blessing of graves, guaranteed that those who had died without living friends to pray for them were not left without the assistance of the community.[64] The embellishment of churches also gathered momentum during the course of the fifteenth century as affluent worshippers sought to minimize their upcoming residence in purgatory through generous giving now. Church decoration together with the donation of funds for vestments, chalices and statues provided the benefactor with a means of keeping his family name before future parishioners who would, it was hoped, continue to pray for the souls of the departed whose names were inscribed on the gifted items.[65]

The late Middle Ages, especially the century after the terrible experiences of the Black Death (1347–9) when upwards of one-third of the faithful perished, was the era of the *danse macabre*, when ubiquitous death was portrayed as a smirking corpse who summoned every person to provisional dissolution. Meant simultaneously to disgust and to spark immediate repentance at all costs, the image of putrefying flesh and the body as food for worms was commonplace in churches and private chapels alike. In England, the double-decker *transi*, or cadaver tombs, were a favourite of ecclesiastics, where on the top deck resided the stone image of the deceased in restful repose and outfitted in full clerical regalia, while beneath lay the contrasting figure of the decaying and repugnant corpse, symbolizing the corruption of all flesh irrespective of earthly station. The observer, it was hoped, would be moved to amendment and preparation for the same fate at the least expected hour, using their material goods for the benefit of others and the greater glory of God. Such was the sombre message set in stone, communicated in funeral sermons and acted out in the productions of dramatists.[66]

Central to one's preparation for death, especially in cases where the final struggle had commenced and the outcome was understood by all, was a cluster of ideas and practices referred to as *Ars moriendi*, or the 'art of dying'. Clergy and laity together were expected to master the process, detailed in an official treatise of the fifteenth century, with the goal of arming the repentant sinner against the expected assaults of Satan at the moment before the end of physical life. Specific prayers and appropriate conduct were assigned to the dying person, family members and caregivers, and attending clergy. The *Ars moriendi* described the deathbed as the setting for the last great struggle with Satan over the fate of the decedent's soul, a spiritual battlefield with the highest stakes imaginable, and the outcome in doubt until the moment of expiration.

Death in the Middle Ages was very much a communal process, with family, friends and priests – the ordained soldiers of Christ – all battling in unison on behalf of the dying penitent. The protocols were explicit, even down to the rank order of intermediaries who were to be called upon for assistance. Christ was always first, his supreme sacrifice a buffer between the sinner and damnation. The Virgin Mary was next in line, traditionally associated with the deathbed, and ally of even the most wayward. The saints were then enlisted, especially John the Baptist and John the Evangelist – both expected intercessors at the Judgement. So popular was this formula that it often found its way into the preambles of wills, where the request for heavenly intercession preceded the disposal of the deceased's worldly goods.[67]

Protestantism and Scriptural Authority

The rich diversity of the Gospels posed a particular problem for sixteenth-century reformers who took exception to important components of medieval Catholic belief and practice, but none was more challenging than the fate of body and soul in the space between death and judgement. The New Testament writings, drawing from a variety of Jewish sources, provided conflicting interpretations. Expecting the imminent return of Christ, the Gospel of John maintained that 'the time is coming when all who are in the grave shall hear his voice and come out: those who have done right will rise to life; those who have done wrong will rise to hear their doom.' Similarly in the parable of the sheep and the goats, St Matthew appears to associate the moment of final adjudication with the second coming of Christ. And St Paul, in words which would lead to considerable debate in succeeding centuries, spoke of death as 'sleep' in the interregnum between death and new life, thereby maintaining the focus of Christian hope on the moment of Christ's return in glory.[68] But Luke's Gospel avers that the dead are already experiencing their final destiny. In the parable of Dives and Lazarus, we find an example of a soul being taken immediately into 'Abraham's bosom', what the early third-century ecclesiastical writer Tertullian described as a sort of antechamber to heaven, while the unrighteous rich man is subject to instant pain and punishment. Similarly, Christ's promise to one of the criminals who was crucified with him that 'today you will be with me in Paradise' appeared to signal that reward and punishment took place immediately upon death.[69]

The early sixteenth-century Protestant abolition of a place where disembodied souls undergo remedial suffering prior to Christ's return was part of a much wider attack upon an elaborate penitential system which seemed to undermine the merits of Christ's sacrifice. Preceded by groups as diverse as the French Waldensians in the twelfth century and the English Lollards of the late fourteenth century, the attack on purgatory was designed to end the perceived abuses which had crept into Roman Catholic teaching during the Middle Ages.

It was an Augustinian monk, ordained priest and professor at the University of Wittenberg in the German electorate of Saxony, who brought the whole architecture of purgatory into question. For years before and after his ordination to the priesthood, Martin Luther (1483–1546) had struggled with the question of how sinful humanity might be saved. Focusing on the writings of the apostle Paul and on the Psalms of the Hebrew Bible, by 1517 he was drawn to the conclusion, shared by a small minority of his fellow theologians, that salvation was never earned but instead came as an unmerited gift from a righteous but loving God. St Paul's declaration that 'the just shall live by faith' now set Luther on a collision course with his superiors in the hierarchy of the Church.[70]

The Catholic position on the importance of good works in the quest for salvation was troubling enough to Luther, but the Church's propensity to align the papal-controlled sale of indulgences with works seemed wholly unwarranted by Scripture. Having begun innocently as charitable contributions in return for the ministry of the clergy, indulgences gradually became associated with penance, the outward sign of sorrow for sins committed. Beginning in the late eleventh century, indulgences had been issued to those who fought to secure the Holy Land for Christianity as a sort of insurance policy against sinful actions committed while in battle. During the thirteenth century the papacy endorsed the notion that Christ and his saints in heaven had accumulated a surplus of merits that might now be made available for the benefit of penitent sinners. Indulgences, it was argued, could be deployed to lessen the pains of purgatory, both for the purchaser and for the benefit of deceased loved ones. There were even some who began to equate the purchase of an indulgence with meritorious good works sufficient for salvation. Once the vast economic potential of such additive practices were realized, the abuses multiplied.[71]

Luther's questioning of indulgences was intended to prompt a serious academic debate among Church leaders. Within weeks of its appearance in Wittenberg, the 'Ninety-five Theses on the Power and Efficacy of Indulgences' was translated from German into Latin while printing presses across the Holy Roman Empire and beyond guaranteed that copies would be available to a wide readership. The Protestant Reformation had begun, its origins rooted in a dispute over the geography of the afterlife and the experiences of the deceased.

In response to the alleged errors of the Roman Catholic Church, Protestant leaders began to reduce the theological significance of the funeral service and instead transformed it into a simple process of disposing of the corpse. In England, the Reformation effort to destroy the cult of personal intercession was reflected in the revised

1552 Book of Common Prayer, where all prayers for the dead were removed, and in the Elizabethan Thirty-Nine Articles of 1563, which declared 'repugnant to the word of God' the doctrine of purgatory, the invocation of the saints and the worship of relics. During the following century, in the midst of a protracted civil war, Puritan opponents of the crown published a Directory of Public Worship (1644) which directed that the dead body be 'decently attended from the house to the place appointed for public burial, and there immediately interred, without any ceremony'. Since prayers, singing and reading before the body 'are in no way beneficial to the dead' the Puritans insisted that such practices be eliminated.[72]

As the Catholic purgatory was removed from the matrix of Reformed Christian thought, the burden upon the individual sinner for the ultimate state of his soul was magnified and the moment of death advanced as the practical occasion for final judgement. Luther's tentative expectation that 'In the depths of the Divine mercy, there may be opportunity to win it [salvation] in the future state' was abandoned by 1530 with the publication of his *Disavowal of Purgatory*. As historian Keith Thomas has pointed out, the living were now freed from responsibility for the fate of the deceased in the afterlife, and all links between the two became solely a matter of honour and remembrance.[73]

Souls Asleep

Despite its harsh view of essential human nature, not all Protestant thought was fixated on the pains awaiting the unrepentant. Luther viewed death as release from sin and a bridge to a more intimate relation with God. He counselled that 'all of us are not only not to fear death but even to wish for it, for death was to Abel, as it is to every righteous man, a door; it is passing over from humanity to divinity, from the world to the father, from misery to glory.'[74] By the middle of the seventeenth century, the English clergyman William Drummond could refer to this passing as 'but a short, nay, sweet sigh; and . . . not worth remembrance,' while the noted liturgist Jeremy Taylor could dismiss the death experience as 'so harmless a thing, that no good man was thought to be more miserable for dying, but much the happier'.[75]

But since it was difficult for Protestants to conceive of immediate elevation to Heaven for the Elect of God, some type of surrogate for the Catholic purgatory seemed unavoidable. During the course of the first century after the break from Rome, one of the more controversial explanations offered involved the rest or sleep of the immortal soul between the time of death and the general resurrection. Luther appears to have flirted with the soul-sleeping position in his early writings, quoting in his commentary on the Epistle to the Hebrews St John Crysostom's (c. 344–407) words that death 'is little more than a sleep'.[76] William Tyndale (c. 1494–1536), the English scholar who first translated the Bible directly from Hebrew and Greek texts into English, agreed with the early Lutheran view. Edward VI's Protestant Archbishop of Canterbury, Thomas Cranmer (1489–1556), felt concerned enough about the dissemination of the soul-sleeping thesis that the 1552 Articles of Religion, which subsequently formed the basis for the official Thirty-Nine Articles of the Church of England (1563), included an affirmation that the souls of the deceased neither die with the body nor sleep in idleness. John Calvin's (1509–1564) firm opposition to soul-sleeping, set out most clearly in his first published work, the *Psychopannychia* (1534), ensured that later English Puritans would be hostile to the concept.[77] By the middle of the seventeenth century, a Puritan-dominated Parliament called for the imprisonment of anyone who claimed that the soul sleeps or dies at the moment of bodily expiration.[78]

Calvin's refusal to entertain such a radical alternative to purgatory as soul-sleeping left him with the unpleasant prospect of working with something akin to Catholic notions of the person after death. As he conceded in somewhat imprecise fashion, the recently departed souls of the Elect must enjoy 'blessed rest, where they wait with joy and pleasure for the fruition of the promised glory' while the damned are 'confined and bound in chains', each state 'being but a foretaste of what will follow in the last day'.[79] Perhaps recognizing the affinity of this position with the Catholic standard, he insisted that 'over-curious inquiry respecting the intermediate state is neither lawful nor useful'.[80]

Lawful or not, the alleged connection between sleep and death found in St Paul's letters to the Corinthians and in the Acts of the Apostles had become by the late sixteenth century 'the most platitudinous of all platitudes' in the language of Elizabethan drama.[81] During the seventeenth century Christian mortalists or conditionalists included the influential English Baptist Richard Overton and the Puritan poet John Milton. They insisted that their position confirmed the integrity of Christian teachings respecting the contingent nature of the soul's survival. The revival or awaking of the soul on the last day, after all, arguably provided the strongest evidence of God's providential work in the gift of continuity.[82] In addition, Christian soul-sleepers maintained that their position reflected early Church teaching, a stand given some support by the fact that none of the Latin Fathers before Augustine had discussed a purgatorial ordeal in a temporary middle place.

But for those Christians who wearied of debates concerning an intermediate stage between death and the final judgement, simple belief in the miraculous resurrection of the body offered the only credible solution to the impasse. The body expires and there is no intermediate stage, no conscious existence, no linear time that must be filled with preliminary purgation of sin: this seemed the most economical formula. And personhood consists of a resurrected body and an immaterial soul, whatever state the latter found itself in after the body expired. Only at the end time does God miraculously recreate each person, just as he created the universe from nothing at the beginning of time. The intellectual tussles of theologians and philosophers could not capture the magnitude of divine wisdom, the choices made by an omniscient being. Only by moving outside and ahead of rational explanation and empirical guideposts could one begin to approach a true understanding of the afterlife promise, the unmerited gift.

Shelter and Certainty

For more than nineteen centuries, most Christians accepted the broad outline of humankind's destiny set for them by Church authorities, Catholic and Protestant alike. Physical punishment and reward always framed the analysis, while acceptance of the divine right of the papacy in the Catholic tradition, and austere authoritarianism in the Protestant – and typically national – churches provided the intellectual setting. During the nineteenth century, despite the corrosive effect of Enlightenment rationalism and the scientific method on non-rational modes of inquiry, church building, religious vocations and church attendance reached new heights. Many of the practices that have come to distinguish modern Christianity, including Sunday schools, Bible classes, and religious publications that common people could afford to own, were products of the nineteenth century.

A new generation of liberal theologians was quick to accept the place of reason, free thought and the discoveries of science, including evolution, as in no way antithetical to the faith journey.[83] Protestantism placed a renewed emphasis on practical ethics, the social gospel, cultural progress and individual virtues like temperance, self-reliance and volunteerism. A more benevolent understanding of divine agency led to the decline of hell as a place of fearful and interminable punishment, a significant shift in perspective that would subsequently influence Catholic thought in the reforms of the Second Vatican Council (1962–5).[84] Not surprisingly, heaven retained its pride of place in both traditions, albeit addressed by clergy and laity alike in more general terms. A divine reality standing over and against our world was confidently assumed, and a new life was respectfully hoped for, even though the details remained elusive.[85]

The more significant shift in Christianity took place during the twentieth century and involved what has come to be described as the 'subjective turn'. Heightened emphasis on individual autonomy, human rights, the questioning of authority and a general restiveness with hierarchical formulas, obligatory creeds and institutional directives produced a sharp decline in attendance and support for most churches in the West.[86] But personal religiosity and spirituality appears to have remained strong. In particular, belief in some type of heavenly destination continues to reassure the anxious, console the grieving, relieve the outcast and placate the distraught. Heaven, it appears, remains a compelling human interest even as its punitive opposite has been relegated to the status of malevolent myth.

The contemporary theologian John Bowker (b. 1935) has written of the religious sensibility as an ancient survival technique, being 'the earliest protective systems of which we have any evidence that create the circumstances in which people are more likely to survive, have children and bring them up to be adults.'[87] Some of the world's religions developed with a focus on truths within, expressed in such varied terms as enlightenment or emptiness, and constitute what are called the 'inversive systems'. Others look outward and concentrate their energies on relationships within community and with external gods or God, the uncreated creator. But all religions, Bowker contends, are cultural systems that provide protection and improve chances for continued existence in this life. They issue templates for behaviours that extend human life; they bind people together in a common enterprise.

For most of human history, religions have been about experiences now in the presence of a higher reality and not, at least early on, about a purported afterlife. There was no compensatory afterlife for Gilgamesh, no eternal bliss in the whole of the Jewish Scripture until relatively late, nothing but agnosticism in Confucius.[88] Today, each of the world's major religious traditions endorses the prospect of continuity beyond the grave in forms ranging from the personal spiritualized body to the non-personal absorption of the single individual identity into a larger reality of being. The need for shelter and the pursuit of certainty remain of great consequence even in the secularized West. For most humans, the process of secularization, while at home in several compartments of life, stops at the approach of unwelcome mortality.

FOUR

Adverse Environments

When the seventeenth-century English divine John Donne wrote that death was 'no extraordinary event', he was referring to its ubiquity, its dominion over every living being. But while the encounter is assured, the circumstances have varied widely over time and place. Prior to the industrial revolution the earth could seem an especially unfriendly host, replete with seasonal terrors, inexplicable natural disasters and mysterious illnesses. Communitarian efforts occasionally deflected the worst assaults of nature, but in the end the built environment and food production were at the mercy of larger forces. The sometimes hostile ecosystem was made more dangerous by an even harsher social environment marked by the propensity of the species to do harm against its own kind. Since the appearance of *Homo sapiens*, personal, family and clan quarrels often led to violent encounters and indiscriminate killing. Unwanted infants were routinely discarded, disrespected neighbours were attacked with impunity and narcissistic monarchs habitually used violence against their own subjects as well as against innocents abroad.

One suspects that in these chronically adverse surroundings people thought about their own mortality more frequently than we do. Death's propinquity, its regularity and immediacy within each and every family and society made the prospect of one's own demise more tangible, more within the realm of the routine. And certainly whatever level of fear was involved had more to do with the process of dying as opposed to the state of being dead. As we have seen, the major faith traditions provided richly embellished road maps concerning the death event and its sequel. But the course of dying prior to the advent of efficacious and palliative medicine in the late nineteenth century often was very painful and protracted. Doctors were unable to cure any grave disorder. At most they offered preventative advice, not curative technique. The sick were obliged to suffer mightily while helpless loved ones – their primary care givers – bore witness to the anguish of the victim. This was especially the case when mystifying disease was the culprit, when enigmatic nature seemed to conspire against both sinner and saint with equal lack of concern.

In more recent centuries powerful nation states have deployed the resources of science and industry both to improve the material quality of life and to destroy it on an unprecedented level, killing with shocking economies of scale. Wars became more lethal as the line between combatants and non-combatants was erased, as powerful secular ideologies drove thousands to their deaths in ever more destructive regional conflicts and global wars. And if death from external state forces was not enough, during the late twentieth century, fully mature capitalist and consumer-based economies in the West contributed to the rise of new, self-inflicted threats to life and limb. Sedentary middle-class lifestyles – once the dream of earlier generations – now began to pose serious and growing health problems worldwide. Environmental degradation, the unintended consequence of industrial prowess and insatiable consumerism, also became an emergent threat to health and longevity. Thus a powerful combination of natural and socially constructed environments diversified the death event far beyond anything known by our earliest forebears, making contemporary life – on the surface a cornucopia of creature comforts – every bit as precarious as earlier centuries.

Nature's Indifference

Although we have no written evidence of the ailments that threatened our ancestors for 4.5 million years before the advent of civilization, archaeological evidence and skeletal remains provide some indication of a relative absence of viral and bacteriological infections that lead to contagious disease. As we observed in chapter One, scattered bands of hunter-gatherers never camped long enough in an area to pile human waste or pollute a water source to the stage where that source could transmit disease. Prehistoric hunter-gatherers in tropical climates did face formidable opponents in shape of microparasites (viruses and bacteria that feed on human tissues), large animal predators and other human bands intent on claiming exclusive control over a specific area.

But social and cultural evolution allowed these early humans to adapt to more temperate (and less disease-prone) climates. Housing improved and insulating clothing in the form of animal skins was introduced, making contact with the elements less direct. Nevertheless, as hunting proficiency increased, herds of large-bodied game declined, placing an inevitable check on human population. One suspects these conditions ushered in recurring periods of malnutrition and early death, which in turn may have intensified both the frequency and the level of conflict between hunting groups. Indeed the fact that population levels never exploded may have more to do with the proclivity of early humans for violent encounters with wild animals and other humans as much as it has to do with debilitating disease.[1] All of this would change once humans stopped chasing after their dinner and began growing it around 12,000 BCE.

Disease and Epidemics

The transition to a sedentary lifestyle and the radical manipulation of the natural environment for human purposes (in other words, the domestication of plants and animals) brought with it unprecedented opportunities for disease agents to find suitable human hosts. Plants and animals offered humankind more abundant and more varied food supplies, providing key nutrients to counter some of the challenges presented by parasites. But this advantage may have been offset by higher rates of infection from animals that were now in regular and close exchange with humans.[2] Simply breaking the sod for cultivation exposed early farmers to new insects and worms. Irrigation farming in the early river valley civilizations brought individuals and groups into contact with water-borne parasites that could penetrate the skin and enter the bloodstream. Dogs, cattle, sheep, goats, horses and poultry shared diseases with humans, while rats and worms, and insects including mosquitoes and lice, all established dangerous relations with their unwitting hosts.

The advent of agriculture may have allowed for soaring birthrates and the invention of the territorial state, but it also brought new and misunderstood causes of death into societies around the globe. With the invention of writing and record keeping, intellectual leaders began to speculate about the origin of rampant sickness and fatal diseases. In Mesopotamia, Egypt, India and China it was conventionally understood that illness was the work of demons, devils and evil spirits.[3] Later physicians, following guidelines set by Galen (c. 131–201) and Avicenna (d. 1037), attributed disease to vaguely defined miasmas or undisciplined lifestyles – anything but tiny living organisms.[4] Malevolent action on someone's part, at least, seemed as plausible an explanation as any. The germ theory of disease had to wait until the dawn of the twentieth century.

By 500 BCE pathogens began to have a sizeable negative impact on populations in major European and Asian civilizations. Microparasites that produce great killers like smallpox and influenza passed directly from human to human without the need for a freeloading carrier. And while populations could over time develop relative immunity to a particular disease, the greater mobility of organized armies and commercial traders meant that lethal diseases were now portable, resulting in widespread plague in previously isolated venues. Combatants were drawn from different epidemiological zones and typically carried infections 'for which the inhabitants of war zones have little or no acquired immunity'.[5] The results were always catastrophic. The Greek historian Thucydides recorded the effects of the plague that befell Athens between 430 and 427 BCE during the early stages of the Peloponnesian War. Himself a survivor of the unknown epidemic (smallpox seems likely), Thucydides described a cruel course of events that subjected most victims to between seven and nine days of intense suffering before death.[6]

Headache, fever, vomiting, painful coughing, uncontrollable spasms, diarrhoea and dehydration, depression and mental confusion merged in ferocious alliance. Some estimates place the mortality rate from this one plague alone at one-third of the city's population, including their leader Pericles. Thucydides described a breakdown in respect for laws and burial customs in the wake of the plague. Family members abandoned loved ones and bodies were thrown on pyres built for others. Medical arts and religious rites proved equally ineffective, leading some to reject conventional social norms. 'No one was enthusiastic over additional hardship for what seemed a noble objective, considering it uncertain whether he would die before achieving it. Whatever was pleasant immediately and whatsoever was conducive to that were deemed both noble and useful.'[7] The epidemic finally passed, but Athens lost the war and never regained its former regional influence.

Of course Athens was not unique. As the Romans conquered much of the Mediterranean world and what became western Europe in the first centuries of the Common Era, epidemics followed in the wake of military advances. The so-called Antonine plague of the mid-second century lasted for fifteen years and probably killed between one-third and half of the population in affected areas, undermining defensive operations – and morale – during the reign of Marcus Aurelius (160–181). Labour costs rose, tax revenues tumbled and large-scale building projects were brought to a standstill. In addition, seasonal malaria appears to have been endemic in low-lying areas of the empire, elevating death rates across entire regions and again interfering with military readiness.[8]

Plague assaulted the Byzantine capital of Constantinople in 541, killing thousands of people each day. The proximity of humans in overcrowded cities always compounded the effects of contagion. When it struck it usually killed 60–80 per cent of those it infected. The grim examples of urban destruction could be multiplied in every civilization. Indeed until fairly recently all cities – those remarkable centres of commerce, culture and intellectual excitement – could not replace their populations lost to recurrent disease without a constant influx of migrants from rural areas. The exhilaration and diversity of the urban lifestyle came at a very high cost indeed, especially for the very young since children were at a particular risk for smallpox and measles.

A Great Dying

The worst recorded natural catastrophe to strike Eurasia was the bubonic plague of the mid-fourteenth century, what contemporaries referred to as the great dying and what the early nineteenth-century physician-historian J.F.C. Hecker hauntingly labelled the 'Black Death'.[9] Most likely originating in China, where large numbers of fatalities were recorded in the early 1320s, the onset and spread of bubonic plague killed millions of people and wreaked havoc with the social and economic fabric of major civilizations. The Muslim chronicler Ibn Battuta arrived in Syria in 1348 and observed that deaths in the city of Damascus numbered 2,400 per day.[10] Between a quarter and a third of the population of the Muslim Middle East perished during the pestilence. Beginning in 1347 the plague entered western Europe from the east by way of Genoese trading ships that had recently returned from a number of Black Sea ports. These ships delivered their cargos (official and unofficial) to Messina, Pisa, Genoa and Marseilles. Goods and disease then proceeded up river valleys and along commercial roads and pathways.[11] And although reports of plague devastating populations in China and India had reached the West the year before, no one was prepared for what was soon to befall Christian Europe.

A rat-borne disease that is transmitted to humans by fleas, bubonic plague withstood weather and seasonal variations. It manifested itself in two forms, the first infecting the bloodstream and causing internal bleeding and the second attacking the lungs and spread by respiratory contact. From the point of the appearance of symptoms – fever, swelling, coughing and the discharge of blood – death was rapid and extraordinarily painful. Rich and poor, urban and rural, priest and layperson – all fell victim. Clerical records from the archdiocese of York in northern England, for example, indicate that 40 per cent of the resident clergy were killed during the first wave of plague.[12] Entire villages disappeared, while universities, monasteries and nunneries were forsaken by the inhabitants. Before its most virulent stage subsided in the early 1350s, approximately one-third of Europe's population, or about 24 million people, had succumbed, with estimates of mortality rates in crowded urban centres even higher at around 50 per cent.[13]

So powerful was the ripsaw of plague in Europe that survivors could not bury the dead fast enough. In the French city of Avignon bodies were thrown into the Rhone river until mass burial pits were dug. In London such pits, covered with quicklime to accelerate decomposition, were at capacity before new ones could be made available. The streets of major cities across Europe were littered with corpses. The Florentine writer Giovanni Boccaccio (1313–1375) introduced his *Decameron* with a harrowing record of the first wave of plague. The dying often had no opportunity to make their confession to a priest or to be administered last rites. Neighbours avoided neighbours, parents abandoned children, spouses departed their partners with no thought of prayers, much less physical comfort, for the dying.[14] In an effort to burnish their learned credentials, the Paris faculty of medicine concluded that atmospheric changes resulting from a rare conjunction of planets was to blame for the plague.[15] But most contemporaries stuck to planet earth and the abode of heaven, interpreting the great dying as the scourge of God, a just if brutal punishment for the myriad sins of humankind. Why else was the behaviour of the pestilence so arbitrary, decimating the population in some areas but skipping over others?

Other observers took a less elevated view and blamed foreign travellers, witches, and alleged well-poisoning by Jews; entire Jewish communities were attacked and some of the accused were burned to death by mobs. So widespread was the anti-Semitic rage that in July 1348 Pope Clement VI (r. 1342–52) felt compelled to declare the Jews innocent of the trumped-up charge of well-poisoning. Whether or not the declaration had a major impact on popular attitudes is uncertain, for the failure of the Church to intervene with an angry and enigmatic God undercut the credibility of priest and pope alike. Sacraments, masses, intercessions, acts of charity, fasting and pilgrimages – nothing was of use in decelerating the colossal rate of mortality. The destruction was unrelenting, and Europe's population did not return to pre-plague levels until the sixteenth century.

Inadvertent Germ Warfare

Infectious diseases were especially virulent killers in the Americas after 1500. Prior to the voyages of Columbus, the American continents had been biologically separated from Europe. But in addition to introducing new plants and animals into the Americas, early sixteenth-century European explorers were the inadvertent carriers of pathogens and parasites against which the indigenous populations had no natural immunity. Diseases like smallpox, typhoid, typhus, bubonic plague, influenza, measles, chickenpox, malaria, whooping cough and diphtheria all wreaked havoc on the Native American population. The historian Alfred Crosby estimates that population densities were roughly comparable around the world in 1500, with perhaps a fifth of the world's population living in the Americas before an unprecedented demographic disaster struck in the century after Columbus. The highland populations of Meso-America and Peru alone fell by 90 per cent during the 1500s. In North America the native population is estimated to have been around 5 million in 1492; by 1800 it had been reduced to 600,000.[16]

This colossal die-off, according to Crosby, helps explain the explosive growth in the transatlantic African slave trade after 1500. Europeans scrambled to fill the labour shortage created by the impact of involuntary bacteriological warfare on Native Americans by accelerating the importation of black Africans. The latter had previously acquired immunity to smallpox through childhood exposure to a weak pathogen.[17] Wherever that immunity was absent, death followed the imperial pathways of the European powers. Writing in the early nineteenth century at the conclusion of his circumnavigation of the globe, Charles Darwin observed that 'death seems to pursue the aboriginal. We may look to the wide extent of the Americas, Polynesia, the Cape of Good Hope, and Australia, and we find the same result.'[18]

The effects of this inexplicable cataclysm on the morale and intellectual well-being of the survivors can only be imagined. Young and old, healthy and frail, prosperous and poor – all succumbed to the microlife epidemics. Administrative centres, often home to the governing elite, were hardest hit, and, in the absence of strong leadership, resistance to the European intruders disintegrated. The victims had recourse to their religious systems, but to no avail, while the Christian newcomers smugly assumed that the expanding charnel house was the dictate of the one true God. Sir Francis Drake's account of the spread of disease after his arrival along the northeast coast of Florida in the 1580s could be repeated in many other contexts. According to Drake the inhabitants 'died verie fast and said amongst themselves, it was the Inglisshe God that made them die so fast'. In New England during the 1630s smallpox devastated the native population. The governor of Plymouth colony, William Bradford, described how those who were infected 'fell down so generally of this disease as they were in the end not able to help one another'.[19] Another Pilgrim settler mused that 'The good hand of God favoured our beginnings . . . in sweeping away the great multitudes of the Natives by the Small Pox.'[20] The Puritan governor of Massachusetts Bay colony to the north of Plymouth concurred with this assessment, remarking that 'the Lord hathe cleared our title to what we possess'.[21] The impenetrable judgement of God had been revealed against native peoples in the most overwhelming fashion.

Persistent Assaults

Recurrences of plague in Europe struck fear and took additional lives with oppressive regularity down until the early eighteenth century. London experienced a virulent plague epidemic in 1665 and 1666. Only a massive fire which destroyed large portions of the central city and levelled many of the unspeakable slums reduced some of the environmental factors that made plague such a powerful killer. As in previous cycles, during the London epidemic those residents with adequate fiscal resources – including many clergy – fled for the salubrious air of the countryside, while the poor were left to die without the benefit of pastoral comfort. Hospitals, where they existed, offered little comfort, for they were not places of healing and treatment but refuge stations where the sick, especially those without family support, went to die.[22] Two centuries later, cholera expanded out of South Asia (a by-product of military and colonial activity) and arrived in industrial Britain, claiming 130,000 residents over five separate surges. But this death toll was negligible compared to cholera's impact in British-controlled India, where over 25 million people perished during the second half of the nineteenth century.[23]

Epidemics continued to haunt developed and underdeveloped countries alike well into the twentieth century. The terrible influenza pandemic of 1918–19, probably originating in the central United States and spread by American soldiers arriving in Europe during the final months of the First World War, quickly reached global proportions. It swept away at least 50 million people worldwide in just two years, easily outpacing the total number of military dead during the First World War. Most of the victims were in the prime of life, with some estimates indicating that as many as 8–10 per cent of young adults around the world perished before 1920.[24]

The response to this pandemic, however, was unprecedented. No longer turning to introspective religious explanations of the disaster, governments and the general public looked instead to the pioneers of medicine to uncover the cause and discover an effective treatment. Beginning in the twentieth century scientific medicine, not extraordinary narratives, would confront the malevolent forces of nature through basic research and the development of vaccines and antitoxins. The victories over disease were many, highlighted by the eradication of smallpox in 1980, after a campaign lasting more than two decades. But at the start of the twenty-first century the confidence of researchers was tempered by the drug-resistant mutations of microorganisms that cause disease, together with the appearance of new and emerging infections that guaranteed an ongoing struggle in an increasingly interconnected world.[25]

Famine

The significance of food crises or famine as a cause of death is difficult to estimate for most of the human past. Pre-industrial peoples worldwide typically lived in a constant state of malnourishment, but famine brings with it the assurance of a protracted and painful death. Prehistoric hunter-gatherers may have been less vulnerable to food crises than subsequent settled farmers, but even they lived in ecosystems marked by uncertainty. The advent of the so-called Columbian exchange after 1500, where foodstuffs from America like potatoes and maize diversified the European diet, seems to have reduced the recurrence of famine and led to a modest acceleration in population growth. But it is only in the nineteenth century that we enter the period of reliable reporting for some areas of the globe. After 1800 peacetime famine was largely eliminated in Europe, with the powerful exceptions being Ireland in the 1840s, Finland in the 1860s and Russia in the early 1890s. One recent scholar estimates the number of famine-related deaths worldwide during the nineteenth century at 100 million.[26]

Famine can be the result of environmental factors like back-to-back harvest failures, volcanic eruption, extended drought or uncontrolled flooding. The Europe-wide famine of 1315, for example, was preceded by heavy downpours and low temperatures during the previous summer. Of course, food crises can also be triggered by human factors like poor governance, economic mismanagement and the effects of war. After the collapse of the Soviet Union, its former client state of North Korea experienced a famine that lasted from 1994 to 1997 and cost the lives of an estimated 1 to 3 million people. On occasion famine has also been deliberately orchestrated as an act of aggression against perceived enemies of the state. In the hands of Stalin from 1929–33, for example, it became a weapon of mass destruction against the peasantry in general and the people of Ukraine in particular when they dared oppose the dictator's collectivization of agriculture. Approximately 14 million subjects of Stalin's terror state perished over a period of time comparable in length to the First World War, a death toll higher than the total for all countries during the First World War, and one where virtually all of the victims were unarmed civilians, young and old.[27] Such acts of calculated brutality strengthen the widely held contemporary view that all famines are preventable and that their occurrence is the result of human malevolence.

This was not always the case. As recently as the late eighteenth century the English economist and Anglican clergyman Thomas Malthus insisted that the failure to regulate family size would lead in the end to recurrent famine, a harsh but natural check on overpopulation. Malthus attributed this inexorable law to divine providence, God's way of objecting to human sexual profligacy.[28] England's poor laws, he insisted, merely compounded the problem of destitution by creating a false sense of economic security that led the poor to produce more children who would suffer acute want in their turn. The Malthusian calculus was not much advanced beyond the description of irritated gods in the *Epic of Gilgamesh*, gods who abruptly cut the population back in an effort to keep the noise down. Such appeared to be the case again during the Irish Famine of 1845–9, when divine providence or the natural check on overpopulation ended the miserable lives of over a million Irish peasants. Those fortunate enough to emigrate did so, always remembering the seeming indifference of imperial authorities to the disaster.[29]

In the mid-nineteenth century Charles Darwin, reflecting on Malthus's *Essay on the Principle of Population* (1798), acknowledged the book's influence on shaping his own revolutionary theory of natural selection. Whatever the theoretical underpinnings, the onset of famine has historically been accompanied by sharply rising food prices, higher levels of infectious disease, popular unrest, involuntary migration and increased property crime. Most tragically, famine calls forward rudimentary instincts of self-preservation, often at the expense of other-regarding behaviours. Long-established friendships collapse, the bonds of family dissolve, leaving husks of humanity to betray their savage impulses.

The Limits of Remediation

The art of medicine is the study and treatment of physical suffering or pathology based on the best available knowledge. Pathology has changed enormously through the centuries, but it has always been anchored in current science as it applies to the structure (anatomy) and functions (physiology) of the human body. The medical practitioner attempts to diagnose the ailment or abnormality (a theory of disease), offer treatment based on reason and experience, and predict likely outcomes. Throughout most of human history the pre-eminent diagnostic accounts focused on external, extraordinary or supernatural factors. At the opening of Homer's *Iliad* a deadly pestilence is lifted after the king releases the daughter of a priest of Apollo who had been held for ransom. And at multiple points in the New Testament we find Jesus healing the sick and raising the dead in a manner that simply defies naturalistic explanation.[30] As we have seen, the terrible plague of the fourteenth century was interpreted by many as punishment for the collective sins of humanity. Disease was widely believed to have moral or spiritual roots, its cause peripheral to the bodily mechanism and intimately connected somehow to events and changes in the wider cosmos. The great chain of being left nothing unaccounted for; even the smallest event, the least significant change, was accomplice to a larger if inscrutable purpose.

Imperfect Interventions

Even so, the alleged connection between a solitary human organism and a deeper moral or physical order did not prevent the earliest healers from making attempts, some even heroic, to alleviate suffering. Archaeological excavations of ancient burial sites reveal efforts to set broken bones and treat severe wounds, and presumably these techniques were taught informally over many generations. The same archaeological record reveals signs of trepanation, or holes drilled through bones, but whether or not such procedures were in response to pain and illness is a matter for conjecture.

Ancient texts from Mesopotamia and Egypt indicate an awareness of symptoms related to disease, while lists of ameliorative drugs were copied and transmitted over hundreds of years. Still, more often than not these texts, when addressing a likely outcome of an illness, revert to supernatural intervention – the anger of a god, spirit or demon always loomed large. Healing rituals and incantations were as important as medicinal herbs and potions or timehonoured physical intrusions.[31]

A competing view, rooted in the Graeco-Roman world, turned its attention to the physical causes of illness and employed treatments that took no account of divinely ordered variables. This is not to say that Greek physicians rejected the role of divine intervention, only that a two-track approach to diagnosis and treatment was employed. Still, before the third century BCE anatomical knowledge of the human body and its internal organs was lacking. Disease was usually associated with an imbalance in what were thought to be the body's four elements or humours: black bile, yellow bile, phlegm and blood. A range of treatments involving baths, diets and bloodletting were deployed in an effort to restore the proper balance. Humoral medicine was embraced by Hippocrates in the fifth century BCE, but its most influential exponent was the Roman physician Galen, who authored what became the standard textbook for medical training in Europe for the next thousand years.

Only in the sixteenth and seventeenth centuries, in the wake of enhanced knowledge of anatomy and physiology, was humoral practice discredited, although its lack of efficacy had been apparent to practitioners and patients alike for a very long time. From this point forward investigation turned exclusively on the body itself, its organs and its systems.[32] Anatomical dissection, which had been disallowed by the medieval Church, only emerged as an essential part of formal medical training during the Renaissance. The great architect, painter, engineer and scientist Leonardo da Vinci (1452–1519) claimed to have practised dissections on human corpses. His hundreds of anatomical sketches represented the powerful intersection between Renaissance art and the emergence of anatomy as a key element in medical science. This empirical turn has proven to be tremendously productive over the course of the last four centuries, in particular since the nineteenth century, allowing researchers and physicians to understand and, on occasion, to conquer disease. But only on occasion. Not until the twentieth century did the art of medicine make a significant impact on reducing mortality. One example, the practice of surgery, will suffice to illustrate the point.

Although invasive surgical procedures took place in the ancient world, it was more often than not a last resort, an act of desperation against all odds. Those surgeries that were successful as a rule involved the exterior body. Wounds, broken bones, tooth extractions, boils and abscesses might be treated successfully with clamps and sutures. But internal surgery involving the abdominal cavity or the brain was very much the exception. Most trained physicians in the ancient and medieval periods left surgery to their social inferiors, men engaged in manual labour rather than a liberal science. The former cut hair and shaved faces for a living, and the only credentials these 'after hours' practitioners held were the recommendations of those who happened to survive their interventions. Prior to the quite recent introduction of anaesthesia (in the 1840s) every invasive surgery was an excruciatingly painful experience. Both surgeon and patient required nerves of steel during a procedure, with the former's professional reputation based largely on speed and accuracy. Caesarean sections, for example, most often proved fatal for the mother.[33] To undergo emergency surgery prior to the mid-nineteenth-century introduction of antiseptics and anaesthetics was to acknowledge that death was standing by, either the result of the procedure itself or through post-operative sepsis (infection).

Childbirth and Infant Mortality

Prior to the industrial age, death was most commonly associated with the very young, not, as is the case today, with the very old. Rates of infant and childhood mortality were particularly high in agricultural societies. Indeed it is estimated that between one-third and half of all children in the pre-modern centuries perished before the age of two. Malnutrition, severe diarrhoea and a variety of infectious and in the end mysterious diseases like measles and smallpox took their cruel toll year after year without remission. So frequent was infant death that a widespread posture of resignation, if not indifference, characterized adult culture. The Roman writer Epictetus (55–135 CE) advised that when parents kiss their child at night 'you say to yourself, "Perhaps it will be dead in the morning."' And Plutarch (c. 46–120 CE) observed that when an infant died, 'people do not stand around long at their funerals or keep watch at their tombs'.[34] In some societies parents refrained from naming babies until there was a reasonable expectation that the child would survive infancy. Why, after all, should a parent invest deep emotional stock in a creature whose chances of survival were so small?

This extraordinarily high death rate for infants posed a significant challenge to Christian theologians who believed that everything that happens in this world is in response to God's will. Bishop Gregory of Nyssa (c. 335–c. 395) was one of the first to investigate the larger problem of evil in a providential world from the perspective of infant death. According to Christian teaching, the child who dies soon after birth presumably has not engaged in any of the thoughts or actions that are determinative of eternal reward or sanction. And denied any opportunity to live a life in accord with the principles of the Gospels, God has no basis upon which to judge them. Gregory's solution to the dilemma involved the construction of a post-mortem middle place where the deceased could grow in knowledge of God in anticipation of a full reward at the Day of Judgement. More specifically, God has withdrawn certain infants from the world because they have been born with an evil disposition that would ultimately lead them away from the true path. Removing them from this world and locating their souls in a middle place is an expression of divine love. The infant's soul is now better positioned to receive the blessing of eternal life after participation in the middle place.[35] For the parents, the death of a child must be understood as a beneficent act and accepted as a comfort and a blessing.

Similarly, St Augustine approached the problem of infant death from the perspective of the Fall story. In the first two books of his spiritual autobiography, *The Confessions*, Augustine argued that all humans, even infants, are born with original sin. A good God would be unjust in taking the life of an innocent child, but no one, irrespective of age, has escaped the impact of Adam's sin in Paradise. Augustine adopted a literalist interpretation of the Psalmist who declared that he was conceived in iniquity and 'sinful from the time my mother conceived me'.[36] Although newborns lack the capacity for understanding or the physical capacity to commit evil acts, their innate selfishness anticipates even greater sinfulness as an adult. The death of an infant affirms God's eternal justice because all have affronted their maker and are in need of Christ's redeeming power: 'It was for their sakes too that their Lord became a baby.'[37]

Such views were hard to square with the overriding narrative of a compassionate deity who takes a special interest in the existential well-being of all creatures, and humans in particular. But there were few alternatives to the Augustinian standpoint prior to the age of scientific medicine. Endogenous causes like congenital anomalies, gestational immaturity and birth complications, together with the exogenous causes, especially those related to injury, nutrition and disease, were not understood and therefore never entered the descriptive vocabulary. In a way that seems unthinkable to us, the death of infants and young children was normative, and although no less wrenching for that fact, such losses were for most of the human experience simply to be endured, one more departure in accord with a superior – and totally unfathomable – strategy.

Unnatural Dangers

The expansive reach of natural threats to human life only began to narrow with developments in scientific agriculture during the eighteenth century, new approaches to public health in the nineteenth century and the remedial and restorative power of medical practice in the twentieth. Still limited, in large part to populations in the developed West, the manipulation of nature for human purposes and an evidence-based approach to illness has relegated most natural dangers to life to a single (albeit expanding) demographic:

the elderly. On the other hand, orchestrated, avoidable death at the hands of other humans has persisted across the centuries and into the contemporary world with distressing regularity. The targets have been altered slightly, with most newborns accorded a right to life that was absent in all but the past two millennia, but in general the overwhelming majority of victims have been innocent, poor and without significant access to either education or political power.

Infanticide

Modern revulsion notwithstanding, the wilful killing of infants has been a ubiquitous feature of human culture throughout history, practised by Palaeolithic hunter-gatherers, by agriculturalists and by educated inhabitants of modern industrial cities.[38] Today the murder of an infant is typically reported as an aberration, carried out by a parent suffering from severe mental illness or depression. Modern contraceptive techniques and legalized abortion in the West have reduced the incidence of infanticide dramatically, and harsh criminal sanctions, together with widespread public disapprobation, provide further controls. But while it has been condemned for centuries in most major civilizations, the practice of infanticide historically served important family, economic, religious and cultural needs. In brief, a newborn's right to life is a rather recent formulation in global culture, emerging alongside improved economic conditions and a more expansive understanding of human rights over the last few centuries.

The calculated killing of a newborn was most often associated with dire material circumstances facing individuals, immediate family and wider society. Following – ironically perhaps – the modern notion that it is better to die than to suffer, the act was most often a method of family planning or birth control, where a decision was made that food and other essential resources were inadequate to sustain an expanding population. In early societies where abortion procedures always endangered the mother's life, infanticide was the only option (absent sexual abstinence) as a method of controlling family size. Female infants were often singled out for elimination since they were thought to be less valuable to the family economy and, in dowry-based societies, sex-selective infanticide released the parents from a future financial burden.

In classical Greece and Rome, the practice of infanticide was met by widespread indifference on the part of society's elite, and one suspects that this attitude was widespread. The child was viewed as an investment, expected to work as soon as they were old enough and to support their parents in the latter's declining years. The Greek concept of *logos* (word, speech, reason) was associated with adult males. Women had the potential for *logos*, but children were believed to be outside the world of reason.[39] In addition to population control, the Greeks would abandon infants to the elements if they were deformed or otherwise deemed unhealthy. Estimates suggest that as many as 20 per cent of infant girls in Athens were abandoned, a practice that was tantamount to a death sentence. The helpless victim might be the product of a wife's adultery or deemed to be somehow defective by the midwives or female relatives present at the birth. In a world where infant mortality from natural causes ran as high as 30–40 per cent, the discarding of unwanted offspring was rarely an event of major social concern.

When married couples were involved, the decision to take the life of a newborn almost always involved the father, for it was he who decided whether or not the infant was to be a member of his family. In a strictly legal sense, children belonged to their fathers, not their mothers. It was left to the latter, however, to carry out the violent act.[40] In the Roman family the first eight or nine days after an infant's birth were critical; if the child was accepted into the family a ceremony was held, the child was named and the register office was informed. This was the point of social birth and juridical personhood, a moment of greater significance than biological birth. According to the first-century Stoic philosopher Seneca, those infants who were rejected were commonly drowned. By the start of the second century a drop in population led Roman authorities in some parts of Italy to encourage the growth of families. Consequently there was a move to curb the practice of exposing infants, but no legal sanctions were applied until the reign of Emperor Valentinian in 384.[41]

Evidence of widespread infanticide in China can be traced to texts dating back to around 1000 BCE. Documents from the Zhou dynasty (c. 1050–256 BCE) express concern over the scale of child abandonment, while prohibitions against abandonment were issued by the Qin (255–206 BCE) and Han (206 BCE–220 CE) dynasties. Legalist philosophers emphasized the importance of strict enforcement of the laws against infanticide and abandonment as a measure of concern for the greater cosmic order, but Confucian thinkers placed greater emphasis on the well-being of the community and equated rising levels of infanticide with the ruler's failure to provide for the whole. In ancient China the newborn's existence was not officially recognized until the third day after birth, thereby allowing a brief period in which the newborn might be rejected. Centuries later, in 1080, the Song dynasty scholar-poet Su Shi wrote to complain to a local magistrate about the drowning of infant girls in the Yangtze River in Hubei Province. 'A baby is often killed at birth by drowning in cold water,' Su Shi reported, 'but in order to do this the baby's parents have to close their eyes and avert their faces while pressing the baby down in the water until it dies after crying a short moment.'[42]

One ancient civilization stood as an exception to the general rule. Egyptians were strongly opposed to infanticide and seem to have recognized the autonomous personhood of the child at a very early stage. Indeed the Egyptian child generally was viewed as free of sin and early transgressions were attributed to ignorance. Even the orphan was treated humanely in a society where economic self-sufficiency was maintained and an optimistic picture of the afterlife shaped religious practice. Abandoned infants were often adopted as foundlings or maintained as household slaves. The Greek historian Diodorus Siculus, writing around 20 BCE, indicated that Egyptian law always protected the unborn child. A pregnant woman who was sentenced to death, he wrote, would not be executed before the birth of the child.[43]

It is perhaps not surprising that the Jewish biblical philosopher Philo of Alexandria (20 BCE–50 CE) argued against both abortion of the foetus and infanticide. His views were echoed more broadly in ancient Jewish culture. Although the exposure of infants was not unknown in Jewish society, the rabbinic tradition held that while there was no specific legal mandate that parents protect all of their offspring, they bear a moral responsibility to do so. This was the position adopted by the early Christian community as well. While the New Testament does not speak directly of infanticide, texts from the second century onwards take a strong stand against the practice. Clement of Alexandria, writing in the late second century, emphasized the natural innocence, simplicity and obedience of children, together with their indifference to worldly affairs. Origen, Irenaeus and Tertullian similarly stressed the child's lack of concern for status and wealth as qualities that ought to be instructive to Christians of all ages.[44] For the early fourth-century Christian author Lactantius (c. 240–c. 320), who served as an adviser to Emperor Constantine, infanticide was 'an especially great impiety', a bold rejection of God's commandment not to take another life. Lactantius was the first Christian author to acknowledge that exposure is often prompted by severe poverty, but he rejected its legitimacy on this or any other grounds.[45]

During Europe's Middle Ages and into the early modern period the common punishment for acts of infanticide was execution. At the close of the fourteenth century in the Belgian city of Namur, for example, the perpetrator was to be tortured before being burned to death. In the Duchy of Luxembourg the convict was buried alive near the gallows, strangled or killed by the sword. But even with strong civil injunctions and the growing influence of the Roman Church, laws against the killing – usually through abandonment – of newborns continued to be widely disregarded. It is difficult to estimate the scale of infanticide in early modern Europe, but it is safe to assume that the extant judicial records capture but a fraction of the killings perpetrated. One scholar has gone so far as to claim that exposure 'was practised on a gigantic scale with absolute impunity', but the quantitative evidence is just not available.[46] Acute material hardship, the censure of peers and shame over the birth of an illegitimate child appear to have been the biggest motivators.

With the expansion of monasteries, convents and abbeys in the High Middle Ages, increasing numbers of infants were abandoned at the doorstep of these Church institutions. The work of the religious who assumed guardianship over deserted infants marked the start of the first orphanages. But serious efforts to halt the practice of infanticide did not really gather force until the nineteenth century.[47] Under the Napoleonic Penal Code of 1810, infanticide was defined as the wilful destruction of a baby at the moment of delivery or immediately afterwards. The letter of the law called for the perpetrator to be sentenced to death for the crime, but over time the courts began to recognize a variety of extenuating circumstances. Fathers were never prosecuted, while married mothers were rarely defendants. The unwed mother, impoverished and powerless, was the usual target of law enforcement. In Belgium, for example, as late as the first half of the nineteenth century between 15 and 18 per cent of all murders committed involved the destruction of newborns. But after 1867 the crime of infanticide was no longer automatically linked with capital punishment for the offender.[48]

The emergence of state-supported foundling hospitals and private charities reduced the numbers of deaths previously associated with abandonment, although mortality rates in these institutions remained high. Legal scholars and court practice began to acknowledge the role of mental illness and diminished capacity in the commission of the crime, especially when the perpetrator was a birth mother living in extreme poverty and lacking the support of family and community. In our own day, organizations like The Society for the Prevention of Infanticide have argued that the decline in the number of reported child killings in the West (approximately one in every 3,000–5,000) is directly related to the growing availability of access to abortion.[49] Without this admittedly controversial option, the historic predisposition of humans to kill their own young, especially whenever adverse personal or economic circumstances arise, would continue to preoccupy our legal systems and our moral consciousness. Today that legal and moral engagement is focused exclusively – and especially in the U.S. – on the practice of abortion.

Warfare

Simply put, war is organized, premeditated violence legitimized by some form of governmental structure and in pursuit of a particular economic or political objective.[50] Over the past three millennia this mass application of lethal force has been instigated by sovereign states governed either arbitrarily or by constitutional means. Throughout prehistory and into the historical era the victims of war were almost always active combatants, but in the twentieth century an alarming blurring of the distinction between combatants and civilian non-combatants occurred. Consequently, the century just concluded was the bloodiest on record in terms of state-sponsored violence, with millions of innocents perishing in wars large and small, regional and global.

While the extraordinary number of humans whose death has been hastened by modern warfare is in part a function of developments in technology, the growth of nationalist sentiment and universalist ideologies, at the end of day humans decide how that technology will be deployed. The very human ingenuity and technical prowess responsible for improving the quality of life over the past 100 years has also allowed us to kill one another more effectively, on a sweeping scale, and at greater distances. It took the U.S. government a mere three years to gather the scientific researchers, invent the technology, build, test and deploy the atomic bomb. Today the deployment of unmanned aerial vehicles (drones or robotic planes) brings the distance factor, the anonymity of killing, into sharp relief, allowing one state to kill its enemies halfway around the world from virtual 'cockpits' located safely on home territory.

Technology and decision-making aside, the impulse to settle disputes between states by war – what the nineteenth-century German military theorist Carl von Clausewitz (1780–1831) mordantly called politics by other means – seems to have remained unbroken since the formation of the earliest states in the ancient Middle East. Golden age Greece, the supposed 'cradle' of Western intellectual life, was a place of bloody and chronic military conflict. City-state rivalries often degenerated into war, and ultimately the city-state ideal gave way before consolidated empire. Much the same can be said of Rome. While the Roman Empire brought military security, fostered urban and commercial life and introduced sophisticated legal systems across western Europe, its leaders also imposed an unrivalled level of organized violence on peoples who resisted the advance of 'civilization'. With the spread of Christianity under Roman auspices and into the Middle Ages, those who had been trained to wield lethal force on behalf of civil authority had to overcome new moral and ethical prohibitions against killing other human beings. This led to the development of 'just war' theory, propositions in favour of the use of lethal force under certain circumstances that were endorsed by religious authorities.

Although an appalling constant in the human experience, organized warfare was not a major cause of death in terms of total population until the advent of mechanized combat in the mid-nineteenth century. There were exceptions, of course, with an estimated 1 million Muslims and Christians killed during the crusades of the High Middle Ages and possibly as many as 7 million combatant and civilian fatalities during the Thirty Years War (1618–48). The earliest mechanized wars, made possible by the development of lethal industrial technology, included the American Civil War of 1861–5, in which over 600,000 lost their lives, and the First World War of 1914–18, which the survivors often referred to, somewhat ironically, as the 'Great War'. Its scale was certainly great, with machine guns, poison gas and artillery bombardments – early instances of death from afar – claiming the lives of approximately 16 million people, of whom 10 million were military personnel and 6 million were civilian non-combatants.

No one expected such devastation in August 1914 when the war began. Indeed most of those who flocked to the recruiting stations (this was a volunteer affair for two years) expected to be home by Christmas after a short conflict featuring pleasant marches, smart uniforms and minimal casualties. Theirs, after all, was a progressive civilization, master of global empires.[51] Most would die in combat on the Western front, sacrificed by arrogant and inflexible commanders who for four years ordered men 'over the top' in head-on assaults against withering enemy fire. During the first four months of fighting alone, 700,000 German, 850,000 French and 90,000 British troops were either killed or wounded. The Battle of the Somme was emblematic. On 1 July 1916 eleven British divisions, 110,000 men, climbed out of their trenches across a 13-mile front and were immediately mowed down by enemy machine guns. More than 60,000 were either killed or wounded on that first day of battle. The cries of the mortally wounded in no-man's-land were heard in the opposing trenches for the next 24 hours.

Long after the Armistice and only a few years before the outbreak of the Second World War, the poet and essayist Edmund Blunden (1896–1974), who had survived the Somme, recalled the initial horror of the assault. 'By the end of the day both sides had seen, in a sad scrawl of broken earth and murdered men, the answer to the question. No road. No thoroughfare. No race had won, nor could win, the War. The War had won, and would go on winning.'[52] The soldier-author Siegfried Sassoon (1886–1967) was even more direct. 'War is hell', he wrote, 'and those who institute it are criminals.' The political and military leadership thought otherwise: the architect of the entire homicidal debacle at the Somme, British commander Sir Douglas Haig, was promoted to the rank of Field Marshall in 1917.

In the Middle Ages, Catholic 'just war' theory sought to identify criteria under which organized killing was morally permissible. Not surprisingly, the theory emphasized the importance of protecting innocent civilians and limiting action to official combatants. But the injunction was often honoured only in the breach as opposing sides sought every advantage in the heat of combat. Today pitilessly lumped under the euphemism 'collateral damage', the killing of civilians during wartime is justified by what one scholar refers to as consequentialist moral theory, the notion that one must prioritize circumstances, costs and benefits. Aerial firebombing of major German cities during the Second World War and the atomic bomb attacks against Japan are two of the most dreadful illustrations of the practice, with civilian fatalities from the former easily exceeding the better-known, and precedent-setting, nuclear assault.

It is estimated that almost half the deaths during the Second World War were civilian, and the percentage continued to increase in regional wars over the remainder of the century. The nation, or in our new age of non-state terrorism, the higher cause, is claimed to absolve those who take the lives of innocent civilians. Ironically, violent death due to war has become a high percentage prospect for non-combatants and a distinctly less likely conclusion for trained warriors. It hardly needs mentioning that most of those civilian deaths since the end of the Second World War have occurred in poor countries, and most of the victims belonged to the most vulnerable groups, those with the most fragile grip on the minimum requirements of physical well-being.

Murder

Outside the sanction of the state and its laws, individuals have been taking the lives of family members, spouses, neighbours, friends and strangers for millennia. And although murder statistically is an uncommon crime, it features prominently in our cultural imagination, the subject of dramatic novels, television programmes, feature films and the print and electronic news media.[53] Murder rates are normally calculated in terms of the number of victims per hundred thousand of population in a given year. Some anthropologists have estimated that in prehistoric stateless societies it was common for upwards of 40 per cent of adult males to die violently. But in the absence of a state which claims a monopoly over the legitimate use of lethal force and erects a legal system to criminalize certain behaviours, one can only speak of killing and not the socially constructed act of murder.[54] For medieval Europe, where state power to control internal violence was limited, the estimated murder rate stood at around 35 per thousand. By the sixteenth century it had fallen to twenty per thousand, and at the close of the eighteenth century it had dropped to five per thousand, where it has remained into our own day. The lower rate may be misleading, however, since many wounds that were fatal prior to the advent of efficacious medicine are now in the category of serious injuries and long hospitalizations.

Why one commits murder has been of intense academic interest to criminologists, psychologists, theologians and philosophers for more than a century. The deliberate taking of another innocent life (and the state's criminalization of this act) has been assigned to innate sinfulness, malevolent dispositions in human nature, diseased minds and burdensome environmental factors, but no single theory has ever gone uncontested. Certainly none of these hypotheses explains the biblical stories of divine enmity against frail humans. In the words of psychologist Steven Pinker, the Old Testament 'is one long celebration of violence'. One son of Adam and Eve murders another; God drowns humanity in the story of Noah and the Ark; later the same God orders Abraham to murder his only son. When Abraham's nephew Lot settles in Sodom, God immolates the entire population of the city – men, women and children. The king of kings kills and gives orders to kill for all manner of perceived offences. As Pinker states, obedience to absolute rule, not respect for human life, is the cardinal virtue in the biblical world.[55]

Throughout the Roman republic the killing of another human being was considered a private act, not a public offence within the purview of the state. According to a recent study, 'republican Romans had neither the capacity nor the inclination to make the essentially private act of malicious and intentional homicide an offense actionable by the government'.[56] During the Middle Ages fatal interpersonal violence was most common among the elite of society, men preoccupied by notions of honour, and its incidence prompted little widespread concern. Indeed for centuries the mastery of personal violence through individualized combat and duels was viewed as a means of enhancing one's social status.[57] And as recently as the mid-1800s, duelling was legal and even normative in many American states. Andrew Jackson killed several people in duels long before he entered the White House as the nation's seventh president. In 1859 editorialists from the Southern states of the U.S. celebrated the acquittal of New York State congressman Daniel Sickles after he had murdered his wife's lover in broad daylight on a Washington street. Supporters called the shooting a justifiable honour killing, the adulterous affair an infringement of Sickles's property rights.[58]

After the start of the industrial revolution, murder migrated from being an activity of the elite and began its current association with the lower classes, especially with economically marginalized males. Today the new narrative of interpersonal conflict ending in violent death follows a disturbingly common set of circumstances: banal arguments between younger male family members, friends or acquaintances – often coupled with the consumption of alcohol and the ready availability of guns – escalate and lead to murder.

At the start of the twenty-first century, the American National Center for Health Statistics identified homicide as the second leading cause of death among young persons aged 15 to 24 (the first was road fatalities).[59] In modern democratic states, murder remains a deep-rooted concern of public officials and citizens at every socio-economic level, calling up images of social fragmentation and alienation, the breakdown of law and order and the callous disregard for the sanctity of human life.[60] Public perceptions of homicide, shaped in large part by the media's proclivity to highlight violent crime, continues to focus our awareness of the possibility of death at the hands of violent criminals and accounts for the significant level of fiscal and personnel resources devoted to detection, prosecution and punishment of those who commit the unforgivable act.

Capital Punishment

States have always used death as a form of punishment for law-breakers, and the practice has only intensified in the modern era despite the parallel rise of human rights claims in the international arena. The ancient code of King Hammurabi in Babylon called for the judicial execution of those found guilty of 25 different crimes, although murder was not one of them. Athens and Rome made ample provision for the death penalty, and sentences were carried out in gruesome fashion, with crucifixion, impalement, drowning and being buried alive all options employed by the agents of the state. Mosaic law allowed for stoning, beheading, hanging and crucifixion, with the last of these only abolished in the early fourth century during the reign of Emperor Constantine.

New torments awaited the condemned, however. During the Middle Ages the emerging states of western Europe permitted the torture of criminals before final execution. These were often extended and vicious affairs, repeatedly bringing the criminal to the brink of unconsciousness before finally putting them out of their misery. During the reign of Henry VIII (1509–47) an estimated 72,000 criminals were executed by the Tudor state and by the early eighteenth century there were more than 200 crimes in Britain which were punishable by death. In the words of one historian, capital punishment 'was a tool of terror: theoretically, that terror inspired by the law maintained order'.[61] Public executions of the lawbreakers were often quasi-religious events, where the condemned person was expected to express his or her remorse and warn others against similar behaviour. At the public hanging of a burglar in colonial Boston in 1773, for example, the estimated 7,000 spectators were able to purchase printed copies of the man's final words of repentance. Early in the nineteenth century such executions turned into raucous public spectacles where souvenirs and alcohol were sold.[62]

Not until the mid-nineteenth century did public opinion turn against public executions, and by the close of the century the punishment was carried out almost exclusively behind prison doors, the event witnessed only by immediate family and state officials. Capital punishment was abolished in western Europe in the second half of the twentieth century, and abolitionism is a strict requirement for membership in the European Union. But it continued to find strong support in many American states, both on the contested grounds of deterrence and in the name of society's obligation to reprise the wrong inflicted on an innocent citizen and against the norms of the wider culture. Gallup poll surveys indicate that more than half of all Americans support the death penalty, although actual executions are few, with a total of 52 taking place in 2009.[63]

Perilous Behaviours

As had been the case for millennia, in 1900 the majority of humans still died as a result of infectious disease. Over the course of the twentieth century there was hope in developed Western countries that this perennial foe would be eliminated as a public health problem, and indeed great strides in diagnosis, treatment and prevention were taken even as dangerous microbes adapted and developed resistance to new drugs. By the second half of the century, however, it had become clear that the early optimism had been misplaced.

In the 1960s new strains of influenza spread around the globe, and during the 1970s sexually transmitted diseases alarmed medical researchers and the general public alike. In the 1970s and '80s, for example, 30 emerging infectious diseases were identified, while growing resistance to vaccines and drug treatments allowed old enemies like malaria and rabies to reassert their destructive power. An avian strain of influenza originating in Hong Kong at the turn of the new century raised fears of a new global pandemic similar in demographic impact to the great influenza of 1918–19.[64] And in a post-9/11 environment, where non-state actors demonstrated the ability to terrorize large populations and inflict significant loss of life, a growing fear of (and preparation for) bioterrorism involving disease-threat agents brought the weaponization of disease into popular consciousness.

Rates of accidental deaths also remained fairly steady across the twentieth century. At the peak of the industrial era in the West, work-related accidents represented a large percentage of deaths in urban centres. The absence of safety regulations in the workplace during the nineteenth and early twentieth centuries contributed mightily to the problem. With the rise of greater safety-consciousness and tighter state regulations after the Second World War, the role of accidental death in overall mortality rates was expected to decline. However new risk factors, largely unrelated to the workplace, have emerged in recent decades, contributing to disturbingly high rates of death by accident in the West's otherwise safety-conscious culture. In 2009, for example, unintentional accidents ranked fifth on the list of leading causes of death for all age groups in the u.s. and stood as the leading cause of death for those under the age of nineteen. Accidental drowning, poisoning, suffocation, property fires, mishandling of firearms and of course road accidents – all took a disproportionate toll on children and teens, while falls and the misuse of prescription medications were leading culprits in the accidental deaths of the elderly.

Lifestyle Diseases

Despite these distressing continuities, mortality data at the end of the twentieth century reflected a fundamental shift in the leading causes of death. What researchers and health experts called lifestyle or chronic, non-communicable diseases (NCDs) now assume the unwelcome status of major killers. In 2010 the American Centers for Disease Control examined the top ten causes of death in the U.S. at the start of the twentieth century and compared these against the present-day top ten. Whereas influenza, tuberculosis and gastro-intestinal infections (together with work-related accidents) loomed large as killers in the earlier period, at the start of the twenty-first century cardiovascular disease, cancer and diabetes rank at the top of the list. Indeed over 60 per cent of the approximately 35 million deaths worldwide each year are now attributable to these three causes alone.[65] Of course everyone must die of something, and an obvious argument can be made that heart disease and cancer are most often correlated with advanced age.

But the data indicate that lifestyle diseases most commonly make their appearance in middle age, a potentially deadly synergy of diets high in sugar and saturated fats, lack of physical exercise, prolonged use of tobacco products and alcohol abuse. Sometimes referred to as the four horsemen of bad health (after the biblical four horsemen of the apocalypse), risky health behaviours have placed an enormous burden on the fiscal resources of modern states. According to the *New York Times*, managing and treating lifestyle illnesses consumed one-seventh of the GDP of the U.S. in 2010. Perhaps more ominously, the editorial board of the American Heart Association projected that health care-related costs in the U.S. from cardiovascular disease alone would triple by 2030 to $800 billion.[66]

Lifestyle diseases are unique insomuch as they are preventable, at least at their developmental stages in youth, early adulthood and middle age. The nineteenth-century shift from predominantly agricultural to industrial economies, and more recently the further transition in some countries from industrial to information-, service- and technology-based economies, has resulted in a number of unintended consequences for human health. Where once most labour involved physical movement and exertion, today an increasing percentage of the workforce is inert, stationed for hours behind computer monitors, retail service desks, or in cars. Immobility at work is coupled with a sedentary home life, with family members – particularly the young – fixated in front of large-screen televisions, game consoles and computer screens. Even simple exercise (when it occurs) has been commodified and commercialized, with fee-for-access health clubs – only accessible via car of course – and salaried 'personal trainers' for those incapable or unwilling to establish and follow their own exercise routine, becoming new growth industries. Western culture, aided by a powerful and sophisticated marketing sector, celebrates our attachment to entertainment technologies, especially the ones masquerading as essential communication tools. We are active but torpid, busy but passive, engaged but increasingly inert. We adopt behaviours that have been shown to shorten our lives and find it difficult to break bad lifestyle habits. We have, in short, chosen to accelerate our own demise.

Environmental Factors

The deliberate and planned manipulation of nature for human purposes, or the process of rapid industrialization which has been the distinguishing feature of Western history over the past three centuries, also produced a variety of unintended health consequences. In one recent estimate 40 per cent of the world's deaths at the start of the new century can be traced indirectly to environmental degradation on multiple fronts.[67] Contaminated water, soil and air, not to mention exposure to dangerous chemicals and materials in the workplace, take their toxic toll on human life in an incremental fashion, with most victims unaware of the dangers and only suffering the consequences years after initial exposure.

Cheap energy, cheap water and rapid population growth over 150 years have powered what the historian J. R. McNeill has called 'a regime of perpetual ecological disturbance', the by-product of 'billions of human ambitions and efforts, of unconscious social evolution'.[68] Unprecedented economic growth in industrialized nations, and the expansion of agricultural productivity through the use of chemical fertilizers and genetic engineering of crops, propelled a dramatic increase in population, not just in Europe but around the world. In 1820, as the industrial revolution was in its initial stages, global population stood at approximately 1 billion. It soared during the twentieth century, reaching 6.5 billion by the year 2000.

But over 50 per cent of this total faced chronic malnutrition, making them more susceptible to a wide range of respiratory infections and diseases like malaria. In 2000, 1.2 billion people were without access to clean drinking water, and since waterborne infections accounted for the majority of infectious diseases, failure to address this basic deficit assured additional deaths. As an illustration, over 2 million infants and children still die each year from diarrhoea, an age-old affliction associated closely with contaminated water – and an entirely preventable state of affairs in light of aggregate global resources. Making those resources available to those most in need appears incompatible with the consumption habits of the world's most affluent states. Nation-state rivalries and conflicts, not to mention internal conflicts and political mismanagement, also contribute their share to the ever-widening chasm between rich and poor states.

Examples of the close relationship between environmental degradation, illness and premature death could be multiplied. The world's ever-growing reliance on heavily polluting, non-renewable fossil fuels to power modern economies, coupled with the interminable growth imperative at the heart of the free market, is perhaps the most familiar case in point. Coal combustion in the late nineteenth and early twentieth centuries, followed more recently by the burning of petroleum products and their resultant emissions, have been linked to respiratory illness and lung cancer. In the U.S.,

20 per cent of lung cancer deaths are caused by particulate matter from vehicle exhausts. The rates are likely higher in developing countries where regulatory codes are absent or unenforced. And those rates will continue to spike as developing states, led by China and India, seek to modernize along the same fossil fuel-dependent lines as their Western predecessors.

In a fascinating review of lead articles appearing over the past century in the prestigious *New England Journal of Medicine*, a team of physician-authors made a case for the social nature of disease, how disease always is defined, experienced and ameliorated within a deeper social and political context. For example, in 1912 articles about tropical infections, syphilis and gonorrhoea featured prominently in the *New England Journal*, the very year when immigration to the u.s. reached its highest level. That same year an editorial rhapsodized over the power of eugenics to supplant evolution in the effort to eliminate the unfit. More recently, articles describing and analysing the negative effects of obesity, smoking, drug abuse, environmental pollution and climate change on health and longevity have been highlighted in the Journal.[69]

All of the above threats to human life elicited public policy approaches to the problems, and all engaged researchers, medical professionals, law enforcement and political leaders at local, regional and national levels. But determining which threats to concentrate on, which adverse environments to address, has always been shaped by cultural expectations and political priorities. The battles against communicable diseases, against those who would harm the youngest and most innocent, and against those who commit singular acts of violence against another person, enjoy broad-based popular support. The more complex battle against self-inflicted harm in the form of lifestyle habits and environmental degradation faces greater obstacles.

The first threat to health and life, arising from lifestyle habits, has become a constituent part of middle-class consciousness and convention. The second threat, environmental degradation, remains a highly contested one, with influential voices still questioning the validity of the evidence in support of environmental decline. In our hasty embrace of consumer culture, our getting and spending in a socially constructed world of planned obsolescence, it is difficult to pause and consider the potential long-term impact of humankind's manipulation of the natural environment. Elected officials and policy makers in the democratic West, like the citizenry that votes them into office, are captives of the short-term fix, advancing the current growth and consumption paradigm that most of us recognize as unsustainable over the long term. The reckoning awaits another generation.

FIVE

Modern Reconsiderations

The poet Philip Larkin died in 1985, at the age of 63, of oesophageal cancer. After an unsuccessful surgery to postpone the finale he told a friend: 'I have at one step passed into the end of life, which of course is always in my mind, but is now real and here, and fills me with dread.'[1] That sense of dread was long-standing for Larkin, as it is for many of us in the early twenty-first century. In 1983 he observed that 'Man's most remarkable talent is for ignoring death. For once the certainty of permanent extinction is realized, only a more immediate calamity can dislodge it from the mind, and then only temporarily.'[2] Larkin's last words to the hospital nurse who held his hand were 'I am going to the inevitable.'[3]

Philip Larkin was not a man of faith and like increasing numbers of western Europeans in the post-Second World War decades he accepted the finality of death. The historic mind–body problem had lost its immediacy for many at the close of the century. Complex thoughts and emotions, it appeared, were best explained as special aspects of physical matter, the intricate by-product of nerves stimulated in the brain. In his poem 'The Old Fools', Larkin expressed a rising sentiment:

> At death, you break up: the bits that were you
> Start speeding away from each other for ever
> With no one to see.[4]

Yet despite this severe appraisal, this return to the wisdom of Lucretius, Larkin was able to affirm the moral significance of life, and to identify a common human imperative that was in alignment with the world's great religious traditions. Most days are filled with misplaced and unrealistic hopes for the future, but if we pause to reflect on the limited possibilities of our brief lives, we are prompted to exercise care and kindness in our dealings with friends and strangers alike. In the face of our ignorance of larger meaning, our recourse must be to one another here and now, avoiding what Sartre described as 'bad faith' and the pursuit of false consolations in prospective goals and relationships.[5]

Western society has reached an impasse on the subject of death. Very few of us look forward to dying and increasing numbers of us have concluded with Philip Larkin that at death we do simply 'break up', our bits 'speeding away' to myriad destinations in a great impersonal recycling project. We turn away from death, banish it from familiar social spaces and assign the unlikeable details to formal institutions and trained professionals in the modern funeral industry. As the prospect of eternity and the world view of traditional religion moves to the defensive for ever-increasing numbers of Westerners, we disown death and struggle mightily to enlarge the present moment. And when the effort fails, as fail it must for everyone, we camouflage the final act, relegating the dying person to places far removed from familiar sights and sounds, detached from the known and the commonplace – our lived context. In removing death from public view, sanitizing it out of society and the home, and by narrowing our exposure to end-of-life situations, we have become more fearful of it. Some 400 years before Larkin, Shakespeare captured the essence of what has become the predominant modern attitude towards death:

> The weariest, and most loathed worldly life
> That Age, Ache, penury, and imprisonment
> Can lay on nature, is a Paradise
> To what we feare of death.[6]

Most of us effuse about the good life and struggle to extend it, but we are loathe to talk about or publicly grieve over the good death, rejecting out of hand that death can be good in any sense. Instead, we have transformed death into the great modern sin, the failure that must be shunted aside and disowned. The Stoic philosopher Marcus Aurelius would be disappointed by contemporary Western culture's embrace of this mirage. But he would be heartened by a minority counteroffensive that began in the 1960s with the goal of empowering the dying person to take control of life's final chapter, to accept his or her place in nature, to be remembered for one's contributions to this world and respected for one's vision of its outcome.

Longevity and its Discontents

In our encounter with death we support and applaud advances in medicine and clinical technology that allow us to cling to life. No one wishes to undergo the harrowing death of Nikolas in Tolstoy's *Anna Karenina*, the captive of terrible suffering.

> There was no position that did not cause him pain, no part of his body that did not hurt and torment him. Even the memories, impressions, and thoughts, within his body now aroused in him the same sort of repulsion as the body itself.[7]

Today physicians enjoy a much-deserved status as compassionate healers, upholding an ancient oath to first do no harm. Billions of dollars are spent annually to forward life-saving and life-extending research, and most citizens view this as a worthy investment of national funds, a priority function of a truly democratic polity. Screening programmes allow for early detection and treatment of many mid-life cancers; advanced cardiology enables us to survive heart attacks; and powerful drug therapies help us to control other system failures.[8] Our consumer-oriented culture, abetted by media images and socially constructed ideals of beauty, promotes the appearance of youthfulness as an essential component of a healthy lifestyle. 'Age management' institutes offer exercise, dietary and pharmaceutical enhancements for those who are determined to remain physically and cognitively vital into their eighth and ninth decades. From over-the-counter cosmetics to under-the-scalpel surgical enhancements, we wish to live longer and look younger no matter the cost – or the facts.[9]

And there's the rub. The facts are immoveable and the costs are without precedent. Moreover, the elusive goal is filled with unintended consequences. First is the compelling evidence – perhaps no surprise to most – that a longer life is no guarantee of a respectable quality of life. The Roman statesman and Stoic philosopher Seneca knew this, of course, but wisdom from the past is rarely appropriated and utilized. We all hope for the good death, quick, painless and preferably while asleep. But increasing numbers are finding the experience prior to death debilitating, lingering and not without anguish. The cognitive plunder associated with Alzheimer's disease in the elderly raises once again the philosophical question regarding the nature of personhood. Is there a core self, an essential 'I' that does not change with age? Next is the untenable economic impact of caring for a rapidly growing elderly sector and the spiralling financial outlay associated with treating chronic illnesses. In the year 2000, approximately 15 per cent of the population of the EU and U.S. was over the age of 65. This figure is expected to double by the year 2050, and ageing populations are major consumers of health care services.[10]

Our current models for supporting extended end-of-life care are simply not sustainable over the long term. The implicit post-Second World War social contract endorsing prolonged medical care for the dying is driving fiscal exigencies in every developed nation at an unprecedented pace. Finally there are the wrenching social and psychological costs associated with inevitable decline and protracted death. Chronic illnesses are most difficult for the victim who loses touch with friends, family and community, and perhaps no less concerning for family members who must cope with a loved one's return to severe dependency. Society struggles mightily to balance the economic consequences of long-term care for a progressively feeble population with its humane commitment to maintaining the dignity and autonomy of the individual.

As we have seen, for most of human history the standard causes of death were as a result of infectious disease, violent activity of one form or another, or complications related to childbirth. Disease was the outsized killer, cutting lives short in what seemed like an instant. Life was fleeting and death was sudden, family and loving relationships ruptured without warning while doctors stood by, ignorant of the causes and helpless to intervene. As late as 1880 approximately 20 per cent of all children born in Western society died before their first birthday and another 20 per cent died before their fifth. In that same year global average life expectancy at birth was around 30 years, a number that had been stubbornly fixed for millennia and seemed unlikely to change. Even in nascent industrialized countries like England, average life expectancy before 1870 was between 30 and 40 years.[11] No more than 5 per cent of men and women lived to see the age of 70 and those who did were on the cusp of experiencing what the sixteenth-century French sceptic Michel de Montaigne referred to as the 'extremist form of dying'. Simply put, while elderly adults could be found in all pre-modern cultures, there were not many of them as a percentage of total population. To be old was to be extraordinary.[12]

There were compensations, however. As we have seen, it was rare in the pre-modern era to die alone or in the presence of strangers. Extended family and friends were nearby and supportive, even if the terminal condition was an extended affair. For working-class families, membership in a burial or friendly society assured a wider network of support. In the absence of efficacious medicine, informal palliative care revolved around the solicitations of loved ones who supervised the patient's personal comfort and emotional well-being. Most importantly, the death event was a spiritual passage given transcendent significance by a widely shared picture of the hereafter and by clergy who supervised the rituals and pronounced the sacred texts long associated with the final departure. Death was the business of religion, the experience and the immediate aftermath framed in spiritual language and under the supervision of those who presumably knew best. As for the economic burdens associated with dying, these were minimal when compared to our own day, largely due to the fact that medical options were limited and because a protracted death from a chronic condition was the exception instead of the rule.

The Medical Turn

Over the past century, and particularly since the end of the Second World War, an unprecedented move towards a longer life has occurred due to advances in public health and sanitation, better nutrition and the triumph of modern medicine (especially vaccines and antibiotics) in addressing myriad internal malfunctions and external pathogens.[13] Where surgery was until recently basically a matter of cutting and removing, the model of continuous repair and replacement is now standard. Technological breakthroughs like computerized axial tomography scans (CAT), magnetic resonance imaging (MRI) and laser microsurgery have greatly enhanced the diagnostic and treatment skill of the physician.[14] Very few people die young now – infant mortality rates fell to 5 per cent in 1920 and below 1 per cent in 2000 – and those children who now survive expect to enjoy the love and nurture of parents, and even grandparents, for many years.

Indeed we now view death before a ripe old age as a defeat, frequently employing the language of 'battle' or 'heroic struggle' in referring to those afflicted with a lethal gene or cancerous growth. The average lifespan in the developed West is now 78 years, and this average increases by two years every decade.[15] As a result we now most commonly die of age-related degenerative diseases and this is often an extended affair since they impair internal organs and cause us to depend on others for basic activities like dressing, eating and bathing.[16] The sufferer gradually loses cognitive and physical functions, becomes socially disengaged and often depressed if living alone. Near the end they experience the humiliation of giving up their personal autonomy and find themselves cared for by well-meaning strangers in an institutional setting.

Statistically confirmed degrees of life, all trending towards greater physical and cognitive impairment as one ages, and all supporting hugely expensive forms of medical technology, pharmacology and residential care, is now the 'new normal' experience of death and dying in the developed West. Taking just one example, in 2009 the U.S. Medicare programme for the elderly paid out 55 billion dollars for doctor and hospital bills for the final two months of patients' lives. The total was greater than annual federal spending for the Department of Homeland Security and the Department of Education combined. It can cost up to $10,000 per day for treatment in an intensive care unit (ICU), where upwards of 20 per cent of all Americans now spend their final weeks and days.[17]

Death outside a hospital setting is increasingly associated with public and private nursing homes, today often referred to as 'skilled care' or 'assisted living' facilities. Between 20 and 30 per cent of the elderly now spend their final months and years in these purpose-designed settings. Beginning with their expansion in the post-Second World War era, the major criticisms of nursing homes have involved patient abuse, poor staffing levels, minimum training and low wages for entry-level nursing assistants, and a patient culture of disempowerment. Governments now do a better job regulating and inspecting these facilities in terms of safety risks and the enforcement of patient rights, but quality of living continues to vary greatly depending on ownership and funding. Church-affiliated, private nursing homes typically offer their residents a wide range of activities and experiences tailored to individual patient need, while state-supported institutions tend to provide a more generic and economical menu of patient options.[18]

Our modern dilemma, possibly the most distressing unintended consequence of modern medicine, was in some ways anticipated in ancient Greek mythology where the handsome mortal Tithonus, son of the king of Troy, becomes romantically involved with Eos, the goddess of the dawn. Eos begs the god Zeus to grant Tithonus immortality but neglects to specify the exact terms. The devious Zeus honours the request, but fails to endow Tithonus with eternal youth. Eventually losing physical strength and slipping into dementia, the babbling Tithonus in time drives Eos to distraction and she turns him into a grasshopper who chirps without cessation. Modern caregivers as a rule exhibit greater empathy and compassion than Eos when it comes to the inevitable decline of an elderly person, but they too are challenged physically, emotionally and economically when the circumstance invades the lives of those we love. Coping with age-related degenerative diseases is gruelling for sufferer and caregiver alike.

Autonomy and Dignity

Of course the laudable mission of physicians and modern hospitals is to alleviate pain, heal the sick and save lives through aggressive interventionist medicine. That is why the final stage of an elderly patient's hospitalization is so often spent in the intensive care unit, where forceful life-saving measures are the norm. In the ICU physicians are now able to deconstruct the dying process, supporting some key bodily functions while deploying technology to replace others. Mechanical ventilators, cardiac pacemakers, intubation (feeding tubes), kidney dialysis machines, drugs to control blood pressure and a host of other sophisticated interventions can keep the body alive where previously the loss of one essential function would quickly mean the end of others. Indeed the development of the first two technologies complicated the traditional cardio-pulmonary criterion for the determination of death, leaving the medical community searching for a new benchmark. Autopsies and the study of cadavers in medical training further objectify and quantify the body, with the variety of organs and not the former person the subject of inquiry.

As a result of the new knowledge and technology, we now have greater control over the timing of death, allowing family and physicians to determine when 'enough is enough'.[19] Making that determination, however, has led to enormous controversy in the field of medical ethics, especially during the past half-century. Central to the debate has been the question of whether or not physicians can assist in the ending of a life, whether prolonging life can sometimes interfere with humane care and the dignity of the dying. In short, when is it appropriate to stop keeping people alive through the power of modern medical skill and technology? Respect for a patient's personal autonomy and desire to avoid the pain and indignities of muscular wastage, incontinence, paralysis and mental deterioration have led in most countries to legal acceptance of the right to take one's own life by refusing treatment, food or hydration. Individual sufferers (or a family member with power of attorney) can decide how aggressively to treat life-threatening conditions, how much pain medication they need and at what point they should be medicated into unconsciousness. It also became legal and morally acceptable for physicians to engage in what is called 'passive euthanasia', hastening a patient's death by discontinuing critical life-support systems, raising dosages of palliative analgesics to expedite death or withholding treatment from an elderly patient with pneumonia.

During the early years of the twenty-first century, public opinion surveys in the u.s. indicated that approximately 70 per cent of citizens believed that physicians should be allowed to assist the terminally ill should the latter desire to end their life.[20] But with the exception of Switzerland, the Netherlands and the State of Oregon in the u.s., active physician-assisted suicide under specific and tightly regulated conditions remained outside the ethical and legal purview of practitioners in the West. Defenders of 'active euthanasia' claimed that there was no moral difference between an act of deliberate omission and an act of commission, that it was inhumane (and a violation of the Hippocratic oath) for a physician to allow prolonged agonies when the means were available to abbreviate them. In the words of one contemporary philosopher, 'Not to do this would be to treat people with less kindness than most pet owners accord to their animals, for it is considered merciful to animals to end their lives swiftly and easily when they suffer without hope of recovery.'[21]

Oregon's path-breaking Death with Dignity Act allowed for terminally ill residents with fewer than six months to live to end their ordeal through the voluntary self-administration of lethal medications prescribed by a licensed physician. Once passed by the state legislature in 1997, opponents feared that Oregon would become a suicide destination for terminally ill Americans. Framed by the national news stories surrounding Dr Jack Kevorkian, the most uncompromising practitioner of physician-assisted suicide in the U.S. during the 1990s, the Oregon experiment attracted widespread attention. But by 2008 fewer than 400 Oregonians, mostly suffering from various aggressive cancers, took advantage of this form of patient choice over end-of-life issues. Clearly in this case the notion that possession of a right entails its subsequent widespread exercise was disproved.[22] But still the conflict of ideas raged on.

Opposition to medically assisted suicide was grounded in strong diagnostic, philosophical and religious claims. Some medical practitioners pointed to the possibility of mistaken diagnosis or the need to explore alternative treatment options, and the challenges associated with knowing when a patient request is rational. For example, how does one eliminate the possibility that a patient is acting under subtle pressure from relatives or insurance companies, making critical decisions based on economic exigencies? Just as philosophers wrestled with the question of when life begins, so too there was an ongoing debate over when it ends and what constitutes legitimate treatment at the end of life.

Religious objections continued to centre on the 'sanctity of life' argument, the insistence that when it comes to humans, only God can determine the moment of death, and that any suffering and pain associated with end-stage chronic illness must be borne bravely.[23] The central argument behind euthanasia, that humans own the right and enjoy the freedom to determine when and how they will die, remained firmly at odds with the mainline Christian understanding of the relationship between God and humanity.[24] Finally, secular critics argued that loosening the legal restrictions on assisted suicide put the most vulnerable at risk: the poor, the disabled, the elderly. At every turn opponents saw the slippery slope of involuntary euthanasia, and with the memory of its most brutal twentieth-century form in the programmed killing of the Nazis, opponents fought vigorously to maintain a firm distinction between killing and letting people die.[25]

Advance care planning and palliative medicine began to make modest progress at the close of the twentieth century, but budget-busting interventions in the ICU continued to be the predominant approach to end-of-life care. In those European countries where the hold of traditional religion waned, the influence of secular medical ethicists expanded. But without the certitudes of traditional religion, these ethicists were obliged to construct their positions on the shifting sands of cultural preference, the currently accepted norms of the majority culture. Try as they might to nudge these norms at the perimeter, in the end the weight of precedent and deep cultural patterns made it difficult to entertain fresh approaches to the end of life involving patient choice.[26]

Defining Death

Throughout most of the twentieth century, physicians defined death as the total stoppage of the circulation of blood and the subsequent cessation of respiration and pulsation. This 'heart–lung' or cardiopulmonary classification of death was fairly easy to establish; checking for heartbeat is the most common method of making a determination of the end of life. But during the 1960s questions concerning forceful resuscitation efforts, advances in biotechnology and the advent of organ transplant surgery complicated the issue, leading to important debates and the emergence of a new academic specialism known as bioethics, or the study of morality in the life sciences. Breakthroughs in biotechnology allowed for mechanical devices to sustain respiration and heart function beyond the carrying capacity of the natural organism. The first human-to-human heart transplant, carried out by South African surgeon Dr Christiaan Barnard in 1967, opened up the possibility of saving lives by harvesting organs of patients on artificial life support. Cardiac transplantation became an option for only a tiny fraction of those suffering from coronary artery disease, but its modest success rate opened new questions about the appropriateness of the cardiopulmonary definition of death.[27]

It was in this climate that a committee of physicians at Harvard Medical School developed an alternative definition of death, one involving the permanent loss of all brain functions. The new designation was proposed in 1968, and in 1981 a u.s. presidential commission affirmed this alternative neurological definition. 'Whole brain death' came to be recognized in the law as an appropriate standard for declaring an end to life, enabling organ transplant teams to move forward, but also generating new philosophical, ethical and public policy concerns.[28] Many critics took the position that artificially sustained life is morally obligatory when the technology is available, even if consciousness – the conventional marker of personhood – is absent.

Still others adopted what has been called the higher brain definition, where the controversial marker of death is the loss of consciousness: a social and psychological, rather than strictly biological, definition of death. Objections to this definition centre on the imprecise and highly contested nature of personhood. Would, for example, Alzheimer's patients be counted as dead as they lack rational capacity? Do patients in a persistent vegetative state lack personhood? Is there a distinction to be drawn between living and merely existing, and if the answer is yes, who determines the dividing line between the two?[29]

Suicide

Physician-assisted death is a relatively new topic of debate and disquiet, whereas the taking of one's own life has over many centuries and across many cultures been one of the most heavily censured of human behaviours. The World Health Organization estimates that over a million suicides take place each year, and in some countries death by suicide is now among the three leading causes of mortality for those between the ages of fifteen and 45. Overall rates of suicide have increased by almost 60 per cent since the late 1960s, with incidents among younger people now displacing the elderly as the major concern.[30]

All of the major religious traditions have condemned self-inflicted death and the work of many modern social scientists continues to be informed by these strictures. One recent sociological study of suicide, for example, purportedly sets out to examine the phenomenon in a balanced manner while the publishing blurb on the back jacket recommends the text for courses in 'psycho-pathology, sociology of deviance, abnormal psychology, and violent crimes'.[31] The assumption remains that in all cases some-thing is wrong with those who willingly take their own lives. Once categorized as sinners and criminals, suicides are now regularly regarded as mentally ill, emotionally unbalanced or socially maladjusted.

Even in the developed West, where notions of individual auton-omy and choice have been at the centre of political and cultural dis-course since the Enlightenment, suicide as rational choice, unlike abortion, is rarely conceded or defended as a legitimate or morally permissible action.[32] Today little serious attention is devoted to suicide as a decision made by thoughtful individuals who take responsibility for themselves and base their decision, after calm consideration, upon judicious evidence. Humans may be capable of reflecting on the meaning of their existence, but the majority culture continues to patronize those who for whatever reason lose the will to live and choose to end their lives voluntarily by accelerating the course of nature. In light of our present-day compulsion to equate all suicide with treatable illnesses, some historical context seems appropriate.

The Long View

We know nothing of prehistoric attitudes towards suicide or the extent of the practice, but we must assume that our earliest ances-tors engaged the question of whether life was worth living. When survival depended upon the effective coordination of group action, it is possible to imagine how voluntary death was not a matter of indifference to the wider society. In the ancient world we encounter a plurality of approaches to suicide. Traditional Hindu practice recognized *sutti* as an appropriate step taken by widows who wished to honour their deceased husbands, and the practice was only outlawed in 1892. Buddhism, while generally opposed to suicide, regarded the action as acceptable under certain circumstances. In China the general who took his own life after a lost battle was admired, as was the deposed statesman who objected to some official policy.[33]

In the Mediterranean world the same variety of approaches existed. Egyptian culture, for example, appears not to have viewed the practice as a violation of existing moral or legal codes, but in ancient Greece self-inflicted death was widely censured as an abandonment of one's duty to the polity and, more importantly, a renunciation of one's status as a servant of the gods. Plato, while in general holding the view that suicide was cowardice, allowed that under certain circumstances, such as extreme personal misfortune or having participated in hugely unjust deeds, the action could be condoned.[34] Aristotle, while also opposed to voluntary death, had less to say on the subject, but neither man was particularly concerned with the well-being or concerns of the suicidal personality. Instead the welfare of the city-state, and the role played by each individual in advancing the polity, always enjoyed primacy.

The Epicureans and Stoics, on the other hand, held that taking one's own life was both morally permissible and an act of liberty when the conditions necessary to a flourishing life (especially rational capacity and health) were absent, irrespective of the impact of such highly personal action on the well-being of the state. For Seneca, whose own life ended in a compelled suicide in the year 65, private good was the crucial factor in the contemplation of self-inflicted death. He insisted that 'mere living is not a good, but living well' and that the wise person 'lives as long as he ought, not as long as he can'.[35] Members of the Roman elite generally accepted self-caused death as a principled action under certain circumstances, and there existed no legal or religious prohibition of suicide for free men. Military commanders who took their own lives when defeat seemed imminent were afforded honourable burials, and common soldiers who faced certain execution at the hands of the enemy brought no dishonour on their family by voluntary death at their own hand or at the hand of a fellow soldier. Suicide was also recognized as a justifiable manner of bringing an end to an intolerably painful illness and was in some cases lauded as a way to demonstrate loyalty to a decedent master or spouse.[36]

Although there is no direct prohibition of suicide in the Tanakh (the sixth commandment, according to one recent scholar, refers to relational – not self – injury), Jewish tradition holds that all human life is sacred and, however painful that life experience might be at a particular moment, one cannot engage in any action that would shorten it. This point is illustrated at the beginning of 2 Samuel, where the mortally wounded King Saul calls upon a young man to kill him 'for anguish has come upon me, and as yet my whole life is in me'. After fulfilling Saul's wishes and faithfully returning the King's diadem to David, however, the young man is ordered to be executed for 'killing the Lord's anointed' – apparently setting a bad precedent for behaviour towards royalty. The Roman-Jewish scholar Josephus described how the garrison at Massada in 73 CE committed mass suicide in the face of Roman aggression, but this was interpreted as an act of heroic martyrdom rather than the wilful taking of one's own life under acute circumstances. Other instances of suicides within the Jewish community during the first and second centuries are similarly framed within the context of martyrdom, a 'greater good' reframing of self-destruction that also informed early Christian attitudes. [37]

In the New Testament John quotes Jesus as saying 'For these sheep I will give my life' and 'No one takes it from me; I lay it down freely myself', but later Church fathers dismissed the suggestion that Christ had taken his own life.[38] During the first centuries of the Common Era, self-inflicted death was regarded by some Christians as a heroic stand against pagan prejudice, but as imperial policy shifted during the fourth century to accommodate Christian practice, an older association of suicide with the betrayal of Christ gained ground around the story of Judas Iscariot, who, according to St Matthew, hanged himself in despair after his act of disloyalty.

The Church's condemnation of what was called self-murder became deeply embedded in its understanding of human life as a precious gift from God. Formal proscription began in the fourth century. The Council of Carthage (348) condemned the practice, and in *The City of God* St Augustine affirmed that 'No man may inflict death upon himself at will merely to escape from temporal difficulties.'[39] Suicide committed out of despair with life was especially reviled because it called into question the Church's authority to pardon sins. During the early Middle Ages Church synods took up the issue and began assigning post-mortem penalties. The official infamy of suicide was institutionalized in both civil and canon law, with local customary law adding special penalties. Most commonly the suicide was excommunicated and burial in consecrated ground was refused. Occasionally, the corpse was hanged and subjected to various acts of torture.[40]

Suicide was even disallowed in cases where a person was suffering inordinate pain in what was clearly a terminal situation. Pain and suffering, it was agreed by Church authorities, were the lot of humans to be endured obediently as preparation for the life eternal. In the thirteenth century Thomas Aquinas cast suicide as a crime for which one could not repent, and in the fourteenth century the poet Dante testified to the staying power of this outlook by relegating suicides to the seventh circle of hell, an abode beneath heretics and murderers. By this point in European history the ignominy associated with suicide was underlined by the practice of dragging the body of the deceased through the streets before being discarded without burial. As an added measure of punishment aimed at the decedent's family, the property and wealth of the sinner was confiscated.

The first serious interrogation of the Church's official position on suicide occurred during the early Renaissance, when so many of the moral certitudes and cultural values of Christian civilization were challenged. Humanists turned initially to the authors of classical antiquity in their wide-ranging critique of medieval Christian conventions, and the rediscovery of examples of heroic self-inflicted death prompted a renewed debate about the limits of individual autonomy. Printed editions and translations of the works of classical authors exposed the literate minority to perspectives on suicide that had for centuries been scorned by Church leaders. Chaucer, Castiglione and other prominent authors wrote sympathetically of suicides who acted out of love and noble motives. In the early sixteenth century Sir Thomas More, Catholic humanist and chancellor to Henry VIII, wrote in his fictional account of Utopia how the inhabitants of the island, when faced with an incurable illness, were permitted to take their own lives.[41] More was executed (or martyred) in 1535 for refusing to accept his monarch's break with the Roman Church, but as the religious divide between Protestant and Catholic intensified across western Europe during the later sixteenth century, both sides hardened their official opposition to voluntary death.[42]

Still there were those who refused to let the matter rest, irrespective of the absolutist claims of the majority of religious voices. Shakespeare's Hamlet encapsulated the central dilemma for his own and every succeeding generation:

> To be or not to be: that is the question.
> Whether 'tis nobler in the mind to suffer
> The slings and arrows of outrageous fortune,
> Or to take up arms against a sea of troubles,
> And by opposing end them.[43]

Shakespeare incorporated 52 cases of suicidal thought and action in his plays, probing lives bounded by ignorance, misfortune, disappointment, injustice, emotional upset and physical pain. But as an observer of the human condition (and not a moralist), his underlying purpose was always to question the great certainties, not to defend those who put an end to their days.[44]

John Donne, writing just ten years after the publication of Hamlet, went much further, setting out to reframe the historic Christian position on suicide. Cautiously avoiding the particulars under which conditions suicide might be permissible, Donne instead challenged the centuries-old Christian consensus that suicide is a sin that merits eternal damnation. 'We think it obvious that suicide is the worst of sins, but if we examine the arguments backing up that seemingly obvious tenet, we find that suicide might possibly not be a grave sin and perhaps not a sin at all.' The law of reason may at times indicate that self-inflicted death is a reasonable act, while God's law as articulated in the Bible nowhere explicitly condemns suicide. Indeed Christ's death, according to Donne, could be interpreted as a deliberate suicide on behalf of real sinners.[45] Recognizing the controversial nature of his ideas, Donne circulated the manuscript among his closest friends but never published it. The treatise, titled *Biathanatos*, finally appeared in print posthumously in 1644, in the midst of a civil war when suicide rates experienced a mild increase.[46]

By the eighteenth century, attitudes towards suicide began to reflect a wider critique of political and religious authority. As calls for an end to absolute monarchy, aristocratic privilege and legal injustices reached a new level of intensity, the intellectual and cultural influence of Protestant and Catholic authorities declined. The language of universal rights, individual autonomy, equality before the law and the amelioration of material conditions for the majority now clashed directly with the medieval counsel of patience in adversity and acceptance of the pains of this life in anticipation of eternal happiness. Now for the first time since the pre-Christian era the subject of suicide was openly discussed and debated – in conversation, in pamphlets and in lengthy treatises. Most of the major Enlightenment figures took a stand against suicide as something unworthy of subjects turned citizens, but they utterly rejected the a priori claim that self-inflicted death was a mortal sin punishable by eternal torment.

During the nineteenth century most of the emerging democratic governments reached back to the position advanced in the classical world by Plato and Aristotle: suicide is an affront to the collective good of the state and to the integrity of the social order. The rise of medical science further advanced the secularization of suicide, but in most cases the professional medical community associated the practice with mental illness. The brains of suicides were sometimes analysed to determine whether acknowledged forms of mental illness were involved.[47] Towards the close of the century, as the claims of aspirant social sciences like psychology and sociology gained a foothold in popular consciousness, the impact of individual pathologies and social factors leading to suicidal behaviour became the object of study.

Émile Durkheim was one of the first to deploy statistical data in his groundbreaking work *Suicide: A Study in Sociology* (1897). He used the data to provide empirical grounding to his claim that the cause of suicide can be reduced largely to key social factors, in particular imbalances in the relation between individuals and their social system.[48] Freud addressed the issue in 1905, attributing suicidal behaviour to a redirection of naturally aggressive instincts usually directed against others that were repressed by society. He later revised this position and claimed that every person had a death instinct that was set in dynamic and constant opposition to the drive for life and reproduction.[49]

During the twentieth century, suicide among the elderly was often prompted by a variety of age-related concerns, including fear of being incapacitated, the loss of mental acuity, declining independence, fatal illness, the death of a long-term spouse or partner and resulting loneliness, a lack of fiscal resources and a desire not to be a burden to one's offspring. These situations led to a view where death seemed like a welcome alternative and suicide an appropriate close to a life well-lived. In the U.S., the elderly now account for more than a quarter of all suicides, and more than three-quarters of those who take their own life visited their primary care physician in the month before their death, suggesting the importance of declining health as a key cause.[50] The psychologist Thomas Joiner has argued that people who die by suicide come to see their departure as a comfort to others and themselves. Feeling themselves to be a burden or alienated from others, the decision to end one's life seems like a rational choice even if they do suffer from a mental disorder.[51]

Today suicide continues to be stigmatized, something unthinkable outside the context of mental pathology or emotional abnormality. Few of us are willing to support self-inflicted death as a matter of individual choice that rational people can make at the close of a productive and happy life. We are prepared to engage the meaning of the life worth living as a thought experiment, but few are prepared to ascribe noble meaning to one's decision, upon measured reflection, to bring a close to one's days. Sartre defended suicide as an appropriate element of radical freedom and responsibility, but mainstream culture does not agree. Instead, we feel obliged in every circumstance to 'combat' suicide as a major public health problem that reflects poorly on the community and betrays the social compact. In this compartment of life, autonomy and choice must be subordinated to the collective self-image of Western society.

The Business of Our Deaths

How the body is treated from the moment of death to the final deposition has varied extensively across time and culture, but some form of preparation and burial or interment of remains has been practised by all peoples for millennia as an appropriate last act on behalf of the decedent. Whether that interment was by inhumation (deposition in the earth), stone envelopment, consignment to the ocean depths or cremation and urn placement, humans have been careful to perform some type of ritual dispatch of the body. The ritual itself has been accepted as of maximum importance, both for the dead and for the community of which the departed had been a member. As we have seen, for early peoples an unburied body was of enormous concern since the dead were sensitive to affronts to their physical remains committed, either wilfully or neglectfully, by their immediate descendants. No one wished to exasperate the departed inasmuch as the quality of life going forward continued to be touched by them. In more recent times the concept of the angry dead has been replaced by the expression of ongoing love and concern for the deceased through an increasingly commercialized post-mortem goodbye.

In the major religious traditions, the form of dignified and reverential preparation and burial reflected specific understandings of the afterlife experience. Hindu and Buddhist cremation practices, for example, affirmed the apersonal nature of being, the oneness of reality into which the departed returns, either to reincarnation in another form or to a final destiny with Brahman. The belief in bodily resurrection for the faithful that informed the later Jewish, Christian and Muslim faith traditions mandated the inhumation of the fully intact (articulate) body. Early on, however, no such precautions applied to the remains of the reprobate. The prophet Jeremiah declared that those who offend God in life 'shall not be lamented; neither shall they be buried; but they shall be as dung upon the face of the earth . . . and their carcasses shall be meat for the fowls of heaven, and for the beasts of the earth'.[52] In the early fourth century Roman officials, in an effort to tamp down Christian veneration of martyrs, ordered that the bodies of the victims be exhumed and deposited in the sea 'lest any, regarding them as actually gods, should worship them as they lay in their tombs'.[53] In our own day we have witnessed similar cautionary practices carried out by state authorities when dealing with the remains of terrorist masterminds in Afghanistan and ruthless dictators in Libya.

Until a few centuries ago most Europeans were 'waked' at home and buried in sanctified Church ground under the direction of Church authorities, with affluent parishioners enjoying a privileged final resting place beneath the floor of the sanctuary. Poorer congregants were typically buried outside in unmarked graves but still in close proximity to the church building. Family gravestones and imposing markers eventually made their appearance in the early modern period, marking the good deeds of the deceased and hopefully keeping the memory of the decedent alive within the community – at least for a generation or two. As churchyards reached capacity, the skeletal remains from old graves were exhumed and the bones placed into an ossuary, making room in the churchyard for more recent decedents. With the dawn of the industrial age, new private cemeteries opened on the outskirts of cities, towns and villages where families could purchase individual sites.[54] The aesthetic appeal of well-manicured private cemeteries with grave sites that would not be repurposed after the incumbent body had properly decayed reflected a growing concern for the health of the living as much as any commitment to the eternal destiny of the deceased.

The turn of the twentieth century witnessed a fundamental change in the physical relationship between the living and the dead. As we have seen, prior to the late nineteenth century death was a constant if unwelcome companion, visiting the young in particular with fixed regularity. One typically died at home, in the social world of the living, and in the presence and with the prayers of loved ones who were supported by neighbours and friends. Doctors, if they had any role to play, treated the dying in the home. There was really no alternative. In 1873, for example, there were fewer than 200 hospitals across the entire U.S. and a quarter of these were reserved for the mentally ill. By contrast in 1923 there were almost 7,000 hospitals in the U.S., an extraordinary increase in just half a century.[55] Death rates were cruelly high before the twentieth century, but at least the moment of death and its immediate aftermath were for most people part of a domestic lived experience.

After 1900 the corpse gradually made its exit from the private spaces of the living. As mortality rates, especially infant mortality, decreased and death became associated with old age, the business of disposing of bodies was redefined as a secular commercial venture. New public health regulations, combined with a striking rise in the number of institutional deaths, resulted in the loss of control by kinsman and Church authorities. The death event no longer enjoyed its primary association with the journey of the indestructible soul and became a matter of hard data and scientific investigation. Church records of births and deaths were replaced by public registers, where categories and statistical analyses were prioritized. If the cause of death was uncertain, post-mortem examinations were carried out by the coroner, pathologists and other forensic scientists, all of whom were agents of the state. One no longer exited this earthly stage merely for having lived or for mysterious reasons associated with the will of God; rational, materialist, medical explanations were now the obligatory order of business.

Bureaucratic rationalization also began to inform the process by which the body was disposed, the work becoming the almost exclusive preserve of a professional funeral industry dedicated to efficiency and orderliness. Ownership of cemeteries passed out of the hands of the churches and into the domain of public municipalities and private companies. Burials and cremations were organized around regular work schedules at these sites and facilities, irrespective of the convenience of mourners.[56] The nineteenth-century undertaker was transformed into the self-styled 'funeral director' who now offered comprehensive services involving the preparation of the body for public viewing, the scheduling of religious services and the final deposition of the body.

Relieving the immediate family of all details related to the handling of the corpse, the secular, for-profit professional in charge of the transition from death to burial commodified the immediate period after the death of a loved one, just as the medical profession was beginning to commodify the days, weeks and months before death. Even death rites in the mainstream Christian churches took on a more sanitized facade, concentrating less on the deceased person's eternal destiny (sin and post-mortem punishment left behind) and more on his or her temporal accomplishments, character and continuing impact on the living.[57]

The great breakthrough for the emerging funeral industry was the practice of embalming. Once widely decried as bodily mutilation, the practice gained support during the American Civil War when the bodies of fallen Union soldiers were embalmed prior to transport north for burial. The embalming of President Abraham Lincoln's body prior to its final journey from the nation's capital to Springfield, Illinois, also led to greater cultural acceptance. Requiring specialized knowledge and training, temporary preservation of the body was both promoted by funeral professionals on public health grounds and requested by an expanding middle class eager to extend the period of visual contact with their deceased loved one. During the first three decades of the twentieth century specialized mortuary schools emerged, offering scientific training in anatomy and chemistry, together with licensure for professional practice.[58] Death professionals were even careful to emphasize the quasi-religious function of their specialized services, allowing friends and family the necessary time to separate themselves from the cosmetically enhanced physical remains of the departed.

In 1963 in her exposé of the professional funeral industry titled *The American Way of Death*, the British-born author Jessica Mitford (1917–1996) disparaged the commercialization of the death event as a cynical exploitation of clients at the moment of their greatest vulnerability. The book became a best-seller and prompted an investigation by the Federal Trade Commission into the business practices of what by the end of the twentieth century had become a $20-billion-dollar industry.[59] A major television network followed Mitford's lead with a documentary called The Great American Funeral and MGM studios hired Mitford as a consultant on the film The Loved One, based on the 1948 novel by Evelyn Waugh and featuring a sleazy casket salesman. Mitford's readers were awakened to the fact of post-war excesses in the industry and encouraged to return to simpler, less expensive paths.[60] The book was updated and reissued in 1998, its critique still relevant within the context of a society where multiple options now exist for consumers who seek alternative means of dispensing with their bodies upon death. One of the alternatives was cremation (discussed below), already widespread in Europe by the 1960s but still rare in the U.S. where cultural norms and the power of the 'body-centred' funeral industry initially discouraged its adoption.

Recent Approaches to Mortality

Throughout the Middle Ages, the role and importance of the self was subordinated to the needs of the wider Christian community and the priorities established by God. The wishes of the individual were insignificant before the requirements of social superiors in the family, the Church and the village or town. Only during the Renaissance did the first signs of individual distinctiveness emerge, a new picture of personal value and potential where each person was viewed as unique and capable of defining their own place in the world. The evidence for a newly assertive sense of self was widespread, from the appearance of the names of authors and artists on texts and paintings, to marked gravestones and Church appointments.

The Reformation amplified this trend, making each individual responsible for their relationship with God, still the most important business in life, without the intermediary role of an ordained clergy. The Enlightenment and late eighteenth-century age of democratic revolution expanded the concept of individual autonomy into the spheres of politics and social opportunity.[61] One important consequence of these longer trends in Western culture was the appearance of more personal, sometimes controversial approaches to the end of life that took little account of traditional narratives, formulas and practices.

Denying Death

For some who lost their allegiance to the traditional religious narratives and faith communities but who still trusted in the reality of a post-mortem existence, a variety of options remained. During the middle of the nineteenth century a movement known as spiritualism became popular among segments of the middle class on both sides of the Atlantic. Especially after the start of the controversy around Darwin's theory of evolution, the spiritualist alternative offered a fresh, and presumably empirical, approach to what had always been one of the chief concerns of Christianity.

Operating on the principle that the spirits of the deceased lived in another realm, spiritualists held that the dead could be contacted through the power of mediators in the setting of the seance. Most of the prominent mediators were typically female, allowing women a rare public role in society, albeit one that was highly controversial. By the 1860s, spiritualist congregations had emerged in America and Europe and thousands were attending seances on a regular basis, hoping to experience at least a moment's connection with a deceased loved one.[62] Prominent figures like Horace Greely, editor of the New York Tribune and, in the early twentieth century, Sir Arthur Conan Doyle, enthusiastically embraced the spiritualist movement.[63] The latter remarked that spiritualism 'is a religion for those who find themselves outside all religions; while on the contrary it greatly strengthens the faith of those who already possess religious beliefs'.[64] Eventually the practice lost favour as evidence mounted of deception and fraud by a number of leading practitioners, but the survivalist theme did have a considerable impact on subsequent twentieth-century paranormal claims.

The term 'parapsychology' refers to the experimental study of psychic or paranormal phenomena and appears to have been coined in the 1880s by the German psychologist Max Dessoir (1867–1947). The field gained academic currency in the English-speaking world thanks to the efforts of the influential social psychologist William McDougall (1871–1938). The Society for Psychical Research was established in London in 1882 under the presidency of Henry Sedgwick (1838–1900), a highly respected Cambridge moral philosopher. Similar societies were soon founded in New York and Paris. Many of the early leaders in psychical research were sons of clergy and prominent intellectuals who had received a secular education. They raised doubts about the faith of their fathers, but accepted the duality of mind and body operating in a purposeful universe.[65]

Coming under the broader heading of the paranormal, or phenomena which cannot be explained in terms of current scientific knowledge of nature, one of the principal focal points of parapsychology was the survival hypothesis. In 1927 McDougall and his younger colleague J. B. Rhine (1895–1980), in collaboration with Rhine's wife Louisa, established a laboratory-based research centre of psychic phenomena at Duke University in Durham, North Carolina. Beginning with the launch of the American *Journal of Parapsychology* in 1937, professional associations and peer-reviewed journals dedicated to research into the paranormal gained new credibility. The biggest step towards the integration of parapsychology into the mainstream of scientific circles occurred in 1969, when the American Parapsychology Association was admitted to the highly regarded American Association for the Advancement of Science.[66]

Despite this recognition, the academic community in general continued to view parapsychology as an injudicious attempt to appropriate the tools of scientific investigation to demonstrate the existence of a non-physical soul. Many viewed parapsychologists as 'new age' evangelists whose minds were made up long before the work of experimental validation began. Interest seemed to peak in the 1970s but funding for research waned in later decades, with research institutes finding it increasingly difficult to win acceptance among their colleagues in more traditional academic departments. Still, within the general population interest in the paranormal remained high. A 1991 Gallup poll in the U.S. indicated that even among the educated, belief in ghosts, communication with the dead and the possibility of an afterlife remained high. Television programmes and feature films tapped into the fascination with the paranormal, skilfully leveraging general interest in a world that defies scientific validation, for commercial advantage.[67]

Perhaps the most unusual symbol of the displacement of religious ideas concerning the end of life and its replacement with secular and scientific formulations involves the fringe movement known as cryonics. Initially championed by an American mathematics and physics teacher, Robert Ettinger (1918–2011), the movement gathered widespread attention with the publication of Ettinger's *The Prospect of Immortality* (1962). His Cryonics Institute pioneered the process of preserving recently deceased human bodies in very cold temperatures in the expectation that future advances in science and technology would allow for the resuscitation of the person.[68]

At the Cryonics Institute in Michigan and at another facility in Arizona, bodies are gradually cooled until they reach the temperature of liquid nitrogen (around minus 200 degrees Celsius). Blood is removed and replaced with a sort of antifreeze that prevents damaging ice crystals from forming and exploding cells. The final step involves the encasement of the body in large, liquid nitrogen-filled tanks. Only a few hundred bodies are in cryonic suspension today, with the waiting list not much longer. Critics are resolute in their assertion that the movement is nothing more than an immoral combination of pseudoscience and unscrupulous business practice.[69] Most of the public seems to agree, for despite Ettinger's efforts to bring the price of the cryonic procedure down to that of a new car, this particular immortality project has never become a growth industry.

From Hospitals to Hospice

Since the 1960s, a distinct but growing minority of Westerners have decided not to have their dying arranged for them. The older norms of the churches and the more recent prompts from the funeral industry were interrogated and rejected by those who argued on behalf of individual self-respect, informed decision-making and freedom of choice. Discussion of the dying process, the death event, funeral or memorial options, and personal forms of grief began to take place in a frank and open manner. Each of these topics became the subject of academic study and resulted in thousands of articles and books by authors from a wide variety of backgrounds and personal perspectives. What the marketers declared most appropriate in terms of the funeral, what the medical and psychological communities defined as 'normal' grief, what the culture endorsed in terms of the proper disposal of the body – all of these efforts to classify, bureaucratize and rationalize death were challenged as examples of arbitrary power in Western society.[70] The goal was to return power to the person doing the dying, to test the limits of what might be possible in one of life's most important and easily most personal event. The hospice movement has been at the forefront of this trend.

Medicine has always been devoted to keeping people alive, but in the new world of degenerative diseases and receding death, questions concerning the quality of life in extreme old age began to assume a new prominence. Since the primary mission of modern hospitals is to heal, their ability to help people achieve a good death is limited. Patients, in addition to being mere shadows of their normal physical selves, are also stripped of the psychological benefits of accustomed surroundings. For more and more people, the process of dying generated as much fear as the event itself, a situation reminiscent of a much earlier period in history when palliative medicine was non-existent.

It was in response to this misalignment that power of attorney documents and advance health care directives or living wills developed out of existing estate law. These new legal records were first employed in the 1960s and permitted a health care proxy to provide direction to medical staff if and when the patient lost the ability to make rational decisions. 'Do not resuscitate' (DNR) orders were commonly embedded in these documents, identifying the specific circumstances under which the patient would decline further medical interventions. By the start of the twenty-first century most health care institutions were required to alert patients to their options under the law. In the u.s. the living will opportunity was given executive-level support when President Obama made known that both he and his wife had drawn up living wills and encouraged all adults to do the same.[71]

Equally significant during the 1960s was the development of modern hospice care. Pioneered in Britain by Dr Cicely Saunders, who had first started working with terminally ill patients in the late 1940s, the movement gained academic reinforcement after Dr Saunders addressed medical students, nurse trainees and social workers at Yale University in 1963. By 1967 Saunders had founded St Christopher's Hospice in a residential suburb of London. Seven years later Florence Wald, former Dean of the Yale School of Nursing, after studying and working at St Christopher's, opened the first American hospice in Branford, Connecticut. Led by medical professionals who had grown disillusioned with the medicalized and institutionalized care of dying patients, and viewing social and psychological support as being equally important to the patient as access to advanced life-prolonging technology, hospice pioneers brought new hope to end-of-life experiences. At the core of hospice was the determination to let the patient follow their own inner compass, not to impose the values or preferences of the caregiver onto those receiving services.[72] Additional key components of the hospice philosophy were the importance of pain relief or palliative care, acceptance of passive euthanasia and opposition to active euthanasia.

The hospice movement gained added prominence with the publication of Dr Elisabeth Kubler-Ross's international best-seller, *On Death and Dying* (1968). In additional to her controversial thesis that all terminally ill patients progress through five distinct stages (denial, anger, bargaining, depression and acceptance), Kubler-Ross made a strong case for the social and psychological value of home care over institutionalization. She wrote persuasively about the importance of patient engagement (whenever possible) in the end-of-life decision-making process, always stressing that the last chapter must be framed by the patient's personal choice.[73]

An important milestone was reached in the u.s. during the early 1980s when Congress enacted legislation making hospice centres eligible for federal funding in support of their work with patients. By the end of the twentieth century hospice had expanded its services beyond residential solace centres to include intensive in-home and day care services, bringing pain control, social companionship and emotional support services into the home setting. Today over 90 per cent of hospice services are delivered in the patient's home.

The doctor–patient relationship also evolved in part thanks to the hospice movement. During the first half of the twentieth century it was customary for loved ones and medical staff to withhold the terminal prognosis from the patient out of fear that the sufferer would lose the will to live and thus hasten the moment of death. The conspiracy of silence was especially hard on family members who were asked to be dishonest in their relationship with a loved one. More recently, dying patients have been informed early on of their prognosis so that they may live their remaining time with a view to meeting any number of personal priorities. Where once the priest or minister scrutinized the soul of the dying and encouraged them to end their life reconciled to God and in a state of grace, more recently in the secularized West the physician, psychologist or other counsellor offers remission of psychological burdens through transparent communication and support. As a result, end-of-life decisions are undertaken by the patient in full knowledge of their imminent demise.[74]

Cremation in a Modern Context

The ancient and widespread practice of cremation regained popular acceptance in western Europe during the late nineteenth and early twentieth centuries. Social attitudes towards incineration modified in response to public health concerns over decaying bodies in over-subscribed cemeteries, especially burial grounds located in the burgeoning industrial cities and factory towns. Improved incinerator technology made the option of cremation attractive to those who applauded the advance of industry and the use of technology to improve all aspects of life, including its end and immediate sequel. There was also a growing trend towards de-emphasizing the importance of the body to a non-material afterlife, especially in light of the growing recognition that both traditional burial and cremation involve decomposition of the body – the latter at a much accelerated pace.

Mainline churches initially stood in opposition to cremation both on theological grounds (the importance of bodily resurrection) and out of concern that Church control over funeral practice, and thus the larger influence of the Church in society, would be undermined. In some cases these fears were not misplaced. In the Soviet Union cremation was advanced as part of a broad attack on the cultural hold of the Orthodox Church while in Communist China cremation was promoted to counter the traditional emphasis on ancestor worship, the latter cultural practice being interpreted by state authorities as a potential threat to the new political order.[75]

Tragic and brutal events during the first half of the century accelerated the trend. During the two World Wars millions of soldiers were killed hundreds and thousands of miles from home. The pulverizing strength of modern weaponry meant that in many cases the remains of combatants were never identified. Other, less mutilated victims of the wars were interred on foreign soil or at sea, never to be visited by loved ones. In many cases there were no burial plots at home where the spouses of fallen soldiers and their children would be buried in due course. It was in these sad circumstances that personal choice about the manner of disposal, coupled with a growing aversion to the class distinctions intrinsic to more traditional memorialization, gathered interest and support.[76]

An important turning point occurred in 1963, when the still-influential Roman Catholic Church ended its opposition to the burning of bodies, a practice that for centuries had been associated with capital punishment for sinners and heretics. At first cremated remains were buried or placed in a memorial site, a requirement that advantaged the funeral industry, but beginning in the 1970s regulations were relaxed and state laws began to allow family members to take possession of cremated remains for personal use or private disposal. In Britain cremation overtook burial as the major form of disposal during the early 1960s and had become the choice of over 70 per cent of the population by the start of the twenty-first century.[77] In the U.S., where in the 1960s fewer than 5 per cent chose cremation, by the close of the century the figure was approaching 25 per cent. Still not quite mainstream, by the 1990s even the nationally renowned American televangelist Bill Graham averred that cremation posed 'no hindrance to the resurrection'.[78]

From Institutional Religion to Autonomous Belief

The more strident predictions of nineteenth-century secularists regarding the demise of organized religion in the face of advancing scientific knowledge and expanding education have not been realized. In the Americas, established religion has maintained its resiliency, especially within evangelical and fundamentalist communities. Catholic and Protestant churches still dot the landscape across Europe, their congregations maintaining traditions that have been buffeted by the cross-currents of modernity. One of those traditions, the public and social transfer of the dead out of the world of the living, continues to serve an important purpose for grieving families, close friends and the wider community.

While the process of dying may have been removed from the home and immediate family, clergy continue to offer consolation and spiritual support during the final phase of life, while the religious service and burial provides an opportunity for family and friends to reconvene. The burial or memorial service shows signs of increased secularization, with poems and stories complementing, or in some cases taking the place of, sacred texts, but religious functionaries still officiate. In some communities, even formal prayers for the dead remain an essential part of the weekly service.

These conventions enjoyed broad support despite the fact that attendance at church services fell dramatically across Europe during the final decades of the twentieth century. A 2004 Gallup poll indicated that even in countries where there was a relatively high level of trust in religious institutions, regular church attendance was in sharp decline.[79] Even Catholic Ireland, rocked by a paedophilia scandal during the first decade of the new century, witnessed a rapid fall-off in church-going and religious affiliation generally. A half-century of peace, better education, rising affluence, a declining birth rate and an overall reluctance to accept established dogmas and practices have all contributed to the downward trend. And bitter internal divisions, especially concerning the role of women in the life of the Church, further undermined the authority and intellectual standing of religious leaders across the Protestant–Catholic spectrum.

One area where there did seem to be a strong measure of consensus involved the centuries-old geography of the afterlife. With remarkably little fanfare or public notice, but with enormous implications for theology, the revised accord demolished one of the essential mainstays of the Christian narrative. Satan's fiery abode, what St Matthew referred to as 'a furnace of fire' where there will be 'wailing and gnashing of teeth', has been quietly detached from the map of eternal habitation.[80] More than a return to the early Greek underworld or the indifferent Jewish Sheol, by the start of the twenty-first century most mainstream churches had cancelled the drama of eternal punishment and restrained the churlish and sometimes capricious God of the Old Testament.

Recompense for the faithful, equality for the downtrodden, hope for the long-suffering: a beneficent deity continued to welcome those who followed the straight path. But what became of the malefactor was anybody's guess. The immaterial, imperishable soul continued its journey after the death of the body, but only the good soul was subject for discussion. Heaven, in the words of Douglas Davies, had become 'more therapeutic than theological'.[81] With the dissolution of hell, or at least its removal from official discourse, traditional Christianity was quietly transformed, the earthly passage downgraded to something other than a period of testing, the judicial apparatus of the great assize at the end of historic time now off limits.

The influential mystic and Trappist monk Thomas Merton (1915–1968) was one of the earliest to capture what for many has become the predominant Christian outlook on the purpose of life.

Merton was repelled by the anthropomorphic God of the Old Testament and New Testament. Emotional, sensitive to neglect, quick to anger and holding grudges, this God was for Merton a reflection of the worst elements of human personality. He found solace in a more abstract and philosophical conception of God as Being, where even the most advanced human efforts to understand his nature fall short. At the close of his 1948 autobiography, *The Seven Story Mountain*, Merton called on his readers to embrace a highly personalized approach to life – and death – in the context of our limited knowledge of God:

> Whether you teach or live in the cloister or nurse the sick, whether you are in religion or out of it, married or single, no matter who you are or what you are, you are called to the summit of perfection: you are called to a deep interior life perhaps even to mystical prayer, and to pass the fruits of your contemplation on to others. And if you cannot do so by word, then by example.[82]

This social gospel for the twenty-first century is now the consensus position of mainline churches on both sides of the Atlantic. Concern with the amelioration of conditions in this life, worship of a tender deity, a more personal approach to life's great questions, belief in the continuity of personal identity after the death of the body and a studied silence regarding the abode of the errant – these are some of the characteristic elements of contemporary Western faith traditions.

New Grief

How we express our sense of loss when death comes for a loved one has changed dramatically over the past two centuries, with cultural norms in Western society reflecting the changing physical location of most deaths, the virtual eradication of infant death and the lessened role of formal religion. During most of the nineteenth century a much more overt, extended and public demonstration of grief and bereavement was accepted by the wider culture. Indeed ritualized grief was embraced as a normal response to loss, a 'condition of the human spirit or soul' rather than a somatic (bodily) phenomenon.[83] This was especially the case with the emerging middle class, where grief was understood as the counterpart of love. Public grief figured prominently in novels, shaped songs and instructional materials for children and guided pastoral counsellors.[84] Informed by the still-predominant Christian world view, the last rites and public viewing of the decedent's body (more likely than not a child) would take place in the home where the emphasis on the prospect of immortality was explicit – as was the fear of hellfire.

The formal expression of grief was assigned to women who would lay out, wash and prepare the body for viewing. Female mourners would dress in black attire both for the funeral service and for many months thereafter. A period of withdrawal from social life was also expected, again with women taking the lead role. In America many middle-class girls received mourning kits for their dolls, the ritual acted out in the world of play.[85] Such procedural expressions of grief were considered healthy responses to the death event. The combination of Christian hope for immortality and personal despondency at the loss of a partner or family member was accepted as a balanced approach to this difficult period.

With the advance of scientific naturalism, improving average lifespan and the sharp decline in infant mortality, the traditional doctrines of hell and eternal judgement began their slow recessional, transforming the conventional pattern of grieving and remembrance throughout the industrialized West. The horrors of the First World War still drove widows into mourning black, but as the number of battle-inflicted fatalities rose, private funeral services became less elaborate. In the absence of so many bodies, nation states turned to the construction of public memorials to fallen patriots, dedicating special days of remembrance and merging mass expressions of grief with allegiance to principles of self-governance and civic loyalty.

By the early 1920s personal displays of grief had become unfashionable and even mildly offensive, and those who engaged in them were thought to be unhealthy or even psychologically unbalanced.

Most end-of-life connections to home were severed, both for the decedent and the family, while the communal aspect of a death observed was reduced to a brief encounter in a formal setting or a note of condolence from a distance. Resignation and emotional restraint became the new convention, with funeral services increasingly focused on the life well lived as well as the prospect of a new eternal life just under way.[86] Periods of public mourning vanished, visits to the final resting place became less frequent and the watchful preservation of the decedent's ashes took place in private.

As the process of dying was removed from the familiar setting of the home, as public expressions of grief and mourning lost currency, and as the disposal of the body occurred in greater privacy, Western culture turned away from thoughts of morbidity with a redoubled commitment to the goods and distractions of this world. Nietzsche compared this with the final moments before the departure of an emigrants' ship, where 'people have more to say to each other than ever, the hour is late, and the ocean and its desolate silence are waiting impatiently behind all of this noise – so covetous and certain of their prey'.[87] But a more positive reading of this cultural transition is also possible. Rather than a denial of death, more circumspect approaches to mourning reflect the twentieth century's remarkable death transition, where the great majority of the population now departs peacefully after having enjoyed a long life. And while the departure is cause for sadness, now more than ever it can be a moment of reflection and thanksgiving for hopes and opportunities realized, contributions made and pleasures experienced across many decades.

There are only two forms of death: the death of another person and our own demise. The former elicits a range of responses on our part: relief and even satisfaction when an evil presence departs; sadness when good and decent humans breathe their last; and emotional upset and grief when a loved one leaves our midst. Seven years before his own passing at the age of 86, the historian Arnold Toynbee (1889–1975) admitted that while he was reconciled to his own death, he found the suffering that death inflicts on the survivor hard to accept. 'If one truly loves a fellow human being, one ought to wish that as little as possible of the pain of his or her death shall be suffered by him or by her, and that as much of it as possible shall be borne by oneself.'[88]

Toynbee's words remind us that generalized, medicalized models of how best to respond to the loss of a loved one continue to be contested in the West, not least because no two people respond similarly when suddenly confronted with a world and relationships that have been altered forever. The quality and duration of the relationship with the deceased, whether or not the death is anticipated or sudden and unexpected, and the influence of cultural factors together play important roles in the grieving process. All major life transitions, including the loss of a loved one, elicit defensive and coping mechanisms that are unique to each person. Some find comfort in limiting their social contacts; others turn quickly to activities that help them to adjust to the new reality of their lives. How long it takes for the person to engage again with a changed reality, or whether that engagement is ever fully restored, cannot be sorted by mechanistic theories of human behaviour.[89] But with public expressions of grief discouraged in the contemporary West – and even associated with abnormal behaviour – the dynamics of loss have been pressed into the realm of the secretive, a giant camouflage amid dominant, socially prescribed behaviours. Older forms of public grieving, however static and ritualistic they appeared to late twentieth-century critics, allowed for the intense grief experienced around loss to be assuaged at some level, allowed survivors to communicate their sorrow in a manner that elicited understanding and support within the wider community.

There remains, of course, our own demise, which still strikes fear in some and serious reflection in the rest of us because it negates the only world we know.[90] For courageous non-believers, death is a non-event inasmuch as there is no 'I' to experience it. It is the physical and mental anguish of dying that causes concern, not a death at which they will play no part. Believers, on the other hand, must hold fast to a world view that makes them part of an orderly and meaningful reality, one that confers deeper purpose on mere temporal encounters and relationships. They still long for a measure of justice too often denied in this world of broken promises and chronic violence. Their various religious narratives, however diluted they have become in the modern age, continue to offer that promise, albeit in a posthumous setting.[91] As long as these needs remain part of our evolutionary heritage, it seems unlikely that bodily death will be accepted by most people as anything other than a prelude.

Conclusion

Humans are unique inasmuch as they are self-aware; they recognize that they will die but also imagine the possibility of living beyond death. For most of the human experience the time allotted to contemplate the whole of being was brief. Death enveloped life at every stage, carrying away newborns and their mothers, infants and their older siblings, husbands and wives, priests and monarchs. Endings were sudden and capricious, nature mysterious and inexplicable. Perhaps this is one reason Socrates urged his listeners to organize their lives in preparation for inevitable death. His advice, along with the Platonic doctrine of the immaterial soul, became key intellectual cornerstones of institutional Christianity during the medieval and early modern periods. Life as a time of trial, a pilgrimage, a divinely authored assessment exercise: this was the believer's manual. In its mythical and theistic form the continuity thesis frames the universe as a process moving ineluctably towards a goal established once for all by a divine being.[1] Humans find themselves centre stage in a great cosmic drama, the final act of which was written long before the auditions took place.

The drama wielded enormous power for good and ill over the centuries, informing social systems, cultural preferences and political priorities, and shaping moral and legal systems based on supposedly revealed texts. Even today, billions worldwide continue to organize their lives around the principle that a higher, more satisfying reality lies just beyond our last breath. This great hope frames action and provides comfort in moments of bereavement when human bonds are shattered by death.

Many of these faithful also welcome the discoveries of modern science, seeing the scientific enterprise as complementary to the ancient religious quest. Both, they would argue, guide us into the reality of an unseen world which sustains the observed one. Both force us to recognize that sometimes our senses and intuitions can lead us astray. We do not, for example, experience the earth spinning on its axis; nor do we feel our planet in dynamic motion around the sun. Instead we see what the medieval Church saw, what Galileo's intolerant accusers saw. Contemporary neuroscience may present important advances in the effort to identify specific areas of the brain with discrete mental activities, but it has yet to explain the overarching question: how can complex bundles of nerve cells within the brains of animals lead to consciousness; how can sophisticated thought be reduced to neurology?[2] The religious sensibility points to an ongoing need for great imaginative leaps, leaps that bring us into alignment with non-empirical, transcendent truths.[3]

A very different view achieved limited currency during the Enlightenment and has gathered strength into our own day. It too traces its roots to the ancient world and can be termed the Epicurean, or mortalist, perspective. Its influence is clearest in western Europe, and while less pervasive in the Americas, even there the questioning of traditional authorities and a heightened sense of individual autonomy has prompted some to re-evaluate their earliest commitments to time-honoured religious imaginings. Simply stated, the mortalist proposal accepts the Copernican and Darwinian dethronement of the species. No longer are humans the centre of the cosmos or the pinnacle of creation; instead they emerge as minor parts of an interrelated whole that takes no interest in the doings, or the dying, of one species.

In light of this severe fact, mortalists invite us to ignore death and focus our attention on the relationships and challenges of this life. Since death is non-being, we have nothing to fear with its arrival, and since living is often hard and unpleasant, who in their right mind would wish to extend it unnecessarily? We can either defeat death by making meaning for ourselves in an otherwise indifferent universe (the path of existentialism), or we can travel the less authentic road of accumulation and consumption in the naive hope that the ephemeral delights of this world will bring us solace at the end of days.

In some respects the mortalist position has become more amenable to contemporary minds in the West due to the mortality revolution of the twentieth century. Death now comes for most of us at the end of a long life. Average life expectancy increased by about two years every decade over the last century, and if the rate of increase were to continue at this pace during the twenty-first century, the aged will become a very large percentage of the population.[4] We shield our young children from exposure to death, minimizing their interactions with terminally ill grandparents and excusing them from attendance at funeral and memorial services. Thanks to rapid advances in public health and medical technology, the death of a middle-aged parent is rare; the death of a youthful sibling or friend rarer still. For children, and indeed for most young adults, death is an abstraction mediated by electronic sources of news and entertainment. It is something that happens to someone else, the stranger, the celebrity, the victim of a faraway civil conflict or natural disaster.

In the meantime, most of the elderly can prepare for death, putting their affairs in order, settling an estate and leaving instructions for the disposal of their body. Those who live longest even experience a series of social deaths before their final retreat into senescence and institutional care. The passing of a spouse, peers and neighbours, lifelong friends, even in some cases one's own children, can all contribute to a sense of loneliness and resulting disengagement from previous interests and connections. And then there is the concluding hospitalization. For increasing numbers of elderly people, it is a slow-motion, medically orchestrated ending at a distinct remove from familiar surroundings, with personal contacts limited to formulaic cultural props and social scripts. The hospital visits, the hushed sidebar conversations with doctors, nurses and other professional staff, the loss of autonomy – these have become the social markers of the death experience in Western society. For the elderly dying person, this entire course of events can appear more burdensome, more frightening, than the prospect of annihilation.

Indeed over the past century death concerns have shifted away from the afterlife experience to focus almost exclusively on the dying process. As we have seen, for 99 per cent of human history, sudden, premature and violent death was the norm, and religious authorities were the foremost professional guides and counsellors in end-of-life matters. Quite suddenly during the twentieth century, medical and therapeutic practitioners came to assume pride of place over religious figures when the subject turned to human endings. Psychologists became grief practitioners, the culturally specific – rather than universal and instinctive – origins of grief and mourning were emphasized, and social norms for emotions, so-called 'feeling rules', were guided in the direction of greater privacy and brevity.[5] Getting through the course of dying became a major source of anxiety and alarm.

Our consciousness of death has always influenced how we live, what we define as meaningful and even obligatory. This is true for the non-believer as well as the believer. It is sometimes suggested that the mortalist is by nature a rather despairing type, sharing with Arthur Schopenhauer and Bertrand Russell the hunch that death negates all human endeavours. But nothing could be further from the truth. For most non-believers death is what gives life its constructive meaning, its singularity and richness. The Somali-born author Ayaan Hirsi Ali (b. 1969), in describing her own harrowing journey from the patriarchal Islam of her youth to the atheism of her adulthood, speaks for many when she affirms that life, however troublesome, carries its own modest rewards. The act of constructing and embracing a personal ethic, refining an individual moral compass, is the essential task and constitutes life's higher purpose. 'Life on this earth,' Hirsi Ali writes, 'with all its mystery and beauty and pain, is then to be lived far more intensely: we stumble and get up, we are sad, confident, feel loneliness and joy and love. There is nothing more; but I want nothing more.'[6]

Still, it may be difficult for many of us, irrespective of our place along the continuity–mortalist spectrum, to live in the 'eternity' of the mundane moment like Ayaan Hirsi Ali. Even if we accept life's ups and downs with equanimity, even if we are grateful for those moments of simple pleasure, we tend not to be satiated by them. Even the rearguard action of modern day psychologists and psychiatrists, trained to ignore the big questions once tackled by theology and philosophy and to focus instead on mechanisms for coping with life, cannot satisfy our needs. We desire, it seems, something more encompassing, something that overwhelms us.

Back in 1926 Carl Van Doren (1885–1950), a distinguished professor of English at Columbia University, offered what is perhaps a fair analysis of this historic quandary: 'Men live so briefly that their plans far outrun their ability to execute them. They see themselves cut off before their will to live is exhausted. Naturally enough, they wish to survive, and, being men, believe in their chances for survival.'[7]

Almost 50 years later the American cultural anthropologist Ernest Becker (1924–1974) published The Denial of Death, a Pulitzer Prize-winning study of the human search for meaning in the face of mortality. According to Becker, everyone engages in what he called an 'immortality project', an undertaking that will outlast our time and connect us with a world of larger values. For many the project revolves around allegiance to a religious system; for others the project might be an artistic or financial bequest that elevates one in the collective memory of society. On a more troubling level, the immortality project may drive one into the morass of death denial whereby we pursue multiple worldly distractions in order to shift attention away from the disquieting fact of inevitable departure.

Most problematic for Becker were those occasions when our chronic need to deny death results in a world filled with dogmatic commitments and the desire to impose these commitments on our fellows. Religious intolerance is the most obvious example, with violence prompted by imagined cultural, national and racial differences coming in a close second. The facile equating of happiness with appropriation and consumption has of course been a failure on the personal front, with the added distinction of having pushed the planet towards long-term environmental impairment. Our need to distract ourselves, it appears, can outpace our individual and collective pursuit of wisdom, foreshadowing a possible premature death for an entire ecosystem. Without a larger shared frame of reference, a cosmic sensibility, or what historian Karen Armstrong has called a 'spiritual revolution', the outlook, many would suggest, is less than propitious.[8]

If Becker is right about the potentially harmful impact of 'immortality projects', then more recent efforts to reframe the meaning of death may prove a welcome antidote. Going a trace beyond the everyday hurt and happiness described by Ayaan Hirsi Ali, the very fact of our ending may serve to distinguish the brief journey as meaningful, both personally and in terms of community well-being. Many elderly people, for example, are able to bounce back quickly from the acute personal losses that increase each year. They are able to find consolation and even pleasure in lives filled with accomplishment and steady purpose, and they face their own impending departure with serene comportment. They are the more fortunate products of the twentieth century's mortality revolution, having lived long and experienced much. Now those myriad experiences have carried them to a welcome finish line, a satisfying point of closure with few regrets.

The theologian John Bowker, who has been mentioned earlier in this book, captured something of this outlook within the context of modern biological processes. In a world where evolution assumes constant change, he writes, death is necessary for the development of every species. For centuries death was understood as a divine malediction or punishment, something alien to human beings. Death, it was thought, was imposed on life by irascible outside forces; it was not a natural part of the human experience. But Bowker reminds us that life itself, the organization of atoms and molecules into particular shapes and the energy absorbed and expended by these multiple configurations, requires our death. In this very basic respect, death is essential to life, a necessary good that gives life ultimate value.

Our personal journeys are significant precisely because they are framed by a beginning and an end. We craft our significance – singularly and in the company of our fellows – between these universal bookends. Without them we lose the sense of urgency, the deadline that propels us to live in a meaningful manner while we are able. When we die we make room for others to pursue the mystery on their own terms, one hopes better prepared, and perhaps even grateful for the fact of our having made a small contribution. 'Try how the life of the good man suits you,' Marcus Aurelius advised, 'the life of one content with his portion of the whole, and with his own just acts and kindly disposition.'[9] For those fortunate enough to end their days having acted in accord with such judicious counsel, the journey's end can be a welcome and much-deserved emancipation.

REFERENCES

Introduction

1 Elaine Minamide, ed., *How Should One Cope with Death?* (Farmington Hills, MI, 2006), p. 5.

2 Bernard N. Schumacher, *Death and Mortality in Contemporary Philosophy*, trans. Michael J. Miller (Cambridge, 2005), pp. 1–2.

3 Blaise Pascal, *Pensées*, trans. W. F. Trotter (New York, 1958), p. 17.

4 For a discussion of the transition from the traditional heart–lung or cardiopulmonary definition of death to the whole brain definition during the 1980s, see Vincent Barry, *Philosophical Thinking about Death and Dying* (Belmont, CA, 2007), pp. 16–18.

5 Marcus Aurelius, *Meditations*, in *Marcus Aurelius and His Times* (New York, 1945), p. 23.

6 For a review of contemporary materialism, see Keith Campbell, *Body and Mind* (South Bend, IN, 1986).

7 Corliss Lamont, *The Illusion of Immortality*, 5th edn (New York, 1990), p. 16.

8 Plato, *The Republic*, trans. Paul Shorey (Cambridge, MA, 1987), Book VII, pp. 119–23.

9 1 Corinthians 15:19.

10 Hans Küng, *Eternal Life? Life as a Medical, Philosophical, and Theological Problem*, trans. Edward Quinn (New York, 1984), p. 52; Coleen McDannell and Bernhard Lang, *Heaven: A History* (New Haven, CT, 1988), p. 1; Arnold Toynbee, 'Traditional Attitudes towards Death', in *Man's Concern With Death*, ed. Arnold Toynbee, Keith Mant and

Ninian Smart (New York, 1969), pp. 59–62.

11 Animal and veterinary literature treats death solely as biological collapse. See Siri K. Knudsen, 'The Dying Animal: A Perspective from Veterinary Medicine', in Allen Kellehear, ed., *The Study of Dying: From Autonomy to Transformation* (New York, 2009), p. 27.

12 R. Albert Mohler Jr, 'Modern Theology: The Disappearance of Hell', in *Hell Under Fire*, ed. Christopher W. Morgan and Robert A. Peterson (Grand Rapids, MI, 2004), pp. 16–41.

13 Tony Walter, *The Eclipse of Eternity: A Sociology of the Afterlife* (Basingstoke, 1996), pp. 1–2.

14 Boyle quoted in Michael Hunter, *Science and the Shape of Orthodoxy* (Woodbridge, Suffolk, 1995), p. 230.

ONE: **Preliminary Patterns**

1 Barbara J. King, *Evolving God: A Provocative View on the Origins of Religion* (New York, 2007), p. 127.

2 William McNeill, *Plagues and Peoples* (New York, 1998), p. 46. L. S. Stavrianos, *Lifelines from Our Past* (Armonk, NY, 1992), pp. 19–22, describes the kinship basis of hunter-gatherer societies.

3 Nicholas Wade, *Before the Dawn: Recovering the Lost History of Our Ancestors* (New York, 2006), p. 9, argues that conflict was normative and that the social institution of warfare was in place by 50,000 BC.

4 Azar Gat, *War in Human Civilization* (Oxford, 2006), pp. 18, 74.

5 Wade, *Before the Dawn*, pp. 68, 140. For a wider discussion of !Kung attitudes towards death, see James Woodburn, 'Social Dimensions of Death in Four African Hunting and Gathering Societies', in *Death and the Regeneration of Life*, ed. Maurice Bloch and Jonathan Parry (Cambridge, 1982), pp. 199–202.

6 Allan Kellehear, 'What the Social and Behavioural Studies say about Dying', in *The Study of Dying: From Autonomy to Transformation*, ed. Allan Kellehear (New York, 2009), p. 4.

7 Chris Scarre, 'The Iceman: A 5000-year-old Murder Victim?', in Brian M. Fagan, *Discovery! Unearthing the New Treasures of Archaeology* (London, 2007), pp. 40–41.

8 Thomas Hobbes, *Leviathan* (New York, 1950), chapter Thirteen, p. 104.

9 King, *Evolving God*, pp. 1–28, discusses this concept under the heading 'belongingness'.

10 Mike Parker Pearson, *The Archaeology of Death and Burial* (College Station, TX, 1999), p. 146.

11 Theya Molleson, 'The Archaeology and Anthropology of Death: What the Bones Tell Us', in *Mortality and Immortality: The Anthropology and Archaeology of Death*, ed. S. C. Humphreys and Helen King (London, 1981), pp. 16–17; Pearson, *Archaeology of Death*, p. 148.

12 Allan Kellehear, *A Social History of Dying* (Cambridge, 2007), p. 15.

13 J. M. Roberts, *History of the World* (Oxford, 1993), p. 16.

14 Pearson, *Archaeology of Death*, p. 151.

15 Timothy Taylor, *The Buried Soul: How Humans Invented Death* (Boston, 2002), pp. 3, 21.

16 J. Woodburn, 'Social Dimensions of Death in Four African Hunting and Gathering Societies', in *Death and the Regeneration of Life*, ed. Bloch and Parry, p. 188.

17 Peter Stearns, *World History in Brief*, 7th edn (Upper Saddle River, NJ, 2010), p. 9.

18 George Bond, 'Living with Spirits: Death and Afterlife in African Religions', in *Death and Afterlife: Perspectives of World Religions*, ed. Hiroshi Obayashi (New York, 1992), p. 15.

19 Miguel de Unamuno, *The Tragic Sense of Life* (New York, 1913), p. 4. See also C. J. Ducasse, *A Critical Examination of the Belief in a Life After Death* (Springfield, IL, 1961), pp. 8–9; William Ernest Hocking, *The Meaning of Immortality in Human Experience* (Westport, CT, 1957), pp. 5–9; W. R. Matthews, *The Hope of Immortality* (New York, 1960), pp. 14–15.

20 Kellehear, *Social History of Dying*, pp. 23–4, 26–7.

21 Stearns, *World History in Brief*, p. 14; Stavrianos, *Lifelines from Our Past*, pp. 51–4, describes the process of social stratification in agricultural society. Cynthia Stokes Brown, *Big History: From the Big Bang to the Present* (New York, 2007), pp. 75–6, emphasizes the role of population pressure in the transition to a sedentary lifestyle.

22 Kellehear, *Social History of Dying*, p. 75.

23 Wade, *Before the Dawn*, pp. 127–8; Mary Settegast, *When Zarathustra Spoke: The Reformation of Neolithic Culture and Religion* (Costa Mesa, CA,

2005), p. 13. See also Ofer Bar-Yosef and Francois Valla, eds, *Natufian Culture in the Levant* (Ann Arbor, MI, 1991), pp. 1–10.

24 Pearson, *Archaeology of Death*, p. 159.

25 McNeill, *Plagues and Peoples*, p. 57.

26 Kellehear, *Social History of Dying*, pp. 81–4.

27 Molleson, 'Archaeology and Anthropology of Death', p. 19.

28 King, *Evolving God*, pp. 157–60. For a general introduction see James Mellaart, *Çatal Hüyük: A Neolithic Town in Anatolia* (New York, 1967).

29 Pearson, *Archaeology of Death*, pp. 125–7.

30 Taylor, *The Buried Soul*, pp. 23–4, 27–8.

31 Jacquetta Hawkes, 'Early Britain: Peoples and Monuments', in Hawkes, ed., *The World of the Past*, 2 vols (New York, 1963), vol. II, pp. 342–62.

32 M. J. O'Kelly, 'Neolithic Ireland', in Dáibhí Ó Cróinín, ed., *A New History of Ireland: Prehistoric and Early Ireland* (Oxford, 2005), pp. 82–5, discusses the Boyne Valley passage tombs.

33 Quoting F. Daniel Frankforter, *The West: A Narrative History* (Upper Saddle River, NJ, 2009), p. 6.

34 A. Leo Oppenheim, *Ancient Mesopotamia: Portrait of a Dead Civilization* (Chicago, 1977), pp. 171–83, cautions against generalizing statements about Mesopotamian religion.

35 Jean Bottéro, *Mesopotamia: Writing, Reasoning, and the Gods*, trans. Zainab Bahrani and Marc Van De Mieroop (Chicago, 1992), pp. 201–31; William H. McNeill, *A World History*, 4th edn (New York, 1999), pp. 16–18.

36 Harriet Crawford, *Sumer and the Sumerians*, 2nd edn (Cambridge, 2004), p. 135; Christopher M. Moreman, *Beyond the Threshold: Afterlife Beliefs and Experiences in World Religions* (Lanham, MD, 2008), p. 12.

37 Jerrold S. Cooper, 'The Fate of Mankind: Death and the Afterlife in Ancient Mesopotamia', in *Death and Afterlife*, ed. Obayashi, p. 21.

38 Benjamin R. Foster, ed. and trans., *The Epic of Gilgamesh* (New York, 2001), p. 75.

39 Ibid., p. 58.

40 Susan Pollock, *Ancient Mesopotamia: The Eden that Never Was* (Cambridge, 1999), pp. 196–7.

41 Alan F. Segal, *Life After Death: A History of the Afterlife in the Religions*

of the West (New York, 2003), p. 29; Jon Manchip White, *Everyday Life in Ancient Egypt* (New York, 1969), pp. 23–5.

42 Steven Snape, *Ancient Egyptian Tombs: The Culture of Life and Death* (Chichester, 2011), pp. 4–5.

43 Ma'at was the goddess of law and truth and the personification of connective justice; see Jan Assmann, *The Mind of Egypt: History and Meaning in the Time of the Pharaohs* (Cambridge, MA, 1992), p. 238.

44 Erik Hornung, 'The Pharaoh', in *The Egyptians*, ed. Sergio Donadoni (Chicago, 1997), pp. 283–313.

45 Roberts, *History of the World*, p. 73.

46 Salima Ikram, *Death and Burial in Ancient Egypt* (London, 2003), p. 23; Dick Teresi, *The Undead* (New York, 2012), pp. 53–6.

47 Segal, *Life After Death*, p. 38.

48 Moreman, *Beyond the Threshold*, p. 15.

49 Ibid., p. 17.

50 Bernardo T. Arriaza, *Beyond Death: The Chinchorro Mummies of Ancient Chile* (Washington, DC, 1995), pp. 1–15.

51 Ibid., p. 151.

52 Roberts, *History of the World*, pp. 148–9.

53 John Iliffe, *Africans: The History of a Continent* (Cambridge, 1995), p. 12.

54 King, *Evolving God*, pp. 10–11.

55 John S. Mbiti, *Introduction to African Religion*, 2nd edn (Oxford, 1991), pp. 117–18.

56 Benjamin C. Ray, *African Religions: Symbol, Ritual, and Community* (Upper Saddle River, NJ, 2000), pp. 102–3.

57 Alexis B. Tengan, 'Death and Afterlife', in *The Oxford Encyclopedia of African Thought*, ed. F. Abiola Irele and Biodun Jeyifo, 2 vols (Oxford, 2010), vol. 1, p. 283.

58 John S. Mbiti, *African Religions and Philosophy* (New York, 1969), pp. 26–7; Laurenti Magesa, *African Religion: The Moral Traditions of Abundant Life* (Maryknoll, NY, 1997), pp. 154–7.

59 Bond, 'Living with Spirits', p. 16.

60 John King Fairbank, *China: A New History* (Cambridge, MA, 1992), p. 32.

61 David N. Keightley, 'The Making of the Ancestors: Late Shang Religion and its Legacy', in *Religion and Chinese Society*, ed. John Lagerwey, 2 vols (Hong Kong, 2004), vol. 1, p. 3.

62 Howard Spodek, *The World's History* (Upper Saddle River, NJ, 1998), pp. 89–90.

63 Kwang-chih Chang, *Shang Civilization* (New Haven, CT, 1980), pp. 31–42, 69–73, 210–11.

64 Julia Ching, *Chinese Religions* (New York, 1993), pp. 26–7.

65 Richard von Glahn, *The Sinister Way: The Divine and the Demonic in Chinese Religious Culture* (Berkeley, CA, 2004), p. 20.

66 Chang, *Shang Civilization*, p. 121; Glahn, *Sinister Way*, p. 24.

67 Wade, *Before the Dawn*, p. 151.

68 Robert L. O'Connell, *Of Arms and Men: A History of War, Weapons, and Aggression* (Oxford, 1989), pp. 226–7.

69 Ibid., p. 4.

70 Jane McIntosh, *A Peaceful Realm: The Rise and Fall of the Indus Civilization* (Boulder, CO, 2000), p. 177.

71 See the articles in David L. Bender and Bruno Leone, eds, *War and Human Nature: Opposing Viewpoints* (St Paul, MN, 1985), pp. 16–45. Lawrence H. Keeley, *War Before Civilization* (New York, 1996) challenges what he views as a recent trend in anthropology to highlight either a 'golden age' of peaceful non-literate cultures or pre-civilized warfare that was limited in scope and consequence.

72 Craig et al., *Heritage of World Civilizations* (Upper Saddle River, NJ, 2005), p. 14; Felipe Fernández-Armesto, *The World: A History* (Upper Saddle River, NJ, 2007), p. 111.

73 Taylor, *The Buried Soul*, p. 4.

74 Nigel Davies, *Human Sacrifice in History and Today* (New York, 1981), pp. 13, 15.

75 Francis Barker, Peter Hulme and Margaret Iverson, eds, *Cannibalism and the Colonial World* (New York, 1998), p. 3. See also Peggy Reeves Sanday, *Divine Hunger: Cannibalism as a Cultural System* (Cambridge, 1986).

76 Taylor, *The Buried Soul*, chapter Three, pp. 56–85.

TWO: **Thinking Things Through**

1 Paul Edwards, ed., *Immortality* (New York, 1992), pp. 1–3.

2 Richard Tarnas, *The Passion of the Western Mind* (New York, 1991), pp. 3–4.

3 Crane Brinton, *Men and Ideas* (Englewood Cliff, NJ, 1950), discusses the variety of the Greek contribution on pp. 29–30.

4 Helen F. North, 'Death and the Afterlife in Greek Tragedy and Plato', in *Death and Afterlife: Perspectives of World Religions*, ed. Hiroshi Obayashi (New York, 1992), pp. 49–50; Alan F. Segal, *Life After Death: A History of the Afterlife in the Religions of the West* (New York, 2003), p. 211.

5 Tarnas, *Passion of the Western Mind*, p. 23.

6 Peter Ahrensdorf, *The Death of Socrates and the Life of Philosophy* (New York, 1995), p. 17.

7 Plato, *Phaedo*, trans. Daniel Gallop (Oxford, 1975), pp. 10–11. See also the interpretation in David Bostock, *Plato's Phaedo* (Oxford, 1986), pp. 21–41.

8 *Phaedo*, pp. 29, 31.

9 Ibid., p. 32.

10 Plato, *The Republic*, trans. Paul Shorey, 2 vols (Cambridge, MA, 1982), vol. I, p. 377; vol. II, pp. 83, 371. See also, Nicholas P. White, *A Companion to Plato's Republic* (Indianapolis, 1979), pp. 127–31.

11 Nancey Murphy, *Bodies and Souls, or Spirited Bodies?* (Cambridge, 2006), p. 13. See also Raymond Martin and John Barresi, *The Rise and Fall of Soul and Self: An Intellectual History of Personal Identity* (New York, 2006), pp. 21–2.

12 Nancey Murphy, 'Human Nature: Historical, Scientific, and Religious Issues', in Warren S. Brown, Nancey Murphy and H. Newton Malony, eds, *Whatever Happened to the Soul? Scientific and Theological Portraits of Human Nature* (Minneapolis, 1998), pp. 4–5.

13 Murphy, *Bodies and Souls*, p. 41.

14 James Warren, *Facing Death: Epicurus and His Critics* (Oxford, 2004), p. 6; George K. Strodach, *The Philosophy of Epicurus* (Chicago, 1963), pp. 76–7.

15 Epicurus, 'Principal Doctrines', in *The Extant Remains*, trans. Cyril Bailey (Oxford, 1926), p. 97.

16 Epicurus, 'Letter to Menacceus', quoted in Linda Trinkaus Zagzebski, *Philosophy of Religion: An Historical Introduction* (Oxford, 2007), p. 169. See also Norman Lillegard, *On Epicurus* (Toronto, 2003), p. 20.

17 Epicurus, 'Principal Doctrines', p. 85.

18 Ibid., p. 99; Geoffrey Scarre, *Death* (Montreal, 2007), pp. 2, 86.

19 Lucretius, *On the Nature of the Universe*, trans. R. E. Latham (Harmondsworth, 1982), pp. 29, 31.

20 Ibid., pp. 113, 121, 122.

21 Ibid., p. 124.

22 Ibid., p. 129.

23 M. Andrew Holowchak, *The Stoics: A Guide for the Perplexed* (London, 2008), pp. 6–11; Tad Brennan, *The Stoic Life: Emotions, Duties, and Fate* (Oxford, 2005), pp. 10–16.

24 Seneca, *On the Shortness of Life*, trans. C.D.N. Costa (New York, 2005), p. 1.

25 Ibid., pp. 16, 17.

26 Ibid., p. 203. We will return to the topic of suicide in chapter Five.

27 Ibid., pp. 23, 25.

28 Marcus Aurelius, *Meditations*, trans. Maxwell Staniforth (Harmondsworth, 1964), pp. 49, 55, 61.

29 Vincent Barry, *Philosophical Thinking About Death and Dying* (Belmont, CA, 2007), pp. 37–9.

30 Herschel Baker, *The Wars of Truth* (Cambridge, MA, 1952), pp. 5–6.

31 Martin and Barresi, *Rise and Fall of Soul and Self*, p. 123.

32 Herbert Butterfield, *The Origins of Modern Science* (New York, 1962) provides a useful overview. See also Arthur Lovejoy's classic statement, *The Great Chain of Being* (Cambridge, MA, 1936).

33 Roland N. Stromberg, *An Intellectual History of Modern Europe* (Englewood Cliffs, NJ, 1975), pp. 31–47.

34 Russell Shorto, *Descartes' Bones: A Skeletal History of the Conflict between Faith and Reason* (New York, 2009), pp. 1–7, provides insight into Descartes' last illness.

35 Descartes, *A Discourse on the Method*, trans. Ian Maclean (Oxford, 2006), p. 17.

36 Quoted in Justin Skirry, *Descartes: A Guide for the Perplexed* (London, 2008), pp. 84–5.

37 Samuel Mintz, *The Hunting of Leviathan: Seventeenth-century Reactions to the Materialism and Moral Philosophy of Thomas Hobbes* (Cambridge, 1962), and John Yolton, *Thinking Matter: Materialism in Eighteenth-century Britain* (Minneapolis, 1983), examine the controversial impact of Hobbes and Locke.

38 Voltaire, *A Philosophical Dictionary*, trans. William F. Fleming, in *The Works of Voltaire*, 21 vols (New York, 1901), vol. VII, p. 270.

39 Will Goetschel, *Spinoza's Modernity* (Madison, WI, 2004), p. 26; Richard H. Popkin, *Spinoza* (Oxford, 2004), p. 83; Andrew Pyle, *Malebranche* (New York, 2003), pp. 96–101; G. MacDonald Ross, *Leibniz* (Oxford, 1984), pp. 96–100.

40 Blaise Pascal, *Pensées*, trans. W. F. Trotter (New York, 1958), p. 17.

41 Ibid., p. 64.

42 Ibid., pp. 65–8.

43 Quoted in Ernest Campbell Mossner, *The Life of David Hume* (Austin, TX, 1954), p. 599.

44 David Hume, 'On the Immortality of the Soul', in *The Philosophical Works of David Hume*, 4 vols (Bristol, 1996), vol. IV, pp. 547, 548.

45 Ibid., vol. IV, pp. 548, 551, 552.

46 Ibid., vol. IV, p. 555.

47 Michael Ruse, *Charles Darwin* (Malden, MA, 2008), pp. 8–20.

48 A. N. Wilson, *God's Funeral: A Biography of Faith and Doubt in Western Civilization* (New York, 1999), pp. 177–202, sets the broader context.

49 Murphy, *Bodies and Souls*, p. 50.

50 Psalms 8:4–5.

51 Schopenhauer quoted in Samuel Enoch Stumpf, *Socrates to Sartre: A History of Philosophy* (New York, 1993), p. 345.

52 Christopher Janaway, ed., *The Cambridge Companion to Schopenhauer* (Cambridge, 1999), pp. 7–8; Robert Wicks, *Schopenhauer* (Malden, MA, 2008), pp. 57–8.

53 Schopenhaur quoted in Herbert Fingarette, *Death: Philosophical Soundings* (Chicago, 1996), p. 144.

54 Dale Jacquette, 'Schopenhauer on Death', in *Cambridge Companion to Schopenhauer*, p. 295; Julian Young, *Schopenhauer* (New York, 2005), pp. 168–73.

55 Alister McGrath, *The Twilight of Atheism: The Rise and Fall of Disbelief in the Modern World* (New York, 2004), p. 54.

56 Feuerbach quoted in Hans Küng, *Eternal Life? Life as a Medical, Philosophical, and Theological Problem*, trans. Edward Quinn (New York, 1984), p. 29.

57 John Bowker, *The Meanings of Death* (Cambridge, 1991), p. 16. See also Brendan Sweetman, *Religion: Key Concepts in Philosophy* (London, 2007), pp. 2–3; Denys Turner, 'Religion: Illusions and Liberation', in *The Cambridge Companion to Marx*, ed. Terrell Carver (Cambridge, 1991), pp. 320–37; Peter Singer, *Marx* (Oxford, 1980), pp. 14–20.

58 Friedrich Nietzsche, *The Gay Science* (1882), quoted in Franklin Le Van Baumer, ed., *Main Currents of Western Thought* (New Haven, CT, 1978), p. 613.

59 Stanley Schneider and Joseph H. Berke, 'Freud's Atonement', *Mental Health, Religion and Culture*, XIV/6 (July 2011), pp. 531–41, discuss Freud's lifelong concern with death. Peter Gay, *Freud: A Life for Our Time* (New York, 1988), provides the most comprehensive survey.

60 Quoted in Simcha Paull Raphael, *Jewish Views of the Afterlife* (New York, 2009), p. 25.

61 Auden quoted in McGrath, *Twilight of Atheism*, p. 76.

62 David Detmer, *Sartre Explained: From Bad Faith to Authenticity* (Chicago, 2008), pp. 153–7, explores Sartre's view of death through the play *Huis Clos* (No Exit). See also Gary Cox, *Sartre: A Guide for the Perplexed* (London, 2006), pp. 153–5. David Sherman, *Camus* (Malden, MA, 2009), pp. 21–37, discusses Camus' understanding of the absurd in postmodern life.

63 Bertrand Russell, *What I Believe* (New York, 1925), pp. 5–6, 13.

64 Richard Dawkins, *The God Delusion* (Boston, 2006) and *The Blind Watchmaker* (Boston, 1986); Stephen Jay Gould, *Rock of Ages: Science and Religion in the Fullness of Life* (New York, 1999).

65 Carl Jung, 'The Spiritual Problem of Modern Man', in *Civilization in Transition*, trans. R.F.C. Hull (Princeton, NJ, 1970), p. 80.

66 Carl Jung, 'The Soul and Death', in *Jung on Death and Immortality*, ed. Jenny Yates (Princeton, NJ, 1999), p. 19.

67 George Santayana, *The Life of Reason: Reason in Religion* (New York, 1905), p. 11.

68 Deborah Blum, *Ghosthunters: William James and the Search for Scientific Proof of Life After Death* (New York, 2006).

69 William James, *Human Immortality: Two Supposed Objections* (New York, 1960), pp. 13–15.

70 Ibid.

71 Percy Bysshe Shelly, *Adonaïs*, in *The Works of Percy Bysshe Shelley*, ed. Roger Ingpen and Walter E. Peck, 10 vols (New York, 1965), vol. II, p. 404.

72 James, *Human Immortality*, p. 17.

73 Ibid., p. 20. See Eugene Fontinell, *Self, God, and Immortality: A Jamesian Investigation* (Philadelphia, 1986).

74 Quoted in Scarre, *Death*, p. 47.

75 Jonathan Swift, *Gulliver's Travels and Other Writings* (New York, 1958), pp. 169–70.

76 Bernard Williams, 'The Makropulos Case: Reflections on the Tedium of Immortality', in *Problems of the Self* (Cambridge, 1973), pp. 82–100.

77 H. D. Lewis and Bernard Williams quoted in Mark Corner, *Death Be Not Proud: The Problem of the Afterlife* (Oxford, 2011), p. 183.

78 Jean-Dominique Bauby, *The Diving Bell and the Butterfly*, trans. Jeremy Leggatt (New York, 2002). I am indebted to Comer, pp. 183–4, for a thoughtful treatment of this memoir.

79 Carl Becker, *The Heavenly City of the Eighteenth-century Philosophers* (New Haven, CT, 1932), p. 142.

80 George Eliot, *Middlemarch*, ed. Rosemary Ashton (London, 1994), p. 838.

81 Aurelius, *Meditations*, p. 59.

82 Leo Tolstoy, *My Confession and The Spirit of Christ's Teaching* (New York, 1887), pp. 23, 27, 30, 46.

83 Ibid., pp. 65, 97, 123.

84 Miguel de Unamuno, *Tragic Sense of Life*, trans. J. E. Crawford Flitch (New York, 1954), p. 13.

85 John Polkinghorne, *The God of Hope and the End of the World* (New Haven, CT, 2002), pp. 104–5.

86 Ibid., p. 106.

THREE: **Extraordinary Narratives**

1 I find compelling the argument of Loyal Rue, *Religion is Not About God: How Spiritual Traditions Nurture Our Biological Nature and What to Expect When They Fail* (New Brunswick, NJ, 2005). According to Rue, a naturalistic account of religious origins is possible.

2 Vincent Barry, *Philosophical Thinking about Death and Dying* (Belmont, CA, 2007), pp. 2–3.

3 Hans Küng, *Eternal Life? Life as a Medical, Philosophical, and Theological Problem*, trans. Edward Quinn (New York, 1984), Coleen McDannell and Bernhard Lang, *Heaven: A History* (New Haven, CT, 1988), and Arnold Toynbee, Keith Mant and Ninian Smart, eds, *Man's Concern with Death* (New York, 1969), are good starting points.

4 A. C. Grayling, *Ideas That Matter: The Concepts that Shape the 21st Century* (New York, 2010), pp. 312–13.

5 Christopher Hitchens, *God Is Not Great: How Religion Poisons Everything* (New York, 2007), stands as his major statement against organized religion. His reference to North Korea was made in a number of talks. See George Eaton, 'Christopher Hitchens, 1949–2011', www.newstatesman.com, 16 December 2011.

6 Karen Armstrong, *The Great Transformation: The Beginnings of Our Religious Traditions* (New York, 2006), pp. 3–48, discusses the Axial Age in detail.

7 Grayling, *Ideas that Matter*, p. 314.

8 Julia Ching, *Chinese Religions* (New York, 1993), p. 63.

9 Judith A. Berling, 'Death and the Afterlife in Chinese Religions', in *Death and the Afterlife: Perspectives of World Religions*, ed. Hiroshi Obayashi (New York, 1992), pp. 182–3.

10 Christian Jochim, 'Chinese Beliefs', in *Macmillan Encyclopedia of Death and Dying*, ed. Robert Kastenbaum, 2 vols (New York, 2003), vol I, pp. 158–9; Christopher M. Moreman, *Beyond the Threshold: Afterlife Beliefs and Experiences in World Religions* (Lanham, MD, 2008), p. 140.

11 Laurence G. Thompson, *Chinese Religion: An Introduction*, 3rd edn (Belmont, CA, 1979), p. 3.

12 H. G. Creel, *Confucius: The Man and the Myth* (London, 1951), pp. 29–65.

13 Mu-chou Poo, *In Search of Personal Welfare: A View of Ancient Chinese Religion* (Albany, NY, 1998), p. 67.

14 Joel J. Kupperman, *Classic Asian Philosophy* (Oxford, 2001), pp. 76–7, 82–4.

15 Ching, *Chinese Religions*, pp. 86–7; Benjamin I. Schwartz, *The World of Thought in Ancient China* (Cambridge, MA, 1985), pp. 186–7.

16 Alan Watts, *Become What You Are* (Boston, 2003), pp. 21–7, offers a useful explanation.

17 Ching, *Chinese Religions*, p. 91.

18 Quoted in Moreman, *Beyond the Threshold*, p. 145.

19 Livia Kohn, 'Ultimate Reality: Chinese Religion', in *Ultimate Realities*, ed. Robert Cummings Neville (New York, 2001), p. 16.

20 Wendy Doniger, *The Hindus: An Alternative History* (New York, 2009), is a recent comprehensive survey. See especially pp. 82–104.

21 David Smith, *Hinduism and Modernity* (Malden, MA, 2003), pp. 33–9.

22 Moreman, *Beyond the Threshold*, pp. 99–101.

23 Vasudha Narayanan, *Hinduism* (Oxford, 2004), pp. 37–47, reviews the sacred texts of the Hindu tradition.

24 Ananda K. Coomaraswamy and I. B. Horner, *The Living Thoughts of Gotama the Buddha* (Louisville, KY, 2001), pp. 1–11, offers a biographical overview. See also Bernard Faure, *Unmasking Buddhism* (Malden, MA, 2009), pp. 11–14.

25 Bradley K. Hawkins, *Buddhism* (Upper Saddle River, NJ, 1999), pp. 42–4. See also Paul Williams, *Buddhist Thought* (New York, 2000), pp. 42–7.

26 Moreman, *Beyond the Threshold*, pp. 120–21; Williams, *Buddhist Thought*, pp. 47–52.

27 Richard H. Robinson and Willard L. Johnson, *The Buddhist Religion: A Historical Introduction*, 3rd edn (Belmont, CA, 1982), pp. 155–97, surveys Chinese Buddhism. See also Peter Harvey, *An Introduction to Buddhism* (Cambridge, 1990), pp. 148–58.

28 Ecclesiastes 9:5.

29 Job 10:21–2. Also Job 20:7, where 'Man will perish for ever like his own dung', and 2 Samuel 14:14, where 'We are like water spilt on the ground which cannot be gathered up again.'

30 Homer, *The Odyssey*, trans. W.H.D. Rouse (New York, 1987), p. 134.

31 A. Seth Pringle-Pattison, *The Idea of Immortality* (Oxford, 1922), pp. 15–17. See also Corliss Lamont, *The Illusion of Immortality* (New York, 1990), pp. 33–4; James McLeman, *Resurrection Then and Now* (Philadelphia, 1967), pp. 21–6; Ray S. Anderson, *Theology, Death and Dying* (Oxford, 1986), p. 39.

32 John Baillie, *And the Life Everlasting* (London, 1941), p. 154.

33 Hosea 6:2; Ezekiel 37:1–10; Daniel 12:2.

34 Russell Aldwinckle, *Death in the Secular City: Life After Death in Contemporary Theology and Philosophy* (Grand Rapids, MI, 1974), p. 113; Clifford Hershel Moore, *Ancient Beliefs in the Immortality of the Soul* (New York, 1963), pp. 66–7; Baillie, *Life Everlasting*, p. 156.

35 John H. Hick, *Death and Eternal Life* (New York, 1976), p. 176; Moreman, *Beyond the Threshold*, p. 38; Joan M. Boyle and James E. Morriss, *The Mirror of Time: Images of Aging and Dying* (Westport, CT, 1987), pp. 28–9.

36 Douglas J. Davies, *Death, Ritual and Belief*, 2nd edn (London, 2002), p. 119.

37 1 John 3:2.

38 1 Corinthians 13:12.

39 Mark 12:24–5. Compare Enoch 109:4 and the Apocalypse of Baruch 51:10. See also Henry J. Cadbury, 'Intimations of Immortality in the Thought of Jesus', in *Immortality and Resurrection*, ed. Krister Stendahl (New York, 1965), pp. 139–40.

40 Matthew 22:13; Mark 9:48; Revelation 14:11. I owe this observation to Anderson, *Theology, Death and Dying*, p. 69.

41 S.G.F. Brandon, *The Judgment of the Dead: The Idea of Life After Death in the Major Religions* (New York, 1967), pp. 99–100.

42 Oscar Cullman, 'Immortality of the Soul or Resurrection of the Dead', in *Immortality and Resurrection*, ed. Stendhal, pp. 9–20. See also Jacques Choron, *Death and Western Thought* (New York, 1963), pp. 42–6.

43 John Donne, *The Sermons of John Donne*, ed. George R. Potter and Evelyn M. Simpson, 10 vols (Berkeley, CA, 1962), vol. II, p. 201. For the Platonic perspective see Moore, *Ancient Beliefs*, p. 71.

44 Kevin J. Madigan and Jon D. Levenson, *Resurrection: The Power of God for Christians and Jews* (New Haven, CT, 2008), traces the connections

between Jewish belief in bodily resurrection and earliest Christian thought and practice.

45 Stephen T. Davis, 'Survival of Death', in *A Companion to Philosophy of Religion*, ed. Philip L. Quinn and Charles Taliaferro (Oxford, 1997), pp. 556–61.

46 Matthew 8:22. For a discussion, see James P. Carse, *Death and Existence: A Conceptual History of Human Mortality* (New York, 1980), pp. 221–4.

47 Leander E. Keck, 'New Testament Views of Death', in Liston O. Mills, ed., *Perspectives on Death* (Nashville, TN, 1969), pp. 33–5.

48 1 Corinthians 15:36–44.

49 1 Corinthians 15:26.

50 Ibid. The roots of St Paul's position can be found in Wisdom 1:13, 'God did not make death neither has he pleasure in the destruction of the living', and in Ezekiel 18:32, 'I have no pleasure in the death of him that dieth, saith the Lord.'

51 Augustine, *City of God*; Whitney J. Oates, ed., *Basic Writings of St Augustine*, 2 vols (New York, 1948), vol. II, pp. 211, 582.

52 See for example Stanton A. Coblentz, *The Answer of the Ages* (New York, 1931), p. 164.

53 Thomas More, 'Four Last Things', in Anton Pegis, ed., *The Wisdom of Catholicism* (New York, 1949), p. 499.

54 John L. Esposito, *Islam: The Straight Path*, 4th edn (New York, 2011), provides a balanced introduction. See also Andrew Rippin, *Muslims: Their Religious Beliefs and Practices*, 4th edn (New York, 2012), and Moreman, *Beyond the Threshold*, p. 78.

55 Malise Ruthven, *Islam in the World*, 3rd edn (New York, 2006), pp. 34–40.

56 John Bowker, *The Meanings of Death* (Cambridge, 1991), pp. 104–5.

57 Moreman, *Beyond the Threshold*, p. 89.

58 Seyyed Hossein Nasr, *Islam: Religion, History, and Civilization* (San Francisco, 2003), p. 73.

59 Jacques Le Goff, *The Birth of Purgatory*, trans. Arthur Goldhammer (Chicago, 1984), provides a detailed survey. See also John Casey, *After Lives: A Guide to Heaven, Hell, and Purgatory* (Oxford, 2009), pp. 225–9.

60 Thomas Aquinas, *Summa Contra Gentiles* quoted in Milton Gatch,

Death: Meaning and Mortality in Christian Thought and Contemporary
Culture (New York, 1969), p. 97; Le Goff, Birth of Purgatory, p. 6.

61 Dante Alighieri, The Purgatorio, trans. Henry Wadsworth Longfellow
(New York, 2005), p. 14.

62 Philippe Ariès, The Hour of Our Death, trans. Helen Weaver (Oxford,
1991), pp. 154–6.

63 Robert Dinn, 'Death and Rebirth in Late Medieval Bury St Edmunds',
in Steven Bassett, ed., Death in Towns: Urban Responses to the Dying and
the Dead, 100–1600 (Leicester, 1992), p. 164.

64 Keith Thomas, Religion and the Decline of Magic (Harmondsworth,
1972), p. 720; Julian Litten, The English Way of Death: The Common
Funeral since 1450 (London, 1991), pp. 6–7; Clare Gittings, Death,
Burial and the Individual, pp. 22–3.

65 Eamon Duffy, The Stripping of the Altars: Traditional Religion in England,
c. 1400–1580 (New Haven, CT, 1992), p. 302. See also Harry
A. Wolfson, 'Immortality and Resurrection in the Philosophy of
the Church Fathers', in Immortality and Resurrection, ed. Stendahl,
pp. 69–72.

66 Duffy, Stripping of the Altars, pp. 310–13; Jean Delumeau, Sin and Fear:
The Emergence of a Western Guilt Culture, trans. Eric Nicholson (New
York, 1990), pp. 40–46. Paul Koudounaris, The Empire of Death:
A Cultural History of Ossuaries and Charnel Houses (New York, 2011),
offers a visual survey of charnel monuments.

67 Duffy, Stripping of the Altars, p. 325. Patrick Geary, Living With the
Dead in the Middle Ages (Ithaca, NY, 1994), pp. 116–24, discusses the
'obligations' of the saints to supplicants.

68 John 5:28–9; Matthew 25:31–46; 1 Corinthians 15:51. The debate
continues in our own day. See, for example, Burton H. Throckmorton
Jr, 'Do Christians Believe in Death?', The Christian Century, LXXXVI
(1969), pp. 708–10. On the tradition of the soul's migration after
death, see Ariès, Hour of Our Death, pp. 247–54.

69 Luke 16:22–3; Luke 23:43.

70 Romans 1:17; Jonathan W. Zophy, A Short History of Renaissance and
Reformation Europe (Upper Saddle River, NJ, 1999), pp. 169–71;
Peter G. Wallace, The Long European Reformation (Basingstoke, 2004),
pp. 75–81.

71 John Bossy, *Christianity in the West* (Oxford, 1985), p. 55; Alister
    E. McGrath, *Christian Theology: An Introduction* (Cambridge, MA,
    1997), p. 64.

72 Litten, *English Way of Death*, p. 151.

73 Thomas, *Religion and the Decline of Magic*, p. 721. See also Carlos
    M. N. Eire, *War Against the Idols: The Reformation of Worship from
    Erasmus to Calvin* (Cambridge, 1986), pp. 9–10.

74 Martin Luther, 'The Commentary on the Epistle to the Hebrews',
    in *Luther: Early Theological Works*, ed. James Atkinson (Philadelphia,
    1962), p. 207.

75 Drummond and Taylor quoted in David Stannard, *The Puritan Way
    of Death* (Oxford, 1979), p. 23.

76 Luther, 'The Commentary on the Epistle to the Hebrews', p. 61. For
    an analysis of Luther's position on soul-sleeping see Paul Althaus,
    The Theology of Martin Luther, trans. Robert C. Schultz (Philadelphia,
    1966), pp. 410–25.

77 Le Roy Edwin Froom, *The Conditionalist Faith of Our Fathers*, 2 vols
    (Washington, DC, 1965), vol. II, pp. 79–87; John Calvin,
    'Psychopannychia', in *Tracts and Treatises in Defense of the Reformed Faith*,
    3 vols (Grand Rapids, MI, 1958), vol. III, p. 413.

78 *Acts and Ordinances* 1:1135, ed. C. H. Firth, quoted in Norman
    T. Burns, *Christian Mortalism from Tyndale to Milton* (Cambridge, MA,
    1972), p. 16.

79 John Calvin, *Institutes of the Christian Religion*, trans. John Allen, 2 vols
    (Philadelphia, 1936), book 3, chapter 25, section 6. See also Francois
    Wendel, *Calvin: The Origins and Development of His Religious Thought*,
    trans. Philip Mairet (New York, 1963), pp. 286–7.

80 Calvin, *Institutes*, 3.9.2; 3.25.6.

81 T. Spencer, *Death and Elizabethan Tragedy* (New York, 1960), pp. 89–90;
    John McManners, *Death and the Enlightenment* (Oxford, 1981), pp. 127–8.

82 Burns, *Christian Mortalism*, pp. 8–9.

83 Linda Woodhead, *Christianity: A Very Short Introduction* (Oxford, 2004),
    p. 95–7. The Enlightenment's critique of religion is discussed in
    Alister E. McGrath, *Historical Theology: An Introduction to the History
    of Christian Thought* (Malden, MA, 1998), pp. 221–3.

84 Piero Camporesi, *The Fear of Hell: Images of Damnation and Salvation*

in *Early Modern Europe*, trans. Lucinda Byatt (University Park, PA, 1990), p. 25.

85 Ted Peters, 'Resurrection: The Conceptual Challenge', in *Resurrection: Theological and Scientific Assessments*, ed. Ted Peters, Robert John Russell and Michael Welker (Grand Rapids, MI, 2002), pp. 297–321.

86 Harvey Cox, *The Future of Faith* (New York, 2009), especially chapter One, 'An Age of the Spirit'.

87 John Bowker, 'The Paradox of Religion', *The Independent* (10 June 2008).

88 Bowker, *Meanings of Death*, p. 33.

FOUR: Adverse Environments

1 Kenneth F. Kiple, 'The History of Disease', in *The Cambridge Illustrated History of Medicine*, ed. Roy Porter (Cambridge, 1996), pp. 16–17.

2 William H. McNeill, *Plagues and Peoples* (New York, 1998), p. 71.

3 Lois N. Magner, *A History of Infectious Diseases and the Microbial World* (Westport, CT, 2009), p. 6.

4 Sheldon J. Watts, *Epidemics and History: Disease, Power and Imperialism* (New Haven, CT, 1997), p. xii.

5 Quoting M. R. Smallman-Raynor and A. D. Cliff, *War Epidemics: An Historical Geography of Infectious Diseases in Military Conflict and Civil Strife, 1850–2000* (Oxford, 2004), p. 5. See also Kiple, 'History of Disease', p. 24.

6 Thucydides, *The Peloponnesian War*, trans. Steven Lattimore (Indianapolis, 1998), pp. 98–9.

7 Jacalyn Duffin, *A History of Medicine: A Scandalously Short Introduction* (Basingstoke, 2004), p. 140; J. N. Hays, *Epidemics and Pandemics: The Impacts on Human History* (Santa Barbara, CA, 2005), p. 6; Thucydides, *Peloponnesian War*, p. 101.

8 Hays, *Epidemics and Pandemics*, pp. 17–20.

9 Philip Ziegler, *The Black Death* (New York, 1969), and John Kelly, *The Great Mortality* (New York, 2005), offer solid treatments. See also Duffin, *History of Medicine*, p. 141.

10 Battuta's experience in Felipe Fernández-Armesto, *The World: A History* (Upper Saddle River, NJ, 2007), p. 453.

11 Watts, Epidemics and History, p. 1.
12 Barbara Tuchman, A Distant Mirror: The Calamitous Fourteenth Century (New York, 1978), pp. 22–3; Fernández-Armesto, The World, p. 452.
13 Watts, Epidemics and History, p. 1.
14 Giovanni Boccaccio, The Decameron, trans. G. H. McWilliam (London, 1972), pp. 53–4.
15 Duffin, History of Medicine, p. 141.
16 Woodrow Borah, 'The Historical Demography of Aboriginal and Colonial America: An Attempt at Perspective', in The Native Population of the Americas in 1492, ed. William M. Denevan (Madison, WI, 1992), pp. 13–34.
17 Alfred Crosby, Germs, Seeds and Animals (Armonk, NY, 1994), pp. 89, 92; Watts, Epidemics and History, p. 84.
18 Darwin quoted in Crosby, Germs, Seeds and Animals, p. 12.
19 Drake and Bradford quoted ibid., pp. 59, 103, 105, 113.
20 Quoted in Andrew Delbanco, The Puritan Ordeal (Cambridge, MA, 1989), p. 106.
21 Winthrop quoted in Alfred Crosby, Ecological Imperialism: The Biological Expansion of Europe, 900–1900 (Cambridge, 1996), p. 208.
22 Daniel Defoe (1661–1731) was one of many contemporaries who described the effects of the 1665 plague; see A Journal of the Plague Year (New York, 1963).
23 David Arnold, Colonizing the Body: State Medicine and Epidemic Disease in Nineteenth-century India (Berkeley, CA, 1993), provides a thorough overview. See also Sheldon Watts, 'From Rapid Response to Stasis: Official Responses to Cholera in British-Ruled India and Egypt, 1860–c. 1921', Journal of World History, XII/2 (2001), pp. 321–74.
24 John M. Barry, The Great Influenza (New York, 2004), pp. 4, 95–7.
25 Scott Chavers and Sten H. Vermund, 'An Introduction to Emerging and Reemerging Infectious Diseases', in Emerging Infectious Diseases, ed. Felissa R. Lashley and Jerry D. Durham (New York, 2007), pp. 3–19.
26 Cormac Ó Gráda, Famine: A Short History (Princeton, NJ, 2009), p. 36.
27 See Robert Conquest, The Harvest of Sorrow: Soviet Collectivization and the Terror Famine (New York, 1986).
28 Thomas Malthus, An Essay on the Principle of Population (London, 1798), pp. 28–9, 74–8.

29 Mike Cronin, A History of Ireland (Basingstoke, 2001), pp. 135–47;
    Christine Kinealy, The Great Irish Famine: Impact, Ideology and Rebellion
    (Basingstoke, 2002), pp. 17–30.
30 Duffin, History of Medicine, pp. 64–8.
31 Vivian Nutton, 'The Rise of Medicine', in Cambridge Illustrated History
    of Medicine, ed. Porter, pp. 46–8.
32 Roy Porter, The Greatest Benefit to Mankind: A Medical History of Humanity
    from Antiquity to the Present (New York, 1997), p. 8.
33 Roy Porter, 'Hospitals and Surgery', in Cambridge Illustrated History
    of Medicine, pp. 205–7.
34 Quoted in Peter Stearns, Revolutions in Sorrow: The American Experience
    of Death in Global Perspective (Boulder, CO, 2007), p. 11.
35 O. M. Bakke, When Children Became People: The Birth of Childhood in Early
    Christianity (Minneapolis, 2005), pp. 75–6.
36 Psalm 51.
37 Augustine quoted in Bakke, When Children Became People, p. 101.
38 The most detailed treatment of this topic is Larry S. Miller, Hardness
    of Heart/Hardness of Life: The Stain of Human Infanticide (Lanham, MD,
    2000). See also Laila Williamson, 'Infanticide: An Anthropological
    Analysis', in Infanticide and the Value of Life, ed. Marvin Kohl (Buffalo,
    NY, 1978), pp. 61–75.
39 Bakke, When Children Became People, pp. 15–16.
40 Sarah B. Pomeroy, 'Infanticide in Hellenistic Greece', in Images of
    Women in Antiquity, ed. Averil Cameron and Amélie Kuhrt (Detroit,
    MI, 1983), p. 207; Pierre Brule, Women of Ancient Greece, trans. Antonia
    Neville (Edinburgh, 2003), p. 136.
41 Bakke, When Children Became People, pp. 30–31.
42 Su Shi quoted in D. E. Mungello, Drowning Girls in China: Female
    Infanticide since 1650 (Lanham, MD, 2008), pp. 4–5.
43 Sander J. Breiner, Slaughter of the Innocents: Child Abuse through the Ages
    and Today (New York, 1990), p. 17.
44 Bakke, When Children Became People, pp. 61, 64, 69.
45 Ibid., p. 114, 128.
46 William Langer, 'Infanticide: A Historical Survey', History of Childhood
    Quarterly, 1/3 (1974), pp. 353–66.
47 Williamson, 'Infanticide', p. 69.

48 René Leboutte, 'Offense against Family Order: Infanticide in Belgium from the Fifteenth through the Early Twentieth Centuries', in Forbidden History: The State, Society and the Regulation of Sexuality in Modern Europe, ed. John C. Fout (Chicago, 1992), p. 35.

49 Julie Wheelwright, 'Nothing in Between: Modern Cases of Infanticide', in Historical Perspectives on Child Murder and Concealment, 1550–2000, ed. Mark Jackson (Aldershot, 2002), pp. 270–85, explores the persistence of concealed pregnancy and infanticide.

50 Robert L. O'Connell, Ride of the Second Horseman: The Birth and Death of War (Oxford, 1995), p. 5.

51 Pat Jalland, Death in War and Peace: A History of Loss and Grief in England, 1914–1970 (Oxford, 2010), p. 16, discusses popular attitudes towards combat in 1914. See also Niall Ferguson, The War of the World: Twentieth-century Conflict and the Descent of the West (New York, 2006), pp. 118–23.

52 Blunden quoted in Paul Fussell, The Great War and Modern Memory (Oxford, 1975), p. 13.

53 Approximately 15,000 murders are reported to federal authorities in the U.S. each year. Tony Waters, When Killing is a Crime (Boulder, CO, 2007), pp. 1, 7. See also Peter Morrall, Murder and Society (Chichester, 2006), p. 158.

54 Waters, When Killing is a Crime, p. 31.

55 Steven Pinker, The Better Angels of Our Nature: Why Violence has Declined (New York, 2011), pp. 4–11. Pamela Barmash, Homicide in the Biblical World (Cambridge, 2005), examines homicide in the Bible within the wider context of Israelite society and ancient Near East culture generally.

56 Judy E. Gaughan, Murder Was Not a Crime: Homicide and Power in the Roman Republic (Austin, TX, 2010), p. 1.

57 Waters, When Killing is a Crime, p. 38.

58 Jon Ledford, 'An Explosive Affair: The Acquittal of Congressman Daniel Sickles', thesis, University of North Carolina, Asheville, 2012.

59 Leonard Beeghley, Homicide: A Sociological Explanation (Lanham, MD, 2003), p. 5.

60 Pieter Spierburg, A History of Murder: Personal Violence in Europe from

the Middle Ages to the Present (Cambridge, 2008), offers the most recent overview. See also Jill Lapore, 'The Rap Sheet', *New Yorker* (9 November 2009).

61 Patrick Calloway, 'Fear, Capital Punishment, and Order', in *Invitation to An Execution*, ed. Gordon Morris Bakken (Albuquerque, NM, 2010), p. 47.

62 Joseph A. Melusky and Keith Alan Pesto, *Capital Punishment* (Santa Barbara, CA, 2011), p. 2.

63 Austin Sarat and Jurgen Martschukat, 'Transatlantic Perspectives on Capital Punishment', in *Is the Death Penalty Dying?*, ed. Sarat and Martschukat (Cambridge, 2011), pp. 1–13.

64 Centers for Disease Control and Prevention, OADPG, 'IV. Infectious Diseases', www.cdc.gov, 30 June 2011.

65 Chris Mihill, 'World Faces Explosion of Lifestyle Illnesses', www.converge.org.nz, 11 May 1997. See also Dr Tim Armstrong of the World Health Organization speaking on lifestyle disease: 'Do Lifestyle Changes Improve Health?', www.who.int, 9 January 2009.

66 Mark Bittman, 'How to Save a Trillion Dollars', www.nytimes.com, 12 April 2011.

67 David Pimentel, S. Cooperstein et al., 'Ecology of Increasing Diseases: Population Growth and Environmental Degradation', *Human Ecology*, 35 (2007), pp. 653–68.

68 J. R. McNeill, *Something New Under the Sun: An Environmental History of the Twentieth Century* (New York, 2000), p. xxiv.

69 David S. Jones, Scott H. Podolsky and Jeremy A. Greene, 'The Burden of Disease and the Changing Task of Medicine', *New England Journal of Medicine*, www.nejm.org, 21 June 2012.

FIVE: **Modern Reconsiderations**

1 Quoted in Andrew Motion, *Philip Larkin: A Writer's Life* (New York, 1993), pp. 517–18.

2 Ibid., p. 520.

3 Rachel Cooke, 'In Search of the Real Philip Larkin', *The Guardian* (26 June 2010).

4 Philip Larkin, 'Old Fools', in The Complete Poems, ed. Archie Burnett (New York, 2012), p. 81.

5 See Philip Larkin, 'The Mower', in Complete Poems, p. 118. See also John Osborne, Larkin, Ideology and Critical Violence (Basingstoke, 2008), pp. 88–9.

6 William Shakespeare, Measure for Measure, III.i.161–4.

7 Leo Tolstoy, Anna Karenina, trans. Louise and Aylmer Maude (Oxford, 1998), p. 501.

8 Allan Kellehear, A Social History of Dying (Cambridge, 2007), p. 213.

9 Matthew Frew and David McGillivray, 'Health Clubs and Body Politics: Aesthetics and the Quest for Physical Capital', Leisure Studies, XXIV/2 (2005), pp. 161–75, explores how modern fitness clubs capitalize on poor body self-image. Rebecca Seal, 'Eternal Youth is an Ugly Obsession', The Observer (11 July 2009).

10 Kieran McMorrow and Werner Roeger, The Economic and Financial Market Consequences of Global Ageing (New York, 2004), p. 9. See also James C. Riley, Rising Life Expectancy: A Global History (Cambridge, 2001), esp. pp. 1–6.

11 Peter Stearns, Revolutions in Sorrow: The American Experience of Death in Global Perspective (Boulder, CO, 2007), p. 81; Pat Jalland, Death in War and Peace: A History of Loss and Grief in England, 1914–1970 (Oxford, 2010), p. 5.

12 Guy Brown, The Living End: The Future of Death, Aging and Immortality (London, 2008), pp. 4, 30. See also Tony Walter, The Revival of Death (1994), chapter Four.

13 Roy Porter, The Greatest Benefit to Mankind: A Medical History of Humanity from Antiquity to the Present (London, 1997), pp. 426–45.

14 Roy Porter, ed., The Cambridge Illustrated History of Medicine (Cambridge, 1996), p. 8.

15 Brown, The Living End, pp. 4, 27, 32.

16 Ibid., p. 93.

17 CBS News, 'The Cost of Dying: End-of-life Care', www.cbsnews.com, 8 August 2010. See also Sharon R. Kaufman, And a Time to Die: How American Hospitals Shape the End of Life (Chicago, 2005), pp. 1–8.

18 Leslie A. Morgan et al., Quality Assisted Living: Informing Practice through Research (New York, 2012), examines issues ranging from patient autonomy, financial realities and the culture of caring. See also

J. Neil Henderson and Maria D. Vesperi, eds, *The Culture of Long Term Care: Nursing Home Ethnography* (Westport, CT, 1995), for patient accounts of quality issues.

19 Stuart J. Younger, 'The Definition of Death', in *The Oxford Handbook of Bioethics*, ed. Bonnie Steinbock (Oxford, 2008), pp. 285–6.

20 John B. Mitchell, *Understanding Assisted Suicide: Nine Issues to Consider* (Ann Arbor, MI, 2007), p. 4.

21 A. C. Grayling, *Ideas That Matter: The Concepts that Shape the 21st Century* (New York, 2010), p. 133.

22 Courtney S. Campbell, 'Ten Years of Death with Dignity', *New Atlantis*, 22 (Fall 2008).

23 Chris Armstrong, 'Christianity Condemns Voluntary Euthanasia', in *Euthanasia*, ed. Carrie L. Snyder (New York), pp. 20–25.

24 Grayling, *Ideas That Matter*, p. 135.

25 Gerald Dworkin, 'Physician-Assisted Death: The State of the Debate', in *Oxford Handbook of Bioethics*, p. 337.

26 L. W. Sumner, *Assisted Death: A Study in Law and Ethics* (Oxford, 2011), while arguing for assisted death as ethically appropriate in certain medical cases, offers a balanced overview of the current debate.

27 Barnard supported and practised passive euthanasia and supported, but did not practise, active euthanasia. See Luis H. Toledo-Pereyra, 'Good Life and Good Death According to Christiaan Barnard', *Journal of Investigative Surgery*, XXIII/3 (2010), pp. 125–8.

28 Leslie Ivan and Maureen Melrose, *The Way We Die* (Pari, 2007), pp. 28–31; Dick Teresi, 'Plight of the Living Dead', *New Scientist*, CCXVI/2887 (2012), pp. 36–8.

29 Elizabeth Price Foley, *The Law of Life and Death* (Cambridge, MA, 2011), discusses the many ambiguities surrounding current legal definitions of death. See also Hans Jones, 'Against the Stream: Comments on the Definition and Redefinition of Death', in *Defining the Beginning and End of Life*, ed. John P. Lizza (Baltimore, MD, 2009), pp. 498–506.

30 World Health Organization, 'Suicide Prevention', www.who.int/mental_health, 12 December 2012. See also Benedict Carey, 'Increase Seen in U.S. Suicide Rate Since Recession', *New York Times* (4 December 2012).

31 Ronald M. Holmes and Stephen T. Holmes, *Suicide: Theory, Practice and Investigation* (Thousand Oaks, CA, 2005).

32 Shelley Kagan, *Death* (New Haven, CT, 2012), pp. 318–44, offers a compelling case for suicide as a rational choice in some circumstances. Jacques Choron, *Suicide* (New York, 1972), pp. 96–101, discusses mitigating circumstances that could constitute valid reasons for committing suicide.

33 Nils Retterstøl, *Suicide: A European Perspective* (Cambridge, 1992), pp. 10–11.

34 Plato, *Laws*, trans. A. E. Taylor (London, 1960), p. 263.

35 Seneca, *Moral Epistles*, trans. Richard M. Gummere, 3 vols (Cambridge, MA, 1917), vol. II, p. 57, epistle 70.

36 Anton J. L. van Hooff, *From Autothanasia to Suicide: Self-Killing in Classical Antiquity* (New York, 1990), provides an excellent overview.

37 Mitchell, *Understanding Assisted Suicide*, p. 33.

38 John 10:15 and 10:18, quoted in Georges Minois, *History of Suicide: Voluntary Death in Western Culture*, trans. Lydia G. Cochrane (Baltimore, MD, 1999), p. 24.

39 Augustine quoted in Minois, *History of Suicide*, p. 27.

40 Alexander Murray, *Suicide in the Middle Ages* (Oxford, 1998), provides a comprehensive survey.

41 Thomas More, *Utopia*, trans. Paul Turner (New York, 2003), p. 83; Minois, *History of Suicide*, pp. 59–66.

42 Minois, *History of Suicide*, p. 68.

43 William Shakespeare, *Hamlet*, ed. A. W. Verity (Cambridge, 1953), p. 60.

44 Eric Langley, *Narcissism and Suicide in Shakespeare and his Contemporaries* (Oxford, 2009), pp. 195–6.

45 John Donne, *Biathanatos* (London, 1700), examines the issue from the perspective of the law of nature and Scripture; Donne quoted in Minois, *History of Suicide*, pp. 95–6.

46 Langley, *Narcissism and Suicide*, p. 218.

47 Stearns, *Revolutions in Sorrow*, p. 74.

48 Émile Durkheim, *Suicide: A Study in Sociology*, trans. John A. Spaulding and George Simpson (New York, 1951), pp. 46–52; Michael C. Kearl, *Endings: A Sociology of Death and Dying* (Oxford, 1989), p. 142.

49 Minois, *History of Suicide*, p. 322.

50 Holmes and Holmes, *Suicide*, p. 58.

51 Thomas Joiner, *Myths About Suicide* (Cambridge, MA, 2010), p. 89.

52 Jeremiah 16:4.

53 Quoted in Richard P. Taylor, *Death and the Afterlife: A Cultural Encyclopedia* (Santa Barbara, CA, 2000), p. 45.

54 Tony Walter, *The Eclipse of Eternity: A Sociology of the Afterlife* (Basingstoke, 1996), p. 98.

55 Gary Laderman, *Rest In Peace: A Cultural History of Death and the Funeral Home in Twentieth-century America* (Oxford, 2003), p. 3.

56 Walter, *Revival of Death*, pp. 10–11.

57 Douglas J. Davies, 'Forms of Disposal', in *Death and Religion in a Changing World*, ed. Kathleen Garces-Foley (New York, 2006), p. 2. See also Ronald G. E. Smith, *The Death Care Industries in the United States* (Jefferson, NC, 1996), p. 9.

58 Laderman, *Rest in Peace*, pp. 6–7.

59 Lisa Takeuchi Cullen, *Remember Me: A Lively Tour of the New American Way of Death* (New York, 2003), p. xi.

60 Stephen Prothero, *Purified by Fire: A History of Cremation in America* (Berkeley, CA, 2001), pp. 165–6.

61 Brown, *The Living End*, pp. 116–17.

62 Jonathan C. Smith, *Pseudoscience and Extraordinary Claims of the Paranormal* (Oxford, 2010), pp. 227–9.

63 John Beloff, *Parapsychology: A Concise History* (New York, 1993), p. 40.

64 Conan Doyle quoted in J. Gordon Melton, ed., *Encyclopedia of Occultism and Parapsychology*, 5th edn, 2 vols (Farmington Hills, MI, 2003), vol. II, p. 1465.

65 Beloff, *Parapsychology*, p. 65.

66 James E. Alcock, *Parapsychology: Science or Magic?* (Oxford, 1981), pp. 4–5.

67 Melton, ed., *Encyclopedia of Occultism and Parapsychology*, vol. II, p. 1184.

68 Jill Lepore, *The Mansion of Happiness: A History of Life and Death* (New York, 2012), pp. 169–88, offers an interesting survey of Ettinger's life and work.

69 Rob Furber, 'Robert Ettinger, the Father of Cryonics, is Gone – For Now', *The Telegraph* (9 August 2011).

70 Walter, *Revival of Death*, p. 10.

71 Arthur S. Berger, *When Life Ends: Legal Overviews, Medicolegal Forms, and Hospital Policies* (Westport, CT, 1995), offers an overview of American practices.

72 Vincent Mor, David S. Greer and Robert Kastenbaum, eds, *The Hospice Experiment* (Baltimore, MD, 1988), explores the American hospice movement. Dick Teresi, *The Undead* (New York, 2012), pp. 13–17, offers a humorous, first-person account of hospice volunteering.

73 Elisabeth Kubler-Ross, *The Wheel of Life: A Memoir of Living and Dying* (New York, 1997), claims that death is an illusion.

74 Walter, *Eclipse of Eternity*, p. 84; Lia Steakley, 'The Importance of Patient/Doctor End-of-life Discussion', *Scope* (Stanford University School of Medicine), http://scopeblog.stanford.edu, 14 November 2012; 'Care at the End of Life', editorial, *New York Times* (24 November 2012).

75 Douglas Davies, *A Brief History of Death* (Malden, MA, 2005), p. 235.

76 Peter C. Jupp, *From Dust to Ashes: Cremation and the British Way of Death* (Basingstoke, 2006), p. 185.

77 Ibid., p. 193.

78 Davies, *Brief History of Death*, p. 235; Graham quoted in Prothero, *Purified by Fire*, p. 189.

79 Robert Manchin, 'Religion in Europe: Trust Not Filling the Pews', www.gallup.com, 21 September 2004.

80 Matthew 13:42.

81 Davies, *Brief History of Death*, p. 58.

82 Thomas Merton, *The Seven Story Mountain* (New York, 1948), p. 458.

83 Lindsay Prior, 'The Social Distribution of Sentiments', in *Death, Dying and Bereavement*, ed. Donna Dickenson, Malcolm Johnson and Jeanne Samson Katz, 2nd edn (London, 2000), p. 332.

84 Stearns, *Revolutions in Sorrow*, pp. 33–4.

85 Ibid., p. 34.

86 Geoffrey Gorer, *Death, Grief, and Mourning* (Garden City, NY, 1965), remains a classic study of this changeover during the first half of the twentieth century in Britain.

87 Friedrich Nietzsche, *The Gay Science*, quoted in Garry Cox,

The Existentialist's Guide to the Universe and Nothingness (New York, 2012), p. 162.

88 Arnold Toynbee, 'The Relation Between Life and Death, Living and Dying', in *Man's Concern with Death*, ed. Arnold Toynbee, Keith Mant and Ninian Smart (New York, 1969), pp. 259–60.

89 Colin Murray Parkes, 'Bereavement as a Psychosocial Transition', in *Death, Dying and Bereavement*, ed. Dickenson, Johnson and Katz, pp. 325–30.

90 Todd May, *Death* (Stocksfield, Northumberland, 2009), p. 6.

91 Dennis Klass, 'Grief, Religion and Spirituality', in *Death and Religion*, ed. Garces-Foley, p. 283; May, *Death*, p. 19.

Conclusion

1 John A. T. Robinson, *In the End, God* (New York, 1968), pp. 27–30.

2 Thomas Dixon, *Science and Religion: A Very Short Introduction* (Oxford, 2006), p. 111.

3 Ibid., pp. 8–9.

4 Guy Brown, *The Living End: The Future of Death, Aging and Immortality* (London, 2008), p. 209.

5 Michael C. Kearl, *Endings: A Sociology of Death and Dying* (Oxford, 1989), p. 470.

6 Ayaan Hirsi Ali, 'How (and Why) I Became an Infidel', in *The Portable Atheist: Essential Readings for the Nonbeliever*, ed. Christopher Hitchens (Philadelphia, 2007), p. 480.

7 Carl Van Doren, 'Why I am an Unbeliever', in *Portable Atheist*, ed. Hitchens, p. 140.

8 Karen Armstrong, *The Great Transformation: The Beginnings of Our Religious Traditions* (New York, 2006), p. xi.

9 Marcus Aurelius, *Meditations*, in *Marcus Aurelius and His Times* (New York, 1945), p. 35.

SELECT BIBLIOGRAPHY

Ahrensdorf, Peter, *The Death of Socrates and the Life of Philosophy* (New York, 1995)

Alcock, James E., *Parapsychology: Science or Magic?* (Oxford, 1981)

Aldwinckle, Russell, *Death in the Secular City: Life After Death in Contemporary Theology and Philosophy* (Grand Rapids, MI, 1974)

Anderson, Ray S., *Theology, Death and Dying* (Oxford, 1986)

Ariès, Philippe, *The Hour of Our Death*, trans. Helen Weaver (Oxford, 1991)

Armstrong, Karen, *The Great Transformation: The Beginnings of Our Religious Traditions* (New York, 2006)

Arnold, David, *Colonizing the Body: State Medicine and Epidemic Disease in Nineteenth-century India* (Berkeley, CA, 1993)

Arriaza, Bernardo T., *Beyond Death: The Chinchorro Mummies of Ancient Chile* (Washington, DC, 1995)

Baillie, John, *And the Life Everlasting* (London, 1941)

Baker, Herschel, *The Wars of Truth* (Cambridge, MA, 1952)

Bakke, O. M., *When Children Became People: The Birth of Childhood in Early Christianity* (Minneapolis, 2005)

Bakken, Gordon Morris, ed., *Invitation to an Execution* (Albuquerque, NM, 2010)

Barker, Francis, Peter Hulme and Margaret Iverson, eds, *Cannibalism and the Colonial World* (New York, 1998)

Barmash, Pamela, *Homicide in the Biblical World* (Cambridge, 2005)

Barry, John M., *The Great Influenza* (New York, 2004)

Barry, Vincent, *Philosophical Thinking about Death and Dying* (Belmont, CA, 2007)

Bassett, Steven, ed., *Death in Towns: Urban Responses to the Dying and the Dead, 100–1600* (Leicester, 1992)

Beeghley, Leonard, *Homicide: A Sociological Explanation* (Lanham, MD, 2003)

Beloff, John, *Parapsychology: A Concise History* (New York, 1993)

Bender, David L., and Bruno Leone, eds, *War and Human Nature: Opposing Viewpoints* (St Paul, MN, 1985)

Berger, Arthur S., *When Life Ends: Legal Overviews, Medicolegal Forms, and Hospital Policies* (Westport, CT, 1995)

Bloch, Maurice, and Jonathan Parry, eds, *Death and the Regeneration of Life* (Cambridge, 1982)

Blum, Deborah, *Ghosthunters: William James and the Search for Scientific Proof of Life After Death* (New York, 2006)

Bowker, John, *The Meanings of Death* (Cambridge, 1991)

Boyle, Joan M., and James E. Morriss, *The Mirror of Time: Images of Aging and Dying* (Westport, CT, 1987)

Brandon, S.G.F., *The Judgment of the Dead: The Idea of Life After Death in the Major Religions* (New York, 1967)

Breiner, Sander J., *Slaughter of the Innocents: Child Abuse through the Ages and Today* (New York, 1990)

Brennan, Tad, *The Stoic Life: Emotions, Duties, and Fate* (Oxford, 2005)

Brown, Guy, *The Living End: The Future of Death, Aging and Immortality* (London, 2008)

Brown, Warren S., Nancey Murphy and H. Newton Malony, eds, *Whatever Happened to the Soul? Scientific and Theological Portraits of Human Nature* (Minneapolis, 1998)

Burns, Norman T., *Christian Mortalism from Tyndale to Milton* (Cambridge, MA, 1972)

Campbell, Keith, *Body and Mind* (South Bend, IN, 1986)

Camporesi, Piero, *The Fear of Hell: Images of Damnation and Salvation in Early Modern Europe*, trans. Lucinda Byatt (University Park, PA, 1990)

Carse, James P., *Death and Existence: A Conceptual History of Human Mortality* (New York, 1980)

Casey, John, *After Lives: A Guide to Heaven, Hell, and Purgatory* (Oxford, 2009)

Ching, Julia, *Chinese Religions* (New York, 1993)

Choron, Jacques, *Suicide* (New York, 1972)

——, *Death and Western Thought* (New York, 1963)

Corner, Mark, *Death Be Not Proud: The Problem of the Afterlife* (Oxford, 2011)

Cox, Gary, *Sartre: A Guide for the Perplexed* (London, 2006)

Cox, Harvey, *The Future of Faith* (New York, 2009)

Crawford, Harriet, *Sumer and the Sumerians*, 2nd edn (Cambridge, 2004)

Creel, H. G., *Confucius: The Man and the Myth* (London, 1951)

Crosby, Alfred, *Germs, Seeds and Animals* (Armonk, NY, 1994)

——, *Ecological Imperialism: The Biological Expansion of Europe, 900–1900* (Cambridge, 1996)

Cullen, Lisa Takeuchi, *Remember Me: A Lively Tour of the New American Way of Death* (New York, 2003)

Davies, Douglas J., *Death, Ritual and Belief*, 2nd edn (London, 2002)

Davies, Nigel, *Human Sacrifice in History and Today* (New York, 1981)

Dawkins, Richard, *The God Delusion* (Boston, 2006)

——, *The Blind Watchmaker* (Boston, 1986)

Delumeau, Jean, *Sin and Fear: The Emergence of a Western Guilt Culture*, trans. Eric Nicholson (New York, 1990)

Detmer, David, *Sartre Explained: From Bad Faith to Authenticity* (Chicago, 2008)

Dixon, Thomas, *Science and Religion: A Very Short Introduction* (Oxford, 2006)

Doniger, Wendy, *The Hindus: An Alternative History* (New York, 2009)

Ducasse, C. J., *A Critical Examination of the Belief in a Life After Death* (Springfield, IL, 1961)

Duffin, Jacalyn, *History of Medicine: A Scandalously Short Introduction* (Basingstoke, 2004)

Durkheim, Émile, *Suicide: A Study in Sociology*, trans. John A. Spaulding and George Simpson (New York, 1951)

Edwards, Paul, ed., *Immortality* (New York, 1992)

Esposito, John L., *Islam: The Straight Path*, 4th edn (New York, 2011)

Faure, Bernard, *Unmasking Buddhism* (Malden, MA, 2009)

Fingarette, Herbert, *Death: Philosophical Soundings* (Chicago, 1996)

Foley, Elizabeth Price, *The Law of Life and Death* (Cambridge, MA, 2011)

Fontinell, Eugene, *Self, God, and Immortality: A Jamesian Investigation* (Philadelphia, 1986)

Froom, Le Roy Edwin, *The Conditionalist Faith of Our Fathers*, 2 vols (Washington, DC, 1965)

Fussell, Paul, *The Great War and Modern Memory* (Oxford, 1975)

Garces-Foley, Kathleen, ed., *Death and Religion in a Changing World* (New York, 2006)

Gat, Azar, *War in Human Civilization* (Oxford, 2006)

Gatch, Milton, *Death: Meaning and Mortality in Christian Thought and Contemporary Culture* (New York, 1969)

Gaughan, Judy E., *Murder Was Not a Crime: Homicide and Power in the Roman Republic* (Austin, TX, 2010)

Geary, Patrick, *Living With the Dead in the Middle Ages* (Ithaca, NY, 1994)

Gorer, Geoffrey, *Death, Grief, and Mourning* (Garden City, NY, 1965)

Hays, J. N., *Epidemics and Pandemics: The Impacts on Human History* (Santa Barbara, CA, 2005)

Hick, John H., *Death and Eternal Life* (New York, 1976)

Hitchens, Christopher, *God Is Not Great: How Religion Poisons Everything* (New York, 2007)

Hocking, William Ernest, *The Meaning of Immortality in Human Experience* (Westport, CT, 1957)

Holmes, Ronald M., and Stephen T. Holmes, *Suicide: Theory, Practice and Investigation* (Thousand Oaks, CA, 2005)

Holowchak, M. Andrew, *The Stoics: A Guide for the Perplexed* (London, 2008)

Ikram, Salima, *Death and Burial in Ancient Egypt* (London, 2003)

Jalland, Pat, *Death in War and Peace: A History of Loss and Grief in England, 1914–1970* (Oxford, 2010)

James, William, *Human Immortality: Two Supposed Objections* (New York, 1960)

Joiner, Thomas, *Myths About Suicide* (Cambridge, MA, 2010)

Jupp, Peter C., *From Dust to Ashes: Cremation and the British Way of Death* (Basingstoke, 2006)

Kagan, Shelley, *Death* (New Haven, CT, 2012)

Kaufman, Sharon R., *And a Time to Die: How American Hospitals Shape the End of Life* (Chicago, 2005)

Kearl, Michael C., *Endings: A Sociology of Death and Dying* (Oxford, 1989)

Kellehear, Allan, *A Social History of Dying* (Cambridge, 2007)

Kelly, John, *The Great Mortality* (New York, 2005)

King, Barbara J., *Evolving God: A Provocative View on the Origins of Religion* (New York, 2007)

Koudounaris, Paul, *The Empire of Death: A Cultural History of Ossuaries and Charnel Houses* (New York, 2011)

Kubler-Ross, Elisabeth, *The Wheel of Life: A Memoir of Living and Dying* (New York, 1997)

Küng, Hans, *Eternal Life? Life as a Medical, Philosophical, and Theological Problem*, trans. Edward Quinn (New York, 1984)

Laderman, Gary, *Rest in Peace: A Cultural History of Death and the Funeral Home in Twentieth-century America* (Oxford, 2003)

Lagerwey, John, ed., *Religion and Chinese Society*, 2 vols (Hong Kong, 2004)

Lamont, Corliss, *The Illusion of Immortality* (New York, 1990)

Langley, Eric, *Narcissism and Suicide in Shakespeare and His Contemporaries* (Oxford, 2009)

Le Goff, Jacques, *The Birth of Purgatory*, trans. Arthur Goldhammer (Chicago, 1984)

Litten, Julian, *The English Way of Death: The Common Funeral since 1450* (London, 1991)

McDannell, Coleen and Bernhard Lang, *Heaven: A History* (New Haven, CT, 1988)

McGrath, Alister, *The Twilight of Atheism: The Rise and Fall of Disbelief in the Modern World* (New York, 2004)

——, *Christian Theology: An Introduction* (Cambridge, MA, 1997)

——, *Historical Theology: An Introduction to the History of Christian Thought* (Malden, MA, 1998)

McLeman, James, *Resurrection Then and Now* (Philadelphia, 1967)

McManners, John, *Death and the Enlightenment* (Oxford, 1981)

McMorrow, Kieran, and Werner Roeger, *The Economic and Financial Market Consequences of Global Ageing* (New York, 2004)

McNeill, J. R., *Something New Under the Sun: An Environmental History of the Twentieth Century* (New York, 2000)

McNeill, William, *Plagues and Peoples* (New York, 1998)

Magesa, Laurenti, *African Religion: The Moral Traditions of Abundant Life* (Maryknoll, NY, 1997)

Magner, Lois N., *A History of Infectious Diseases and the Microbial World* (Westport, CT, 2009)

Martin, Raymond, and John Barresi, *The Rise and Fall of Soul and Self: An Intellectual History of Personal Identity* (New York, 2006)

Matthews, W. R., *The Hope of Immortality* (New York, 1960)

Mbiti, John S., *Introduction to African Religion* (Oxford, 1991)

——, *African Religions and Philosophy* (New York, 1969)

Mellaart, James, *Çatal Hüyük: A Neolithic Town in Anatolia* (New York, 1967)

Miller, Larry S., *Hardness of Heart/Hardness of Life: The Stain of Human Infanticide* (Lanham, MD, 2000)

Mills, Liston O., ed., *Perspectives on Death* (Nashville, TN, 1969)

Minamide, Elaine, ed., *How Should One Cope with Death?* (Farmington Hills, MI, 2006)

Minois, Georges, *History of Suicide: Voluntary Death in Western Culture*, trans. Lydia G. Cochrane (Baltimore, MD, 1999)

Mitchell, John B., *Understanding Assisted Suicide: Nine Issues to Consider* (Ann Arbor, MI, 2007)

Moore, Clifford Hershel, *Ancient Beliefs in the Immortality of the Soul* (New York, 1963)

Moreman, Christopher M., *Beyond the Threshold: Afterlife Beliefs and Experiences in World Religions* (Lanham, MD, 2008)

Morrall, Peter, *Murder and Society* (Chichester, 2006)

Mungello, D. E., *Drowning Girls in China: Female Infanticide since 1650* (Lanham, MD, 2008)

Murphy, Nancey, *Bodies and Souls, or Spirited Bodies?* (Cambridge, 2006)

Murray, Alexander, *Suicide in the Middle Ages* (Oxford, 1998)

Obayashi, Hiroshi, ed., *Death and Afterlife: Perspectives of World Religions* (New York, 1992)

O'Connell, Robert L., *Ride of the Second Horseman: The Birth and Death of War* (Oxford, 1995)

——, *Of Arms and Men: A History of War, Weapons, and Aggression* (Oxford, 1989)

Ó Gráda, Cormac, *Famine: A Short History* (Princeton, NJ, 2009)

Pearson, Mike Parker, *The Archaeology of Death and Burial* (College Station, TX, 1999)

Peters, Ted, Robert John Russell and Michael Welker, eds, *Resurrection: Theological and Scientific Assessment* (Grand Rapids, MI, 2002)

Pinker, Steven, *The Better Angels of Our Nature: Why Violence has Declined* (New York, 2011)

Polkinghorne, John, *The God of Hope and the End of the World* (New Haven, CT, 2002)

Porter, Roy, *The Greatest Benefit to Mankind: A Medical History of Humanity from Antiquity to the Present* (New York, 1997)

——, ed., *The Cambridge Illustrated History of Medicine* (Cambridge, 1996)

Pringle-Pattison, A. Seth, *The Idea of Immortality* (Oxford, 1922)

Prothero, Stephen, *Purified by Fire: A History of Cremation in America* (Berkeley, CA, 2001)

Raphael, Simcha Paull, *Jewish Views of the Afterlife* (New York, 2009)

Ray, Benjamin C., *African Religions: Symbol, Ritual, and Community* (Upper Saddle River, NJ, 2000)

Retterstøl, Nils, *Suicide: A European Perspective* (Cambridge, 1992)

Riley, James C., *Rising Life Expectancy: A Global History* (Cambridge, 2001)

Rippin, Andrew, *Muslims: Their Religious Beliefs and Practices*, 4th edn (New York, 2012)

Robinson, John A. T., *In the End, God* (New York, 1968)

Rue, Loyal, *Religion is Not about God: How Spiritual Traditions Nurture Our Biological Nature and What to Expect when they Fail* (New Brunswick, NJ, 2005)

Sanday, Peggy Reeves, *Divine Hunger: Cannibalism as a Cultural System* (Cambridge, 1986)

Scarre, Geoffrey, *Death* (Montreal, 2007)

Schumacher, Bernard N., *Death and Mortality in Contemporary Philosophy*, trans. Michael J. Miller (Cambridge, 2005)

Schwartz, Benjamin I., *The World of Thought in Ancient China* (Cambridge, MA, 1985)

Segal, Alan F., *Life After Death: A History of the Afterlife in the Religions of the West* (New York, 2003)

Settegast, Mary, *When Zarathustra Spoke: The Reformation of Neolithic Culture and Religion* (Costa Mesa, CA, 2005)

Shorto, Russell, *Descartes' Bones: A Skeletal History of the Conflict between Faith and Reason* (New York, 2009)

Smallman-Raynor, M. R., and A. D. Cliff, *War Epidemics: An Historical Geography of Infectious Diseases in Military Conflict and Civil Strife, 1850–2000* (Oxford, 2004)

Smith, Jonathan C., *Pseudoscience and Extraordinary Claims of the Paranormal* (Oxford, 2010)

Smith, Ronald G. E., *The Death Care Industries in the United States* (Jefferson, NC, 1996)

Snape, Steven, *Ancient Egyptian Tombs: The Culture of Life and Death* (Chichester, 2011)

Spencer, Theodore, *Death and Elizabethan Tragedy* (New York, 1960)

Spierburg, Pieter, *A History of Murder: Personal Violence in Europe from the Middle Ages to the Present* (Cambridge, 2008)

Stannard, David, *The Puritan Way of Death* (Oxford, 1979)

Stearns, Peter, *Revolutions in Sorrow: The American Experience of Death in Global Perspective* (Boulder, CO, 2007)

Stendahl, Krister, ed., *Immortality and Resurrection* (New York, 1965)

Sumner, L. W., *Assisted Death: A Study in Law and Ethics* (Oxford, 2011)

Tarnas, Richard, *The Passion of the Western Mind* (New York, 1993)

Taylor, Richard P., *Death and the Afterlife: A Cultural Encyclopedia* (Santa Barbara, CA, 2000)

Taylor, Timothy, *The Buried Soul: How Humans Invented Death* (Boston, 2002)

Toynbee, Arnold, Keith Mant and Ninian Smart, eds, *Man's Concern With Death* (New York, 1969)

Van Hooff, Anton J. L., *From Autothanasia to Suicide: Self-Killing in Classical Antiquity* (New York, 1990)

Wade, Nicholas, *Before the Dawn: Recovering the Lost History of Our Ancestors* (New York, 2006)

Walter, Tony, *The Eclipse of Eternity: A Sociology of the Afterlife* (Basingstoke, 1996)

——, *The Revival of Death* (London, 1994)

Warren, James, *Facing Death: Epicurus and His Critics* (Oxford, 2004)

Waters, Tony, *When Killing is a Crime* (Boulder, CO, 2007)

Watts, Sheldon J., *Epidemics and History: Disease, Power and Imperialism* (New Haven, CT, 1997)

Williams, Bernard, *Problems of the Self* (Cambridge, 1973)

Wilson, A. N., *God's Funeral: A Biography of Faith and Doubt in Western Civilization* (New York, 1999)

Yates, Jenny, ed., *Jung on Death and Immortality* (Princeton, NJ, 1999)

Yolton, John W., *Thinking Matter: Materialism in Eighteenth-century Britain* (Minneapolis, 1983)

ACKNOWLEDGEMENTS

There is a wealth of excellent scholarly work on the subject of death and dying in the Western tradition, and this short survey relies heavily on the labour of many specialists in the field. Theologians, medical ethicists, philosophers, sociologists, psychologists and care-givers have contributed to the creation of a truly interdisciplinary area of study. Some of the leading works are listed in the select bibliography, but the relevant literature is enormous and growing all the time due to new demographic challenges facing modern Western societies. I wish to thank the reference and circulation specialists at my home institution, the University of North Carolina at Asheville, in particular Helen Dezendorf, Leith Tate and Anita White-Carter, for assisting with the inter-library loan process and with bibliographical suggestions. My colleagues Bruce Greenawalt and Rodger Payne offered helpful advice at the early stages of the project. Aimee Selby, my editor at Reaktion Books, improved the final draft with a number of careful suggestions and made the production process flow smoothly and efficiently. The governing board of the Council of Public Liberal Arts Colleges has been generous in allowing me to combine occasional writing with daily administrative duties. Margaret Carlin and Claire Bailey reviewed the entire typescript and provided timely advice on a wide range of topics. As with earlier projects, my wife Nancy Costello provided quiet support through the gifts of time and patience. The book is dedicated to the memory of my caring and gentle cousin Edward.

INDEX

abandonment 38, 69, 109, 151, 152, 153, 180
Abelard, Peter 67
abortion 60, 149, 151, 153, 179
Abraham 98, 119, 125, 158, 189
accidental death 161–2
Adam and Eve 98
agnosticism 9–10
agricultural revolution 24–7, 42
Alzheimer's disease 72, 88, 170, 178
American Civil War 155
American Parapsychology Association 192
Analects (Confucius) 102
ancestral spiritual realm 101
annihilation 38, 61–2, 72–4, 83, 92, 95, 115, 208
anthropomorphism 61, 83
Antonine plague 136
Aquinas, Thomas 54, 60, 61, 67, 121, 182
Aristotle 59–62, 68, 71, 180, 184
Ars moriendi 124
Assyrian Empire 47
Atman (Hinduism) 108–10
Auden, W. H. 83
Augustine, St 54, 60, 67, 117, 129, 147–8, 182
Aurelius, Marcus 9, 66, 91, 136, 169, 211
Axial Age 13, 97–9
Ayran invaders 46
Ayrans 106

bacteriological warfare 139
Barnard, Christiaan 177
Becker, Carl 90
Becker, Ernest 209
Biathanatos (Donne) 184
Bible 77, 124–5, 125–6, 144, 152, 158, 181, 184, 199, 200
   Book of Daniel 112
   Book of Genesis 111
   Book of Revelation 117
bioethics 177
biological death 9, 13, 16, 41, 105, 111, 116
biotechnology 83, 177
bioterrorism 161
Black Death 123–4, 137–9
Boccaccio, Giovanni 138
Book of the Dead 38
Bowker, John 131, 210
Boyle, Robert 13
Brahe, Tycho 69
Brahman 107, 108, 112, 186
Brahmins 107–8, 109
Brinton, Crane 53
bubonic plague 137
Buddhism 14, 109–11, 179–80, 186
   Chinese 111

Calvin, John 128
Camus, Albert 84
cannibalism 48–9
capital punishment 159–60

cardiovascular disease 162
Çatalhöyük 27
Catholic Church 14, 60, 121, 126
Catholicism 14, 30, 60, 121, 122–3,
    124–5, 126, 127, 128–9, 130, 156,
    184, 197, 198, 199
cave art 23
childhood mortality 146
China, ancient 42–4
Chinchorro people 38–9
Chinese cosmology 50
cholera 141
Christian mortalists 129
chronic illness 170
City of God, The (Augustine) 67, 182
Clausewitz, Carl von 154
Clement of Alexandria 152
communicable disease 15
Confessions (Augustine) 148
Confucianism 14, 97 102–4, 110, 116,
    131, 151
Copernicus, Nicolaus 69
Council of Carthage 181
Cranmer, Thomas 128
cremation 7, 28, 107, 108, 120, 186,
    188–9, 190, 196–8
Crosby, Alfred 139
cryonics 193
Cullman, Oscar 115
cultural evolution 31, 134

danse macabre 123
Dante 11, 122, 182
Darwin, Charles 77, 78–9, 80, 82, 83,
    139, 143
Dawkins, Richard 85
Death with Dignity Act 175
death, definition of 13, 177–8
death, denied 10, 168–9, 191–3
Decameron (Boccaccio) 138
Democritus 62
Denial of Death, The (Becker) 209
Descartes, René 70–72
Descent of Man, The (Darwin) 77
dharma 108
Dialogues of the Dead (Lucian) 89

Discourse on the Method . . . (Descartes) 71
Divine Comedy (Dante) 122
divine intervention 145
Diving Bell and the Butterfly, The
    (Bauby) 90
do not resuscitate 194–5
dolmens 29
Dolni Vestonice 22
Donne, John 115, 132, 183
Dowth 29
Drake, Francis 140
Drummond, William 127
dukkha 109
Durkheim, Émile 185

Egypt 12, 30, 35–9, 47, 48, 85, 112,
    118, 135, 145, 151, 180
Eliot, George 90–91
end-of-life care 169–74
Enkidu 33–4
Enlightenment 16, 54, 75–7, 90, 130,
    179, 184, 191, 206
environmental degradation 163–6
Epicurus 9, 62, 63
eschatology 93
eschaton 116
euthanasia 176
    active 175, 195
    passive 175, 195
evolutionary biology 13, 81
execution 117, 152, 159, 160, 180
exposure 29, 139, 152, 163, 168, 207

famine 26, 142–3
Fang people 40
Feast of All Souls 123
Fertile Crescent 24
Feuerbach, Ludwig 81
fideism 114
final deposition 186
First World War 141–2, 155, 201
Freud, Sigmund 82–3, 185
friendly society 171
funeral industry 16, 168, 185–90, 194,
    197
Future of an Illusion, The (Freud) 83

Galen 70, 135, 145
Galilei, Galileo 69, 206
Gassendi, Pierre 72
genetics 83
germ warfare 139–40
Gilgamesh 33, 34, 131, 143
Golden Rule 99
Gould, Stephen Jay 85
Greece 10, 12, 55, 65, 111–12, 150, 154, 180
Greek ontology 54
Gregory of Nyssa 147
grief 200–04

Haddenham, Cambridgeshire 28–9
Hadith 119, 120
Hadza people 22
Hamlet 12, 17, 183
Hammurabi 33
Harvard Medical School 177
Hawkes, Jacquetta 30
heaven 37, 40–41, 43, 67, 76, 81, 103–5, 109, 125–26, 130, 138, 187
Hebrew Bible (Tanakh) 32, 113, 114, 125, 158, 181, 199
Heidegger, Martin 61
hell 12, 76, 109, 118, 122, 130, 156, 182, 199–201
Herodotus 36
Hinduism 14, 107, 108, 109, 110, 112, 179, 186
Hirsi Ali, Ayaan 208, 209
Hobbes, Thomas 20, 72
Homer 55, 112, 144
homicide 158, 159
Homo neanderthalensis 21
Homo sapiens 18, 21
hospices 193–6
Hume, David 75, 77
humoral medicine 145
hunter-gatherers 18–20
hylomorphism 59, 60

Iliad 56, 144
immortality 10, 34, 37, 41, 55–9, 66, 72, 74–7, 81, 83–4, 87, 89–92, 107, 114–15, 173, 201, 209–10
indulgences 126
Indus River Valley 30, 46
infant death 146–8, 200
infanticide 20, 99, 149–53
infectious diseases 139
influenza 135, 139, 141, 161–2
interventionist medicine 174
Irish Famine 143
Islam 10, 14, 98, 109, 118–21, 155, 186, 208

Jackson, Andrew 158
James, William 86–8
Jaspers, Karl 97
Jericho 26, 27
Jerome, St 60
Jesus 98, 114–19, 144, 181
Jewish Bible see Hebrew Bible
Joiner, Thomas 185
Judaism 14, 98, 111–14, 116, 117, 118, 119, 124, 131, 138, 152, 181, 186, 199
Jung, Carl 85–6
just war 155

karma 108, 110
Kepler, Johannes 69
Knowth 29
Kubler-Ross, Elisabeth 195
!Kung 19–20
Kush 33, 106

Lactantius 152
Lamont, Corliss 9
Laozi 97, 104
Larkin, Philip 167–8
Le Goff, Jacques 121
Leibniz, Gottfried Wilhelm 73
lifestyle diseases 162–3
living will 195
Locke, John 72
long-term care 170
Lucretius 63, 64, 168
Luther, Martin 125–8

McNeill, J.R. 164
Mahabharata 108
malnutrition 26, 147
Marx, Karl 80–82
materialism 61–4, 83–5
Mencius 104
Mendel, Gregor 78
Mersenne, Marin 72
Malebranche, Nicolas 73
Massada 181
materialism 13, 53, 72
medicine, modern 172, 173
Meditations (Aurelius) 66, 211
Mencius 104
Mende people 41
Merton, Thomas 199–200
Mesopotamia 12, 30, 31–6, 47,.118, 135, 145
metempsychosis 56–7
microparasites 134
Milton, John 129
mind–body problem 70–72
Mitford, Jessica 189–90
moksha 108
Montaigne, Michel de 171
More, Thomas 118, 183
mortalism 9, 76
Mosaic law 159
Muhammad 119–20, 121
murder 15, 98, 149, 157–9, 181
Myth of Sisyphus, The (Camus) 84

Natufians 25
natural philosophy 13, 68
Neolithic practices 24, 25–6, 29–30, 42, 45
New England Journal of Medicine 165
Newgrange 29, 30
Newton, Isaac 69, 77, 81, 83
Nietzsche, Friedrich 82, 83, 202
nominalists 67, 68
nursing homes 7, 16, 173

Odyssey 55, 56, 112
On the Origin of Species (Darwin) 77
oracle bones 43–4

Origen of Alexandria 60
Osiris 37, 38
Ötzi 20
Outsider, The (Camus) 84
Overton, Richard 129

Palaeolithic culture 22–4, 49, 149
palliative analgesics 175
palliative medicine 14, 133, 177, 194
parapsychology 17, 192
Pascal, Blaise 8, 73–4, 77
Paul, St 10, 114, 117, 125, 126, 129
Pericles 136
persistent vegetative state 178
personal autonomy 172, 175
personhood 16, 41, 54–6, 89–90, 93, 129, 150–51, 170, 178
Phaedo (Plato) 57, 58
pharaohs 36, 37
Pharisees 113, 114
Philo of Alexandria 151
philosophes 13, 54
Pinker, Stephen 158
plague 135–40, 144
Plato 9, 57–9, 71, 79, 89, 115, 180, 184
Polkinghorne, John 93–4
positivism 13
pre-Socratics 55–7
private cemeteries 187
private grief 203
Protestant Reformation 14, 54, 68, 126–7, 190
Protestantism 14, 54, 121, 124, 125, 126, 127, 128, 130, 183, 184, 198, 199
Psychopannychia (Calvin) 128
purgatory 118, 121–3, 125–8
Puritanism 127, 128, 129, 140
Pythagoras 56

Qur'an 119, 120, 121

realism 67
reincarnation 10, 186
Renaissance 13, 68–9, 145, 182, 190

Republic, The (Plato) 22, 58
resuscitation 93, 94–5, 177
Roberts, J. M. 22
royal burials 33
Russell, Bertrand 17, 84, 208

sacrifice, human 47–8
Sadducees 113
St Christopher's Hospice 195
salvation 54, 60, 78, 82, 105, 118, 121–2, 126
sanctity of life 176
Santayana, George 86
Sartre, Jean-Paul 84, 185
Satan 120, 124, 199
Saunders, Cicely 195
Scarre, Geoffrey 63
Schopenhauer, Arthur 79
Second Vatican Council 130
Second World War 16, 48, 84, 156–7, 161, 167, 170–73
sedentism 26
Segal, Alan 37
Seneca 65–6, 150, 170, 180
sepsis, post-operative 146
Shang dynasty 43, 44, 47–8, 100, 103
Sheol 112, 199
Siculus, Diodorus 151
slavery 44
smallpox 135, 137, 139–41, 147
Smith, Adam 75
Society for Psychical Research 192
Socrates 57, 58, 71, 115, 205
soul sleeping 127–9
Spinoza, Baruch 73
spiritualism 191
Stoicism 64–6
Sub-Saharan Africa 39–42
suicide 16, 31, 65, 75, 92, 99, 175–6, 178–85
Suicide: A Study in Sociology (Durkheim) 185
surgery 146, 167, 172, 177
sutti (Hinduism) 179
Swift, Jonathan 89

Talmud 113
Tao-Te-Ching 104
Taoism 104–6, 110
Taylor, Jeremy 127
Taylor, Timothy 28
teleology 14, 69
Tertullian 60, 125, 152
Thirty-Nine Articles 128
Thirty Years War 155
Thomas, Keith 127
Thoughts on Death and Immortality (Feuerbach) 81
Thucydides 135, 136
Tithonus 173
Tolstoy, Leo 91–2
Totem and Taboo (Freud) 83
Toynbee, Arnold 202
Tragic Sense of Life, The (Unamuno) 92
transmissive power 87
Tyndale, William 128

Unamuno, Miguel de 23, 92
Upanishads 80, 97, 108, 109
Utopia (More) 183

Van Doren, Carl 209
Vedas 107, 108
Vries, Hugo de 78

Wade, Nicholas 45
war 15, 45–7, 99, 102, 154–7
whole brain death 178
William of Ockham 68
Williams, Bernard 89
World as Will and Representation, The (Schopenhauer) 79
World Health Organization 178

Yangshao culture 42
Yanomamo people 19
Yombe people 23
Yoruba people 40

Zeno of Citium 65
Zhuangzi (Zhuang Zhou) 104, 105